Merry Christmas 2018

A gift from Doug & Lamond Banks

Executive Presbyter
Chicago Region

I have read the book *The Master Mentor* and feel that Marvin Gorman has done an excellent job writing about the precious ministry of the Holy Spirit and explaining and illustrating His invaluable gifts and mighty works. As Gorman explains, the gifts, power, and anointing of the Spirit are for all of God's leaders and people. So, if you long to know more about the Holy Spirit, His gifts, and His ways…if you hunger for Him to flow more powerfully through you now and in the days ahead, stop and take time to read this book!

—DR. GEORGE WOOD
GENERAL SUPERINTENDENT OF THE ASSEMBLIES OF GOD

Pastor Marvin Gorman writes from a depth of both spiritual revelation and personal experience. This work flows from a lifetime of learning and living. It will "pull and push" each reader to evaluate their relationship with the Holy Spirit. I believe this book will help bring balance in an age of abuse and abandonment of Holy Spirit teaching. As many grow further away from sound doctrine, Pastor Marvin strategically communicates on this much-needed topic. This book blazes a path to return to Spirit-filled living and Spirit-led leadership. It's more than a book to be read, it's a lifestyle to be lived.

—SCOTT HOLMES
LOUISIANA ASSEMBLIES OF GOD DISTRICT SUPERINTENDENT

The hallmark of Marvin Gorman's ministry has always been, and always will be, his powerful preaching and teaching concerning the Holy Spirit. His new book, *The Master Mentor*, is a treatise being handed down to an Elijah generation that is yearning to be mentored.

—JOHN A. KILPATRICK
FOUNDER AND SENIOR PASTOR OF CHURCH OF HIS PRESENCE
DAPHNE, AL

What an incredible book on the power of the Holy Spirit in our lives. Everyone that wants to live a Spirit led, overcoming life should read this book.

—TROY DUHON
EXECUTIVE PRODUCER OF THE MOVIES GOD'S NOT DEAD
AND DO YOU BELIEVE?

The Master Mentor

Marvin Gorman
With Judy Doyle, PhD

CREATION
HOUSE

THE MASTER MENTOR by Marvin Gorman with Judy Doyle, PhD
Published by Creation House
A Charisma Media Company
600 Rinehart Road
Lake Mary, Florida 32746
www.charismamedia.com

Unless otherwise noted, all Scripture quotations are from the King James Version of the Bible.

Scripture quotations marked AMP are from the Amplified Bible. Old Testament copyright © 1965, 1987 by the Zondervan Corporation. The Amplified New Testament copyright © 1954, 1958, 1987 by the Lockman Foundation. Used by permission.

Scripture quotations marked NKJV are from the New King James Version of the Bible. Copyright © 1979, 1980, 1982 by Thomas Nelson, Inc., publishers. Used by permission.

Scripture quotations marked NIV are from the Holy Bible, New International Version of the Bible. Copyright © 1973, 1978, 1984, International Bible Society. Used by permission.

Scripture quotations marked NASB are from the New American Standard Bible®, Copyright © 1960, 1962, 1963, 1968, 1971, 1972, 1973, 1975, 1977, 1995 by The Lockman Foundation. Used by permission.

Design Director: Justin Evans
Cover design by Bill Johnson

Visit the author's website: www.marvingorman.com

Library of Congress Cataloging-in-Publication Data: 2015909617
International Standard Book Number: 978-1-62998-468-1
E-book International Standard Book Number: 978-1-62998-469-8

While the author has made every effort to provide accurate telephone numbers and Internet addresses at the time of publication, neither the publisher nor the author assumes any responsibility for errors or for changes that occur after publication.

First edition

15 16 17 18 19— 987654321
Printed in the United States of America

*Now concerning spiritual gifts, brethren, I would not have you ignorant. For to one is given by the Spirit **the word of wisdom**; to another **the word of knowledge** by the same Spirit; to another **faith** by the same Spirit; to another **the gifts of healing** by the same Spirit; to another **the working of miracles**; to another **prophecy**; to another **discerning of spirits**; to another **divers kinds of tongues**; to another **the interpretation of tongues**; but all these worketh that one and the self-same Spirit, dividing to every man severally as He will.*

—1 Corinthians 12:1, 8–11

DEDICATION

To my wife Virginia who supports me as I devote numerous hours to Bible study, prayer, fasting, and ministering to others because she, too, understands the call of God upon my life.

TABLE OF CONTENTS

ACKNOWLEDGEMENTS

THIS BOOK WOULD not have been published without the amazing efforts and untiring hours that my wife, Virginia, gave to see this book become a reality.

Only eternity will reveal the contribution that Dr. Judy Doyle, coauthor of The Master Mentor, has made with her prayers, endless efforts of research, and splendid journalism. I am personally appreciative of her exhaustive and extensive assistance.

I would like to express my sincere thanks to Carl and Ellen Rice, who furnished me a lovely office in Shreveport, LA, so I could begin the launching of this project. It was there that I dictated the message of my heart that is the meat of this book. I thank Carl and Ellen for their financial assistance as well.

A special thank you goes to Missionary Kerby Rials, who assisted in the first edit of this book so that it could become available for publication.

Lastly, I want to extend my heartfelt gratitude to the excellent staff of Creation House for their assistance in pushing this project forward.

INTRODUCTION

I HAVE PREACHED THE Word of God for more than sixty-three years. From the time God called me as a young man in Arkansas, God imparted to me a compassionate love for humanity.

I was elected to serve for eight years as the Louisiana Assemblies of God Youth Director. I also served on various committees and boards within the state of Louisiana. I was elected as one of thirteen Executive Presbyters of the Assemblies of God.

For approximately forty years, my wife Virginia and I pastored churches. One of those pastorates was First Assembly of God in New Orleans, LA, which grew from a modest 100 members to well over 6,000. We also began a radio and television ministry outreach, whose programs were broadcast daily throughout the United States, as well as overseas.

In 1985, I established Foundation for Human Helps. This organization was formed to effectively increase my ability to reach out to humanity around the world. My heart-cry has always been to see the lost come to Jesus Christ, to bring healing to the sick and restoration to those who are broken.

I have conducted leadership conferences throughout the United States and in many parts of the world. These included providing specific training for national pastors and leaders.

I am actively involved in projects for missions around the world and serve as a spiritual father for several churches throughout the United States, Mexico, Central America, and Africa.

I know what it is to reap the devastating consequences of sin. I was at the highest peak of my ministerial career when my world was turned upside down because I had allowed myself to become involved with a person of the opposite sex. It was not a long, drawn-out affair, as I have explained in my book, *The Road to Repentance*, but I did sin and repented of it to God, my wife and children, and also publicly.

I went through several sessions of godly counseling. Among those who counseled me was Dr. Richard Dobbins. It was a process of repentance and emotional healing that I had to accomplish. It didn't come easy.

Following that, I resumed pulpit ministry and allowed God to restore me. I mention this because if there are those reading this book who have experienced any kind of failure, you can be assured that through proper counseling, repentance, and dwelling in the Word, you and your ministry can be completely restored. I am enjoying some of the most fruitful days of my ministry at the present time. Thank God!

My purpose in writing this book is to draw attention to the importance of the Holy Spirit and His ministry. As I travel in ministry, I am made aware that many churches are void of the operation of the Holy Spirit and His gifts. This book, *The Master Mentor*, is written in an effort to challenge ministers, as well as laity, to recognize that your greatest friend is the person of the Holy Spirit. *He is the Master Mentor!*

PREFACE

I T IS LIKELY, were the apostle Paul to visit many Christian gatherings today, that he would ask the same question he asked in Acts 19, inquiring whether they had received the Holy Ghost since they believed.

This is because he would see the same absence of power that he saw in the Ephesian men. He would see the same absence of the gifts of the Spirit—no prophetic ministry, no miracles, no signs, no speaking in tongues. The good news is that the solution he offered to them is still available to us today: an infilling and overflowing of the Holy Spirit!

It is my prayer and hope that this book will spark a personal Pentecost in your life. I know you are reading it because you are hungry for more of God. And there is more for you! I wish with all my heart that you will be filled with the same power of the apostles. They healed the sick, cast out demons, and raised the dead.

This is not something far away and unattainable, although the devil would like you to think that! He does not want to see you "endued with power from on high" (Luke 24:49). What trouble you would cause for his kingdom of darkness!

The Holy Spirit wants to shine on this world through you. As noted by theologian Donald Gee, the phrase "manifestation of the Spirit" in 1 Cor. 12:7 is in Greek *phanerosis*, which means a shining forth. The gifts of the Holy Spirit are the light shining through the lantern.[1]

As you join with me in this study of the gifts of the Spirit, I would like to ask you to look at 1 Cor. 14:26 as it has a special message of encouragement for you: "What then shall we say, brothers and sisters? When you come together, each of you has a hymn, or a word of instruction, a revelation, a tongue or an interpretation. Everything must be done so that the church may be built up" (NIV).

Note the word *everyone*. That means you! These powerful gifts of the spirit are not just for the pastor, or the evangelist, or the elder, but for each one of us.

These gifts are for you and for those to whom you minister. Jesus prophesied that these gifts would follow all those who believe in him (Mark 16:17–18).

As Jesus taught us in Luke 11:9, 13 regarding the Holy Spirit, "Ask, and it shall be given you; seek, and ye shall find; knock, and it shall be opened unto you....how much more shall your heavenly Father give the Holy Spirit to them that ask him?"

—MARVIN GORMAN

Part 1

THE HOLY SPIRIT, THE MASTER MENTOR

- Strangers to the supernatural

- Long lost treasure

- Our need for a mentor

Chapter 1

STRANGERS TO THE SUPERNATURAL

Y OU MAY NEVER have heard of Smith Wigglesworth, but please let me tell you a little about him to show what God can do in our day, and in your life, through the power of the Holy Spirit.

Wigglesworth had a worldwide ministry with extraordinary gifts of healing, but he began as a simple tongue-tied plumber in England.

He worked in plumbing full-time for decades, sharing the gospel in his spare time. Public speaking was very difficult for him, however, so his wife Polly did the preaching. But at the age of forty-eight, something happened. Smith was baptized in the Holy Spirit. He suddenly had a new anointing that enabled him to preach with power. Even his wife was amazed at the transformation. The signs and wonders accompanying his ministry included restoration of hearing and sight, the creative formation of missing limbs, the disappearance of goiters and cancerous growths, casting out demons, the recovery of mental wholeness by the violently insane, and the raising of around twenty people from the dead.[1] Smith's ministry of signs and wonders spanned several decades until his death in 1947. He was no stranger to the supernatural.

What a testimony of the power of the Holy Spirit in the life of a simple Pentecostal plumber!

But today in the United States millions of Pentecostals are Pentecostal in name only. This is despite the fact that more people say they are Pentecostal than at any other time in the nation's history. Far too many—leaders and laity alike—readily admit that they have become complacent and comfortable. They are *strangers to the supernatural.*

Once mighty movements and on-fire churches are becoming mere monuments. Yes, we do have paved parking lots, tall steeples, costly chandeliers, and stained glass windows. We have well-equipped church kitchens, spacious fellowship halls, and our own gymnasiums.

We have state-of-the art media equipment, expensive sound systems, and padded pews. We are no longer the shabby church on the wrong side of the railroad tracks.

But something is missing. Because I preach in Pentecostal churches all over the United States, I've gotten a pretty good view of the overall picture. And it's not what we've *got* that's troubling me. It's what we *haven't* got.

What's happened to the intercession and travail we used to have around our altars? Where are the healings and miracles? Where are the signs and wonders? What's with these polished, three-points-and-a-poem sermons? We don't need pretty little *sermons*. We need anointed *messages*! We don't need to hear men quoting other men. We need to hear from God! We don't need Sunday-as-usual services that are so structured, so predictable, that everybody knows exactly what's going to happen before service even begins. "Decently and in order" isn't supposed to mean "dead as a doornail"!

Where are the tears? Where are the joyful testimonies? Where are the precious gifts of the Holy Spirit? The body of Christ is suffering because these gifts are not operating in our midst as God intended. Somebody had better sound the wakeup call because without the powerful operation of the gifts of the Spirit in our midst, we can never fulfill our destiny. We neglect the Holy Spirit and His gifts at our own peril.

According to Ephesians 3:20, "[God] is able to do exceedingly abundantly above all that we ask or think, according to the power that works in us" (NKJV). Is God still able?

Jesus said, "... He who believes in Me, the works that I do he will do also; and greater *works* than these he will do, because I go to My Father" (John 14:12, NKJV). Is Jesus' promise no longer valid?

What's going on? What has happened? Has God changed? Or have our own faith and experiences diminished to the point that we no longer expect the greater works that Jesus promised?

I've spent a lot of time on my knees, analyzing the problem. As I see it, there are at least nine reasons why many churches are rapidly becoming Pentecostal in name only. Take a few minutes to read and meditate on them. See if your spirit bears witness with what I'm saying.

NINE REASONS WHY MANY CHURCHES ARE BECOMING PENTECOSTAL IN NAME ONLY

1. The main reason the gifts of the Spirit are rarely manifested in many Pentecostal services is that we have become satisfied without them. This is the first and most important reason many of our churches are not living up to the name on their sign.

   We may say that our church is Pentecostal because it belongs to a denomination or a movement that had its beginnings in a powerful outpouring of the Holy Spirit.

   However, if we've become content without the power and anointing of God, something has gone wrong. If we're satisfied even though the gifts of the Holy Spirit are rarely, if ever, manifested in our midst, are we *truly* Pentecostal, or are we Pentecostal in name only? Merely attending a Pentecostal church and believing in the book of Acts doesn't make us Pentecostal any more than being born in a cookie jar makes a mouse a cookie. The book of Acts never would have been written if the apostles and those early Spirit-filled believers hadn't *acted*! And those acts weren't completed with the Apostles. The acts and ministries of God's church are still being recorded in heaven today. Is anything being written about *you*?

2. We are substituting complacency for sacrifice. God is the rewarder of sacrifice, but He is the judge of complacency. Smith Wigglesworth used to say, "You need to *live* ready. If you have to stop to get ready when the opportunity comes, by the time you're ready, the opportunity has gone."[2]

3. We are substituting confession for repentance. Confession soothes our conscience, but repentance takes out of us that which makes us rebellious and disobedient. Repentance changes us from the inside out. Every day you or I don't repent is like eating out of the same plate without washing it.

4. We are substituting praise for prayer. The powerful
   prayer meetings of the past are becoming obsolete.
   In 1906, a woman gave a prophecy at Azusa Street
   regarding the last days and the Pentecostal movement. The prophecy warned that people will place a
   great emphasis on *praise* to a God they no longer *pray*
   to. Why? Because it's easier to celebrate than to ago-
   nize. The Spirit of God is calling the church back to her
   knees, back to her altars.

5. We are substituting pious "propriety" for the supernatural ministry of the Holy Spirit. Today in many of
   our churches, if people desire to receive the baptism in
   the Holy Spirit they are not invited to come to the altar
   for prayer lest visitors in the service misunderstand or
   become "offended" by emotional outbursts or speaking
   in tongues. Therefore, people desiring to receive the baptism in the Holy Spirit are taken to a private room for
   prayer or instructed to come to a meeting held at another
   time or place for that purpose.

   However, this erroneous line of reasoning is demol-
   ished by the events recorded in Acts chapter two. On
   the day of Pentecost, a crowd of God-fearing Jews from
   many different nations came together in bewilderment
   when they heard the followers of Jesus in the Upper
   Room declaring the wonders of God in languages
   unknown to those speaking, yet clearly understood by
   those who heard them. Peter explained that they must
   repent and be baptized in the name of Jesus Christ for
   the forgiveness of their sins, and that they, too, would
   receive the gift of the Holy Spirit. "For the promise
   is unto you, and to your children, and to all that are
   afar off, even as many as the LORD our God shall call"
   (Acts 2:39). Rather than being offended and driven
   away because Jesus' followers spoke in tongues when
   they were baptized in the Holy Spirit, over 3,000 people
   accepted Peter's message, were baptized, and added to
   the fellowship of believers that very day (Acts 2:41). Are

ministers today more wise and mannerly than the Holy Spirit? God forgive us.

6. We are substituting glitter for gold. Many of our churches are becoming Pentecostal in name only because we are substituting the *sensational* for the *supernatural*.

   Because many men and women of God are relying upon the natural and the sensational to do the work that only the supernatural can do, manifestations of the gifts of the Spirit are becoming increasingly rare in many congregations today. Yet in the early church, manifestations of the gifts of the Spirit were considered a necessity, not a luxury. Are *we* less needy than *they*? When we try to substitute the sensational for the supernatural, we are robbing the body of Christ!

7. Many ministers do not allow the gifts of the Spirit to move in their services because they're afraid the gifts might be misused in ignorant or carnal manifestations. As a result, many ministers are quenching the move of the Spirit. But just how sound is that logic? Why don't they apply that pious-sounding argument to some other things and see how long it lasts. Have they ever abused the privilege of having a driver's license by speeding? Most likely. Did they park their car in the driveway and walk everywhere from then on? Very unlikely. As Donald Gee, the well-known British Pentecostal teacher and author, used to say: "The cure for abuse is not '*disuse*': it's *proper* use!" Sound, biblical teaching and wise, balanced correction are the remedies for ignorance and abuse—not shutting down every move of God and quenching the Holy Spirit.

8. Preaching or teaching about the Holy Spirit and his gifts makes many ministers uncomfortable because they know if they *preach* it, they've got to *produce* it. I wonder if this is not why many ministers of the gospel are turning away from preaching about the gifts, manifestations, and power of the Holy Spirit even though

they know that the power and demonstration of the Spirit brings people to Jesus Christ.

Let me return to my hero Smith Wigglesworth so that we can understand what it takes to not only preach on the Holy Spirit, but to move in the power. He once confided to a friend, "There's never a waking half hour that I don't speak to the Lord at some time…I go to bed speaking in tongues, and I get up speaking in tongues." He didn't get to that place overnight, and neither do we. But as we hunger for more of God, the Holy Spirit enriches, deepens, and matures our walk with him.

9. We are substituting education and degrees for the gifts and power of the Spirit. At the risk of sounding critical and judgmental, I must point out still another reason many of our churches are becoming Pentecostal in name only. Thank God what I am about to say certainly does not apply to all! But it cannot be denied that many ministers preaching in our pulpits, as well as many men and women serving as leaders or teachers in our colleges and universities, have rarely, if ever, been used in deliverances, healings, or gifts of the Spirit. As a result, some have minimalized or discredited the gifts and power of the Holy Spirit and attempted to substitute degrees and education instead. It's as if the attitude is, "We don't need the Holy Spirit as much as we once did. We have education now."

SHORTCUTS AND SUBSTITUTIONS

Well, we got what we wanted and now we don't want what we got. It's time we faced the fact that because of reasons I've just mentioned, many of us have lost battle after battle with the enemy. We've lost our focus. We've compromised our dreams and taken spiritual short-cuts. And so, we are weary of standing behind a pulpit, service after service, delivering pretty sermons that *inform* but don't *transform,* and watching people walk out the door unchanged.

Oh, we still believe in divine healing, but we're frustrated and confused because hardly anybody we pray for gets healed. We still believe in the other gifts of the Spirit, but those gifts are rarely manifested in our midst. I'm not saying that we don't work hard. But when we spend much more time working *for* God than spending time *with* God, the Holy Spirit is grieved.

If we measure success by the size of buildings, congregations, and budgets, some of us are highly successful. We've got awards, degrees, and diplomas, and I sincerely applaud all of that. But many are awakening to the fact that human effort, acclaim, and education can never take the place of being *empowered, anointed, and taught* by the Holy Spirit.

THE SCHOOL OF THE SPIRIT

Let me illustrate what I mean by the School of the Holy Spirit with a story. Dr. Judy Doyle grew up in an Assemblies of God church and was saved under my ministry at a Louisiana youth camp. She went on to work full-time for the Lord and then enrolled in seminary. After much work, she earned her master's degree and her doctorate.

Shortly after graduating, Judy was standing in a crowded church one Sunday during worship. As the people around her sang, Judy raised her hands and closed her eyes, basking in the presence of God. Suddenly, she had a vision of herself as an eleven-year-old girl. She saw that she was standing with her arms filled with books, ready for school. Behind her stretched the long, dirt lane she walked each day to catch the school bus. Suddenly a voice spoke deep in her spirit: "You have sat at the feet of men. Now I am enrolling you in the school of my Spirit, and you will be taught of the Lord."

In a flash, she understood. According to the world, she was Dr. Judy Doyle, with diplomas on her office wall to prove it. But when it came to the power and demonstration of the Holy Spirit, she was just an eleven-year-old schoolgirl standing with her arms full of books, about to be enrolled in the school of the Spirit and taught of the Lord!

Each of us needs to be enrolled in this school of the Holy Spirit.

THE POWER OF THE SPIRIT AND HIS GIFTS

First Corinthians 12:1 informs us that God does not want us to be *ignorant* concerning spiritual gifts. But many believers *are* ignorant— woefully, shamefully, dangerously ignorant—regarding the mighty, supernatural gifts with which God has equipped his church. As a result, we are victims when we should be victors. Losers when we should be winners. Followers when we should be leaders. Captives when we should be more than conquerors!

The greatest unused energy in the world today is not electrical energy or atomic energy. It's not found beneath the surface of the earth in vast deposits of oil and coal. No, the greatest unused power in the world today is found *within the church* of the Lord Jesus Christ: the mighty Holy Spirit and His gifts. But God cannot do things *through us* until we will let Him work *in us*!

You don't have to remain a stranger to the supernatural. If you're hungry, if you're ready to immerse yourself in the things of God and obey whatever He says, *you* can be enrolled in the school of the Spirit. *You* can be taught of the Lord. Like Smith Wigglesworth, *you* can become a tool in His mighty hand!

Chapter 2

LONG-LOST TREASURE

But we have this treasure in earthen vessels, that the excellency of the power may be of God, and not of us.

—2 CORINTHIANS 4:7

TRUE TO HER usual routine, Elizabeth Gibson was on her way to get coffee when she noticed a large, colorful painting jammed between bags of garbage on the street. She took a closer look. Something about the painting was overpowering. Elizabeth took it home and hung it on her living room wall.

One day she took it down and examined the back. She noticed stickers from art galleries in Manhattan and Paris, so she contacted an art expert. It turned out it was a stolen masterpiece, worth an estimated $1 million! She got more than $15,000 for returning this painting to the owner, who had purchased it for his wife.[1] The painting in the cheap frame wasn't trash. It was a long-lost *treasure*!

SPIRITUAL PARALLELS

The story of that valuable painting struck a chord in my heart. Just as the painting was a gift to a man's bride, Jesus Christ gave the gift of the Holy Spirit to His bride, the church. And just as the painting was seen as practically worthless, today we as believers often miscalculate the value of the gift of the Holy Spirit.

Jesus Promised He Would Send a Comforter

Jesus promised the gift of the Holy Spirit:

> But when the Comforter is come, whom I will send unto you from the Father, *even* the Spirit of truth, which proceedeth from the Father, he shall testify of me
>
> —JOHN 15:26–27

The giving of the Holy Spirit was for a purpose—to strengthen us against the coming persecutions and to empower us to overcome. Right after Christ's promise of the Comforter, he warned of persecution and martyrdom that would follow: "These things have I spoken unto you, that ye should not be offended. They shall put you out of the synagogues; yea, the time cometh, that whosoever killeth you will think that he doeth God service" (John 16:1–2).

But Jesus also gave His disciples another powerful promise. In Matthew 16:18 Jesus declared: "…I will build my church; and the gates of hell shall not prevail against it."

His pronouncement tells us that:

- Jesus Christ *will build* his church in this world.

- His church will be battled by the world and by the strongest powers and principalities of hell itself.

- In spite of everything, the church of the Lord Jesus Christ shall continue and prevail!

Christ's Command to Wait

Christ promises us victory, but victory must have seemed very far away for the tiny group of followers that He left behind after His resurrection. How were they to overcome? And how are we? Christ did not forget them or us. He has not left us alone, weak, and comfortless. He promises the Holy Spirit. This was so critical, that before He ascended, He commanded His followers not to leave Jerusalem, but to wait in prayer for the coming of the Holy Spirit whom the Father had promised (Acts 1:4–7). This was a priority to get the power they needed:

> But you shall receive power (ability, efficiency, and might) when the Holy Spirit has come upon you, and you shall be My witnesses in Jerusalem and all Judea and Samaria and to the ends (the very bounds) of the earth.
>
> —ACTS 1:8, AMP

Did Jesus' followers have any idea how much hinged upon their obedience to His command? Probably not, but thank God, they obeyed! The apostles, the women, Mary the mother of Jesus, his brothers, and the few remaining disciples—about 120 believers in all—went to an upstairs room in Jerusalem. For ten days they prayed for the Holy Spirit, and their prayers were answered on the Day of Pentecost, 33 AD, in Jerusalem. That was when the Church—the bride of Christ— was called into life and began to be built through the Spirit's powers and gifts, just as Jesus promised. Luke relates what happened:

> And when the day of Pentecost was fully come, they were all with one accord in one place. And suddenly there came a sound from heaven as of a rushing mighty wind and it filled all the house where they were sitting. And there appeared unto them cloven tongues like as of fire, and it sat upon each of them. And they were all filled with the Holy Ghost and began to speak with other tongues, as the Spirit gave them utterance.
> —Acts 2:1–4

You Shall Receive Power!

Like the rush of a mighty wind, Christ's promised gift of power from on high blew into the Upper Room. They were all filled with the Holy Spirit. It was as if a great flame from God enveloped them, set them on fire, and they became living torches! A radical new love and a revolutionary new courage and zeal consumed them. From that moment on, they became new men and women.

You Shall Be My Witnesses!

God-fearing Jews from every nation under heaven who were staying in Jerusalem at that time rushed together to see what was happening. They listened in awe as they heard in their own languages glorious words declaring God's plan of salvation and His purposes for the future.

Luke tells us that it was Peter who stood up and addressed the astonished crowd, saying:

> But this is that which was spoken by the prophet Joel: And it shall come to pass in the last days, saith God, I will pour out of my Spirit upon all flesh: and your sons and your daughters shall prophesy, and your young men shall see visions, and your old men shall dream dreams: And on my servants and

on my handmaidens I will pour out in those days of my Spirit;
and they shall prophesy.

—ACTS 2:16–18

At the conclusion of Peter's message, the crowd cried out:

Men and brethren, what shall we do? Then Peter said unto
them, Repent and be baptized every one of you in the name
of Jesus Christ for the remission of sins, and ye shall receive
the gift of the Holy Ghost. For the promise is unto you, and to
your children, and to all that are afar off even as many as the
Lord our God shall call.

—ACTS 2:37–39

Notice that Peter did not say that the gift of the Holy Ghost was just
for the 120 in the Upper Room. He did not say it was only for the 3,000
who had just heard his message. Peter said, "The promise is unto you,
and to your children, and to all that are afar off, even as many as the
Lord our God shall call" (Acts 2:39).

Just as Jesus had promised, His followers received power after His
promised gift of the Holy Ghost came upon them, and they became
His witnesses. The Bible records that after Peter's message that day,
about *3,000 people* believed and were added to their number!

SUPERNATURAL EMPOWERMENT IS PROMISED

Through the influence and empowerment of the Holy Spirit, a church
developed which was endowed with supernatural callings and powerful spiritual gifts. As more and more of Christ's followers received
the Holy Spirit and his gifts, the Lord was able to manifest himself and
his ministry through his church.

The powerful witness expanded and soon included the Gentiles.
The Word of God documents that wherever the leaders and people of
the early church went, widespread manifestations of the Holy Spirit
took place—sudden conversions, tongues, miracles, exorcisms, resur-
rections of the dead, and signs and wonders.

THE SUPERNATURAL CONTINUES

After Christ bestowed the power of the Holy Spirit upon the church, the signs, wonders, and supernatural manifestations didn't stop. They didn't stop with the book of Acts. They didn't stop with the deaths of the apostles and the end of the apostolic age. They didn't stop when the New Testament was completed. No unbiased scholar of church history can examine all the evidence and truthfully argue otherwise. As we are about to see, all down through history, scattered manifestations of the spiritual gifts and various supernatural signs and wonders continued to play a pivotal role in the expansion of the church.

If that is true—and church history verifies that it is—then why did the gifts of the Holy Spirit, signs and wonders, and supernatural manifestations decrease and sometimes disappear from mainstream Christianity?

I would like to answer that by returning to the story about the million-dollar painting put out with the garbage. A similar thing has happened with the multi-billion dollar gifts of the Holy Spirit.

As the early church grappled with infighting and political controversies, one after another, she gradually moved away from her original focus. Spiritual gifts began disappearing from the daily life and witness of ordinary believers, as well as from the worship and ministry of the church. These things were, in effect, put out on the curb. It seemed the church had more important things to do!

The apparent absence of the gifts of the Spirit (*charismata*) led church leaders to believe that they had ended. They taught that they ended with the apostles, or with the completion of the New Testament. In the wake of this false teaching, the manifestations and operations of the supernatural were stolen away from mainline Christendom for centuries.

However, the gifts of the Spirit did not cease. They continued in scattered, supernatural "power surges" throughout church history, as documented in several studies.[2]

So we find ourselves in a situation in which the gifts of the Spirit are available, but many, even today, reject them. In the light of the scriptural and historical evidence, why do Christians today reject the Spirit's gifts for us? It is for the same reasons Elizabeth Green almost rejected the million-dollar painting she found in the trash.

Questionable surroundings. The painting in the garbage
seemed certainly out of place. Just so, the gifts of the Holy
Spirit are often manifested in strange locations— in rough
neighborhoods, among alcoholics, among the poor, rarely
among the rich and beautiful. As scripture says, "God has
chosen the foolish things of the world to shame the wise, and
God has chosen the weak things of the world to shame the
things which are strong and the base things of the world and
the despised God has chosen, the things that are not, so that
He may nullify the things that are, so that no man may boast
before God" (1 Cor. 1:27–29 NASB).

Lack of interest. The woman who found the painting had
never been a fan of modern art and wasn't sure she wanted
an example of it. Just so, some have never acquired a taste for
the miraculous. They are just not interested. But dear ones,
it is not a question of what we want, but what God wants, as
Christ prayed in the garden, "Not my will, but thine be done."
What God wants was expressed by Christ when He said, "wait
in Jerusalem until you are clothed with power from on high."

Overcrowding. The woman didn't want the painting because
her apartment was so full. There was little room for anything
else. What a parallel to our lives today! How full they are! We
have so many labor-saving and time-saving devices, but we
seem to have less time than ever before. Our time is eaten up
with television, computers, Facebook, text messages, Netflix,
hobbies, and what have you. If we, dear reader, want to move
into the realm of God's supernatural, it may be necessary to
remove some of the distractions and overcrowding in our
schedules. As someone once said, if you are too busy to pray,
you are too busy!

The cheap frame. The woman thought the painting had little
value, or it wouldn't have been mounted in such a cheap
frame. Right? Many people have walked away from the
miraculous because of the "cheap frames" in which they have
been displayed. Maybe they couldn't see past the country
preacher in the cheap rumpled suit. Maybe the service was
wild and undignified. Certainly, genuine movements of the

Spirit have sometimes been devalued by their "cheap frames" of fanaticism, extreme physical manifestations, sinful life-styles, bizarre teachings, or emotionalism. At other times, the "frames" have been spiritual awakenings that were criticized by society as strange, and by mainline denominations as unscriptural. Sometimes the gifts of the Spirit have been framed in poor and uneducated faces and unfamiliar traditions. As a result, many have rejected and walked away from the long-lost treasure of the Spirit, deeming it beneath their dignity and unworthy of their attention.

An Important Reminder

The Lord knows how easy it is to miss the treasure in the trash, and so He has given us His word as a precaution so we don't get distracted by the cheap frames. As Paul reminded us so poignantly, "...We have this treasure in earthen vessels that the excellency of the power may be of God, and not of us" (2 Cor. 4:7). The Holy Spirit has seen fit to manifest himself in jars of clay through imperfect people. Therefore, as we undertake this study of the Holy Spirit and His supernatural gifts and miraculous gifts and miraculous manifestations, may we remember that even the finest and best of men and women are only *"cheap frames"* displaying the spiritual treasure inside. May God help us look past the frames, however flawed or tawdry, and recognize and cherish the priceless treasure contained within!

Chapter 3

OUR NEED FOR A MENTOR

I WANT YOU TO stop and think about something with me.

What do you suppose would happen in your life if you had the daily help of someone very successful, someone who has already done the things you want to do?

This person (called a mentor) would do everything he could to advise and help you succeed in your job and in your relationships. With someone like that, it would be practically impossible to fail! He has already done it. He knows where the shortcuts are, and will help you avoid the pitfalls.

The good news is that you *have* such a mentor. He is the Holy Spirit.

The word *mentor* comes from Greek mythology. Mentor was a faithful friend of Odysseus. When Odysseus went to fight the Trojans, he left his son with Mentor to be taught and advised. Today, the word *mentor* means a wise and trusted adviser, counselor, teacher, guide, or tutor.

History shows us the value of having a mentor like that.

SOME FAMOUS MENTOR PAIRS IN SECULAR HISTORY

Here are just a few:

- NFL coach Bill Walsh mentored quarterback Joe Montana, who won four Super Bowls with the San Francisco 49ers.

- NBA coach Phil Jackson mentored Michael Jordan, five-time NBA Most Valuable Player—considered the greatest basketball player of all time.

- Greek mathematician Archimedes mentored Italian scientist Galileo, who then invented the modern telescope and discovered that the planets revolve around the sun.

- Former slave trader John Newton became a clergyman and wrote the famous hymn *Amazing Grace*. He mentored William Wilberforce, the British politician who led the movement to abolish slavery in Great Britain.

- Economist Ludwig von Mises mentored former U.S. President Ronald Reagan, who challenged Soviet leader, Mikhail Gorbachev, to "tear down this wall!" Months after the end of his term, the Berlin Wall fell, and the Soviet Union collapsed soon thereafter. President Reagan was among the greatest presidents we have known.

- Teacher Anne Sullivan mentored Helen Keller, a blind, deaf, and mute girl who later graduated from college and became a world-famous author and speaker.

SOME FAMOUS MENTORING PAIRS IN THE BIBLE

Although the word *mentor* is not in the Bible, we do find many successful mentoring relationships.

- Moses wrote the first five books of the Bible and delivered Israel from slavery in Egypt. He mentored Joshua, who led the children of Israel into the Promised Land and conquered Canaan.

- The Israelite widow Naomi mentored Ruth, her Moabite daughter-in-law, who, as a result, married her kinsman-redeemer Boaz and became an ancestor of King David and Jesus Christ.

- Elijah, the loftiest and most wonderful prophet of the Old Testament, mentored his attendant and disciple Elisha. He received a double portion of Elijah's anointing and judged Israel for sixty years.

- Elizabeth, mother of John the Baptist, mentored Mary, the mother of Jesus.

- Jesus mentored His disciples.

- The prophet and teacher Barnabas mentored former persecutor Paul, who went on to found many churches and wrote half of the New Testament.

- Paul mentored his son in the faith, Timothy, who served as his assistant and later became an evangelist, pastor, and regional leader.

THE NEED FOR A MENTOR

Why did I take the time to tell you about those famous mentors? What would have happened without the influence of those mentors in science, media, politics, and athletics? What about the mentors in the Bible that I mentioned? Would we ever have heard of those they mentored otherwise? Maybe. Maybe not.

Would the world ever have heard of Helen Keller if Anne Sullivan had not devoted her life to mentoring this angry, confused, blind, deaf, and mute girl? Would Helen have discovered her gifts and fulfilled her higher destiny? I don't think so. A *mentor* made the difference!

I'm convinced that multiplied thousands of sincere Christians feel as frustrated and helpless as that little blind, deaf, and mute child when it comes to understanding the things of the Spirit. Something inside them is restless and discontented. They've advanced about as far as they can on their own.

Perhaps that is your case. You don't want to go backward, but you don't know how to go forward. You know that God has more for you, but you feel like a blind person groping along, trying to find the steps that will lead you higher. You know that God wants to speak to you, but it's as if you are deaf to His still, small voice. And like Helen Keller, you may feel mute when it comes to knowing how to minister the gifts of the Holy Spirit.

I minister to a lot of people, and I *rejoice* when they talk to me about going deeper with God. Some of them have a rich Pentecostal heritage passed down from former generations of their family, but they're not satisfied with *memories of yesterday*. They're crying out to God for *manifestations today*!

On the other hand, many Christians I minister to have little, if any, Pentecostal background. But some of them have heard about Pentecostal pioneers who walked in the miraculous. They've read about old-timers who were called "prayer warriors"—faithful believers who were willing to shoulder another's burden, travail in the Spirit for the answer, and persevere until they prayed through. They've been told about amazing miracles that took place when those men and women of faith prayed for the sick. They've heard testimonies of how God spoke to their forerunners and led them supernaturally. What they've heard has created *a holy hunger* inside them, and they're crying out for more! However, few of those powerful people from former generations are still around to teach them.

And so people come to me during an altar call or after a service and say, "I'm so hungry for the supernatural! I want to hear God's voice speaking to *me*. I want to be equipped to help others, but I don't know how or where to start. I need somebody to guide me, to teach me. I need a *mentor*, Brother Gorman!"

God Honors Perseverance

I can identify with that hunger for God and His supernatural gifts! When I was a young Christian, I read of the miracles that took place in Bible days, and I also wanted supernatural demonstrations of God's power. I began setting aside hours to pray and wait before God so the gifts of the Spirit would be manifested through my life.

When I was sixteen, Pastor Tanner, from First Assembly of God in Camden, Arkansas, invited a well-known healing evangelist, at that time, to conduct a crusade at his church. Pastor Tanner's son served as the church's minister of music and associate pastor. He asked me to play my guitar in the orchestra. Therefore, I had a front-row seat to the numerous manifestations of the Holy Spirit night after night.

I saw for myself the supernatural operation of the gifts of the Spirit. I began to understand their tremendous value. Believers were strengthened, exhorted, edified, and comforted. The gifts of the Spirit confirmed God's Word; demonstrated His love, mercy, and power; and healed the sick. They served as signs to unbelievers, drew the lost to Jesus, and unmasked and triumphed over demonic spirits. Supernatural words of wisdom and knowledge came when they were needed. As a result, I began asking God for the nine supernatural gifts of the Spirit:

> But the manifestation of the Spirit is given to each one for
> the profit of all: for to one is given the word of wisdom
> through the Spirit, to another the word of knowledge
> through the same Spirit, to another faith by the same Spirit,
> to another gifts of healings by the same Spirit, to another
> the working of miracles, to another prophecy, to another
> discerning of spirits, to another different kinds of tongues,
> to another the interpretation of tongues. But one and the
> same Spirit works all these things, distributing to each one
> individually as He wills.
>
> —1 CORINTHIANS 12:7–11, NKJV

At the close of this meeting, I had such an intense hunger in my
heart that I spent several days fasting and praying. Since I had not
grown up in such an atmosphere, I had no idea how to approach God
to receive these gifts. I did not understand that when I had been baptized in the Holy Spirit, the potential for these gifts operating through
my life was placed at my disposal. However, I knew that Paul said to
Timothy, "Do not neglect the gift that is in you…" (1 Tim. 4:14, NKJV),
and reminded Timothy to "stir up the gift of God which is in you…"
(2 Tim. 1:6, NKJV). Paul told the Corinthians to "earnestly desire the
best gifts" (1 Cor. 12:31). He said, "Since you are zealous for spiritual
gifts, let it be for the edification of the church that you seek to excel"
(1 Cor. 14:12, NKJV).

I began praying that God would allow me to give a message in
tongues. This went on for several weeks. Suddenly, in one of the services, something rose up inside me that was so powerful it was difficult to contain. A powerful message in tongues burst forth, and
the pastor gave the anointed interpretation. I had told God that if he
would just let me give a message in tongues, I would be content. Little
did I realize that once I gave a message in tongues, the desire for other
gifts would intensify.

Next, I began praying that God would allow me to interpret
a message in tongues. Finally, that day came. I will never forget
how I stood trembling and weeping uncontrollably after I gave
the interpretation. After that, I focused on the gift of healing, fervently praying that God would let me pray for someone and that the
person would be healed.

We had seen people healed when a group of us gathered around them and prayed. Now I asked the Lord to let me pray for someone and to let them be healed without any other Christian being present. I didn't pray that because I was on an ego trip; I just wanted to know with certainty that God was using me.

It wasn't long until God allowed me to pray for a person and see them miraculously healed. This only fueled my desire for more gifts. As a result, I kept praying that way for about a year, and God answered! I can truthfully say I personally witnessed all nine gifts listed in 1 Cor. 12:8–11 operating through my life. I didn't stop there. The desire to be used by God in the gifts of the Spirit has stayed with me from that day to this.

God heard and honored my earnest prayers to minister to people, and He will hear and answer *your* prayers, too, for He wants to bless and empower the body of Christ. God is no respecter of persons. He doesn't play favorites. He honors the obedience, faith, and persistence of His children.

ASK WITHOUT FEAR

As you seek these gifts, I would like to encourage you to read Matthew 7:7–11 about persistence in prayer. Present imperatives are used in the Greek text here, indicating that Jesus is speaking of *constant, persistent* asking, seeking and knocking when we pray. He is telling us to ask *and keep on* asking; seek *and keep on* seeking; knock *and keep on* knocking. Please slow down and meditate on that as you're reading the verses from the Amplified Bible:

> Keep on asking and it will be given you; keep on seeking and you will find; keep on knocking [reverently] and [the door] will be opened to you. For every one who keeps on asking receives, and he who keeps on seeking finds, and to him who keeps on knocking [the door] will be opened. Or what man is there of you, if his son asks him for a loaf of bread, will hand him a stone? Or if he asks for a fish, will hand him a serpent? If you then, evil as you are, know how to give good and advantageous gifts to your children, how much more will your Father Who is in heaven [perfect as He is] give good and advantageous things to those who keep on asking Him!
>
> —MATTHEW 7:7–11, AMP

When we ask God for gifts, we don't have to fear that He'll give us something harmful. God's gifts are good, and they are to be received and used for good. That's why I confidently urge *all* Spirit-filled believers—not just the lay people in the congregation, but also the ministers on the platform—to earnestly, persistently *ask* and *expect* God to manifest the precious, powerful gifts of the Holy Spirit through them according to His sovereign will and purposes.

JESUS KEPT HIS PROMISE

As the end of Jesus' earthly ministry was approaching, He said to His disciples: "I tell you the truth; It is expedient for you that I go away: for if I go not away, the Comforter will not come unto you; but if I depart, I will send him unto you" (John 16:7).

Now that's the way it reads in our King James Version. But if we look up the meanings of the words *expedient* and *Comforter* in that verse, what Jesus was saying to His disciples becomes much clearer. He was saying:

> It is expedient [to your advantage: better, good, profitable] for you that I go away: for if I go not away, the Comforter [*parakletos*—par-ak'-lay-tos: *intercessor, consoler, advocate*] will not come unto you. But if I depart, I will send Him unto you.
> —JOHN 16:7, WITH STRONG'S CONCORDANCE NUMBERS

That must have been incomprehensible to Jesus' disciples! How could the *spiritual presence of the Holy Spirit* be preferred to the *physical presence of the human Jesus*? Surely they would be impoverished, not enriched, by Jesus' physical absence!

The disciples couldn't imagine how Jesus' absence from them could be anything except tragic! They had no way of knowing that Jesus' physical absence would mean His intimate presence on a higher plane.

This was because during His earthly life, Jesus was limited geographically by His physical body. He couldn't be in two places at once. Think about it. If He was busy teaching the multitudes on a mountainside, Jesus couldn't be standing by the seashore talking to Peter, James, and John at the same time, could He? Let's say that Andrew wanted to ask Jesus a question, yet Jesus was in another location ministering to the woman at the well. Either Andrew was going to have to go to where Jesus was, or he was going to have to wait until Jesus returned to where Andrew was.

During Jesus' earthly ministry, was He with each disciple every hour of the day, every day of the week? Of course not. There were times when Jesus chose to be alone. There were times when only the disciples that He selected accompanied Him to certain places. Every disciple could not personally be with Jesus all the time.

So, Jesus was geographically limited by His physical body. Furthermore, Jesus' influence on the disciples was from the *outside* in. When Jesus walked the earth with His disciples, He didn't live inside them. But when Jesus ascended to His Father in heaven and the Holy Spirit—the promised Helper, Advocate, Paraclete—was given, Christ's physical presence was exchanged for His omnipresence.

The Holy Spirit is omnipresent. He isn't limited by having a physical body. No matter where the people of God may be scattered across the face of this earth, no matter what they need, the Holy Spirit is equally accessible to us all. Furthermore, the Holy Spirit is an internal presence, not an external presence. Therefore, it is from *inside* the regenerated human heart that the Holy Spirit carries on His work through us.

Jesus told His disciples that it was to their advantage that He go away, for if He did not go away, the Comforter would not come.

Who was this Comforter? Why was it so advantageous that He come? Jesus promised that if He went away, He would send us an intercessor, consoler, and advocate…a supporter, backer, promoter to be *in* us— another Helper constantly on call right there at our side!"

OUR NEED FOR A MENTOR

I know in my spirit that multitudes of believers in the Body of Christ today feel trapped in a purposeless, unfulfilling, wasteful existence. They're realizing their desperate need for a mentor who can open the world of the Spirit to them. I declare to them right now that they already *have* a mentor. He is the Holy Spirit, *the Master Mentor!*

You don't have to wait any longer. Close your eyes. Lift your hands. Open your heart. Begin to worship Him aloud from the depths of your soul. Joyously, hungrily embrace Him and all He is for you. Follow the Master Mentor into a whole new life!

Part 2

INTRODUCING THE GIFTS OF THE SPIRIT

*Now concerning spiritual gifts, brethren, I
would not have you ignorant.*

—1 CORINTHIANS 12:1

IT IS THROUGH the power of the Holy Spirit that the church of
Jesus Christ becomes an invincible force, stronger than any power
on earth. The Bible prophesies of this power in Daniel 2:44: "In the
days of those kings the God of heaven will set up a kingdom which
will never be destroyed, and that kingdom will not be left for another
people; it will crush and put an end to all these kingdoms, but it will
itself endure forever."

The power of the Holy Spirit is revealed in the church through the nine gifts listed in 1 Corinthians 12:1–11. These may be divided into three categories—Revelation, Power, and Inspiration:

THREE GIFTS OF REVELATION	THREE GIFTS OF POWER	THREE GIFTS OF INSPIRATION
These reveal something.	**These do something.**	**These say something.**
Word of wisdom	Faith	Prophecy
Word of knowledge	Working of miracles	Unknown tongues
Discerning of spirits	Gifts of healing	Interpretation of tongues

- **The three revelation gifts** (the word of wisdom, the word of knowledge, and discerning of spirits) are the vehicles God uses to reveal things to His people that they could not know about in the natural or by way of their physical senses.

- **The three power gifts** (the gift of faith, of the working of miracles, and of healings) are God's artillery of signs and wonders used to destroy the works of the devil!

- **The three inspirational (or vocal) gifts** (the gifts of prophecy, unknown tongues and interpretation of tongues) are the vehicles God uses to supernaturally build up, strengthen, and encourage His people.

In the following section, we will examine the revelation gifts, starting with the word of wisdom.

Chapter 4

THE GIFT OF THE WORD OF WISDOM

To one is given by the Spirit the word of wisdom.
—1 CORINTHIANS 12:8

THE WORD OF wisdom is a manifestation of the Holy Spirit and is the first and greatest of the nine gifts of the Spirit—divine wisdom from heaven. The word of wisdom has nothing to do with our wisdom, any more than the gift of tongues has any correspondence with a linguistic gift, or the gift of healing has any relationship with the medical profession. We must draw the line as clearly as possible between what is natural and what is supernatural, for there are natural gifts and there are supernatural gifts.

Howard Carter emphasizes several important points concerning this gift. First, notice that it is not *a gift of wisdom*. There is no gift of wisdom promised in the Bible; God only offers us the gift of "a word of wisdom."[1]

Second, the word of wisdom has always been *directive*. Whenever God speaks to a man directly—as when He spoke to Jonah and said, "Go to Nineveh"—He is giving him a word of His wisdom.[2]

Third, the word of wisdom can come to a child (as in the case of the boy Samuel, I Sam. 3:1–21), because it is God's wisdom and not the child's wisdom.

The gift of the word of wisdom is also *predictive*. Harold Horton states that the gift of the word of wisdom is the supernatural revelation, by the Holy Spirit, of God's divine purpose. It is the supernatural declaration of the mind and will of God. It is the supernatural unfolding of His plans and purposes concerning things, places, people, individuals, communities, and nations.

Horton continues: "In a word, *the word of wisdom* is expressed not only in foretelling events, but in those commands and instructions which God gives men arising out of His knowledge of those future events."[3]

The gift of the word of wisdom is the revealing of *the prophetic future* under the anointing of God. For instance, in addition to the above, the word of wisdom is given by the Spirit when a situation arises that requires supernatural wisdom. For example, in a time of severe persecution of Protestant Christians in a foreign country, the story is told of a young woman who was on her way to secret Bible study one evening when she was stopped by soldiers.

"Where are you headed?" the men demanded angrily. Terrified, but refusing to lie, she shot a prayer heavenward for help, and it was answered as God gave her a word of wisdom.

"I am on my way to hear the reading of my elder brother's will," she responded. Satisfied, the soldiers let her proceed unharmed.

The gift of the word of wisdom is not the natural wisdom of James 1:5. The word of wisdom is a supernatural revelation by the Spirit of God concerning the divine purpose in the mind and will of God that is going to take place in the future.

> The Gift of the Word of Wisdom is both directive and predictive. It is expressed not only in foretelling events, but in those commands and instructions which God gives men, arising out of His knowledge of those future events…
>
> Many also believe that, in addition to the above, the word of wisdom is a fragment of divine wisdom imparted by the Spirit when a situation arises that requires supernatural wisdom.

SOME EXAMPLES OF THE GIFT OF WISDOM IN THE OLD TESTAMENT

Lester Sumrall points out that all the prophets of the Bible were endowed with the spiritual gift of wisdom. They were seers of the future, making known God's wisdom about what would come to pass. For example, it was through this gift that Moses received the Ten Commandments and the ceremonial ordinances of Leviticus. It was also a word of wisdom that conveyed God's specific instructions when He commanded Elijah to anoint Hazael, Jehu, and Elisha, or when He gave Jonah his decree to Ninevah—a message that was a prophecy, a threat, and an exhortation. The power motivating and inspiring men like Noah (Gen. 6:12–13), Ezekiel (Ezek. 38 and 39), Daniel (who saw great visions of empires coming into existence and the nature of those empires), David (Ps. 2 and 22), Joel (Joel 2:28), and Isaiah (Isa. 53), etc., is the same power that inspires and motivates us today: the power of the Holy Spirit. Sumrall emphasizes that we should expect the gifts of the Spirit to function in our lives just as they did during Old Testament times.[4]

When discussing manifestations of the word of wisdom in the New Testament, Sumrall calls attention to the fact that the ministry of the Lord Jesus Christ was foremost among those demonstrating the word of wisdom in the New Testament. In Matthew 24, Luke 21, and Mark 13, Jesus foretold the destruction of the temple in Jerusalem, which came a few years later, and the signs that would accompany His return to earth for His church. Many of these things are coming to pass in our generation. Some of them have yet to come to pass. All this is what the word of God's wisdom is—a revelation of the future.[5]

Sumrall also calls attention to other examples of the word of wisdom in the New Testament. For example, in several epistles to the church, the apostle Paul revealed things that would come to pass in the last days. Also, the apostle Peter was very emphatic about signs that would come to pass before the Lord Jesus returned. The gift was functioning for the apostle Paul in Acts 23, when Paul almost lost his life at the hands of an angry Jewish mob. When it looked as if he would die, the Lord spoke to him by the word of wisdom and said: "Be of good cheer, Paul: for as thou hast testified of me in Jerusalem, so must thou bear witness also at Rome" (Acts 23:11). Paul had no way of knowing he would ever speak for God in Rome, but God revealed the future to him. That was the word of God's wisdom.[6]

HOW THE WORD OF WISDOM IS MANIFESTED

Harold Horton explains that the Holy Spirit can convey the word of wisdom in many ways. For example, the word of wisdom, in our day as in times past, may be manifested through the *audible divine Voice*, by *angelic visitation*, by *dream* or *vision*, or through the spiritual *gift of prophecy*, or the *gift of tongues* and *gift of interpretation*.[7]

However, Howard Carter explains that a word of wisdom may be included when one gives an interpretation of a tongue only if the one who is interpreting possesses the gift of the word of wisdom. To further clarify, Carter states:

> It may come, as some have suggested, in a message in tongues
> and interpretation, but it cannot come, let it be clearly

understood, unless the one who is interpreting has the word of wisdom. If he/she possesses nothing more than the interpretation of tongues, then nothing more will be manifested in the utterance of tongues but the simplest inspired utterance, which will be to edification, exhortation or comfort, for it should be stated that tongues with interpretation are the equivalent of prophecy, the sixth gift of the Spirit.[8]

Carter also explains that the word of wisdom might come in the simplest form of inspired prophecy, if the person who is prophesying possesses this greatest of all gifts.[9]

In *The Gifts and Ministries of the Holy Spirit*, Sumrall sheds light upon ways the word of wisdom may be manifested by the Holy Spirit, as is reiterated below:[10]

Through the Interpreting of a Dream

When Joseph was seventeen years old, God showed him through a dream and its interpretation that he would be a great leader and that his own brothers would bow down to him. Joseph's father and brothers did not believe his dreams, but they came to pass (Gen. 37:5–11; Gen. 42:6–9; Gen. 45).

By a Night Vision

Daniel received wisdom by a night vision. It was the word of wisdom projected into the future (Dan. 7 and 8, for example.).

By Being Caught Away in the Spirit

Ezekiel was caught away in the Spirit for a revelation (Ezekiel 8).

By Receiving a Revelation when We are in the Spirit

While the apostle John was in the Spirit on the Lord's Day, the entire book of Revelation flashed before him.

By Being Caught up into "the Third Heaven"

When speaking of visions and revelations of the Lord, the apostle Paul describes how he was caught up to the third heaven and heard unspeakable words which it was not lawful for him to utter. Paul says that whether it happened in the body or out of the body, he did not know (See 2 Cor. 12:1–4).

By Angelic Visitation

In Daniel 10, the prophet tells how an awesome angel appeared to him in a great vision to make him understand what would befall his people in the latter days.

By an Audible Voice

When Moses went into the tabernacle after it was first erected, he heard the voice of One speaking to him from the mercy seat.[11]

God Can Speak to us However He Wants To

Sumrall stresses that in this matter of choosing to reveal a word of wisdom, God can speak to us however He wants to.

> God has no set way of dealing with the problems of this world. He unveils hidden mysteries and the wisdom to execute His counsels in the way He considers best at that time…Many times we think Jesus can do things only one way, but that is not true. The same is true with the word of wisdom. It does not have to function the same way each time…God has many ways to do things. He can work with you in a unique way—a way He has not operated in before. He can do whatever He wants to do.[12]

THE DIFFERENCE BETWEEN THE GIFT OF PROPHECY AND THE WORD OF WISDOM

How can we distinguish between the operation of the simple inspiration of the gift of prophecy and the gift of the word of wisdom? By noting that there is no element of revelation associated with the gift of prophecy.

1 Cor. 14:3 states the full measure of the blessings of prophecy: "But he that prophesieth speaketh unto men to edification, and exhortation, and comfort." Note that revelation is not mentioned when it comes to the gift of prophecy. As Sumrall explains:

> Any person who speaks out in church, foretelling the future, has left his simple gift of prophecy and has moved into the greatest and foremost revelation gift—the word of wisdom—whereby he foresees the future. The prophet of either the Old Testament or the New Testament is a seer. He sees into the future and possesses the gift of the word of God's wisdom to tell the future.[13]

SOME SCRIPTURAL EXAMPLES OF THE
USE OF THE WORD OF WISDOM

Horton lists some scriptural examples of the use of the word of wisdom
to help demonstrate how indispensable this gift is to mere mortals.[14]

**To Warn and Guide People Concerning Future Judgment or Peril,
Delivering Them out of Danger**

"And God said unto Noah, The end of all flesh is come before Me…I
will destroy them…Make thee an ark" (Gen. 6:13–22).

"And the men said unto Lot, Hast thou here any besides? Bring them
out…for we will destroy this place…" (Gen. 19:12–13).

"And being warned of God in a dream that they should not return to
Herod, they departed into their own country another way" (Matt. 2:12).

To Reveal God's Plans to those He is Going to Use

"And Joseph answered Pharaoh, it is not in me: God shall give
Pharaoh an answer….What God is about to do He sheweth unto
Pharaoh…Famine…look out a man discreet and wise….lay up
corn….And Pharaoh said, Can we find such a one….In whom the
Spirit of God is? See, I have set thee over all the land of Egypt" (Gen.
41:16, 28–41).

To Assure a Servant of God of His Divine Commission

Forty years in the Midian desert. Eighty years old. How was Moses
to know he must yet deliver his brethren? A Shekinah-illumined
bush and the voice of God: "Come now therefore, and I will send
thee unto Pharaoh, that thou mayest bring forth my people out of
Egypt" (Ex. 3:10).

"I heard a voice speaking unto me, and saying in the Hebrew tongue,
Saul, Saul why persecutest thou me? It is hard for thee to kick against
the pricks…But rise, and stand upon thy feet: for I have appeared
unto thee for this purpose, to make thee a minister…" (Acts 26:14, 16).

To Reveal the Acceptable Order and Manner of Divine Worship

How shall God's people, now grown into a nation, lately come from
idolatrous influences in Egypt, with no written word for a guide—
how shall they know in what way Jehovah may be approached in His
awful holiness by the sin-stained children of men? Moses receives the
whole, mighty scheme of redemption in detail in an object lesson—the

tabernacle with its blood-stained way into the presence. "And look that thou make them after their pattern, which was shewed thee in the mount" (Ex. 25:40).

To Unfold to a Prejudiced, Religious, Legalist God's Universal Offers of Grace

How can Peter, a fanatical Judaist, be convinced of the glorious truth that Jehovah loves godless Gentiles and died for even them? God gave him a vision of a sheet let down from heaven containing animals, both clean and unclean. Jews were forbidden to eat unclean animals. God used this vision to show Peter that His gifts of salvation and the Holy Spirit are for the Gentiles as well as the Jews. The Gentiles were considered unclean. "What God hath cleansed, that call not thou common" (See Acts 10:13, 15). A word of wisdom was opened unto the outcast Gentiles.

To Assure of Coming Deliverance in the Midst of Calamity

A helpless ship was mercilessly driven and tossed before a tempestuous wind. No sun by day. No star by night. Exhausted mariners. Bursting planks and splintering masts. All hope was gone. An angel of God appeared to Paul and said, "Fear not, Paul; thou must be brought before Caesar: and, lo, God hath given thee all them that sail with thee" (Acts 27:24, 14–24.).

To Reveal the Will of God in all His Commands and Ordinances

Every "Thou shalt" or "Thou shalt not" is really a gracious unfolding of eternal purpose, a prophecy of blessedness, appropriateness, and relevance to take us where God would have us go.

To Declare God's Future Acts and Providences and His Eternal Mysteries

How can we learn the secret things that belong to the Lord? Only by words of divine wisdom. By revelation Paul can confidently announce, "Behold, I show you a mystery," concerning the sleeping and living saints at the coming of the Lord (1 Cor. 15:51). By revelation, the apostle John saw the great white throne judgment and the dead, small and great, standing there as the book of life and the other books were opened (Rev. 20:11–15).

To Give Assurance of Blessing to Come

Jacob saw the angels of God ascending that night in Haran, revealing the constant presence of his fathers' God, and was assured: "The land whereon thou liest, to thee will I give it and to thy seed...I will not leave thee until I have done that which I have spoken to thee of" (Gen. 28:10–15).

MORE MODERN DAY USES OF THE GIFT OF THE WORD OF WISDOM

To Warn an Individual of Approaching Danger and to Deliver from Harm

Horton shares a story a lonely old woman of God told him about the terrible days in Ireland when to be out on the streets after curfew was to invite the flying bullets and the flashing knives of the lawless. The hardworking old woman, who single-handedly ran a little kitchen bakery from her home, recalled how God spoke and warned her of danger:

> I was counting my week's takings on a Friday afternoon, a matter of perhaps twelve pounds. Sitting on that chair, I was. A voice plainly said, "Put that money away!"
>
> I looked round. Nobody in the room. I stepped to the door. Nobody in the street. I went on counting and making up my little book.
>
> The voice again, louder. "Put that money away!" I looked round again. No person near. "Yes, Lord," I said, recognizing His warning voice, "I am just finishing now."
>
> Then louder than ever, "Put that money away!"
>
> I got afraid and pushed the money quickly under a cushion on that couch when immediately two roughs came in at the door.
>
> "Hullo, Auntie!" said one; "We have come to see you."
>
> "You are not my nephews," I said.
>
> Then one took me by the throat and, pressing me back into a chair, put a pistol to my forehead, saying, "Where is your money?" The other man was searching all the drawers in the room.
>
> "I am a child of God," I said, "and that pistol will never go off!"
>
> Then the Spirit of the Lord got hold of me, and I shouted,

"In the name of the Lord Jesus I command you to leave this house!"

Without another word they both took to their heels and I have never seen or heard of them from that day to this. What a blessing I didn't put the money in the drawer! Whoever would have thought of looking for money under a cushion on that old couch! Praise the Lord![15]

To Make Known or Confirm a Missionary Call

Horton relates the following true story:

> A young woman in Wales received a missionary call from the Lord. How should she know the precise field of her future labors? She waited on the Lord in prayer. In a vision, she boarded a great ship and arrived at a strange port. Unaccustomed houses all of one sort: flat-topped. A great company of little children ran to her and clung to her arms and clothing. As they lifted their heads, she saw under their conical hats yellow faces and almond eyes. China! A few years later she landed on the shores of the Orient and saw the exact houses of her vision and the same group of little children clinging to her arms and garments.[16]

To Tell of Blessing or Judgment to Come

In regard to a word of wisdom foretelling judgment, Horton tells of an occasion in a testimony meeting when a stranger arose to give his testimony, but he was lying. The leader of the meeting stood and spoke by the Spirit that unless the stranger repented, he would be lying dead within three weeks. The man did not repent. Within three weeks of that date, he was killed by a bullet in the war.[17]

On the other hand, Howard Carter got a word of wisdom foretelling blessing—"heaps upon heaps" of money:

> It was the year 1919. Six of us were gathered together for an hour of prayer in a pastor's home in the north of London. The Lord spoke to us, "Gather My people together, saith the Lord; gather from the north, and from the south, from the east and from the west, and build for Me. It shall come upon horses and mules, camels and dromedaries, chariots and wheels, a great company, and ye shall build for Me, and there shall be

heaps of money, heaps upon heaps." I suppose living by faith
has gone out of fashion in these days, but living by faith, as
we understood it then, was having no fixed income; the pastor
had a ministry box at the door in his church, and I had a
box at the door in my church. So, to hear the Lord talking
about heaps of money was something thrilling. That evening the pastor and I had an invitation to supper at a friend's
house in the country. About nine o'clock I said to the pastor,
"We shall need to tell our host we must be going." Our host
said, "Wait a minute, don't go yet; I have something to tell
you." He said, "You know, I am a businessman, and I have
not paid my tithes to the Lord for a long time. God spoke to
me and said, 'Lay the money at the apostles' feet.'" My friend
said, "How much do you think it will be?" "I am not quite
sure; it will be something more than 2,000 pounds" (Formerly,
about $9,600). Our host said, "Well, here's the first heap," and
he gave us 2,400 pounds. (Formerly, about $11,500). A pound
was worth more than it is today—a lot more! "Ah," you say,
"that was wonderful!" Yes, it was wonderful, but mark the
message had three parts to it. The first part said, "Gather My
people together from the north, and from the south, from the
east and from the west." Then part two: "It shall come upon
horses and mules, and camels and dromedaries, and chariots
and wheels." Then the third part: "There shall be heaps and
heaps of money." Within twelve hours the third part of the
message was partly fulfilled: we got the first heap. We could
not see how the first part would be fulfilled, and we waited.
Then it came. In 1921 a call came for me to take charge of the
Pentecostal Bible School in London, and the students came
from the north and from the south, from the east and from
the west. From that Bible school in Hampstead, where I was
principal for over twenty-seven years, there are students ministering in over twenty different countries of the world where
there are camels, dromedaries, horses, chariots, and wheels.
The word of wisdom is always specifically and marvelously
fulfilled when it is from God. His plan for us in 1919 was to
gather together and send out young men, and we should have
heaps of money to do it with.[18]

A WORD OF ENCOURAGEMENT TO YOU

Sometimes we may think that the word of wisdom is something very mysterious and almost unattainable—like it is for the super spiritual and the saintly only. However, that is not what scripture says—it is a gift, and it comes by faith, not by works lest any man should boast!

As the apostle Paul said, "Did you receive the Spirit by the works of the Law, or by hearing with faith?" (Gal. 3:2, NASB). It is by faith, of course. We don't deserve them, and we can't earn them.

Note that the gifts of the spirit (1 Cor. 12) can't be bought or worked for, as the apostle Peter told Simon the sorcerer: "Thy money perish with thee, because thou hast thought that the gift of God may be purchased with money" (Acts 8:20). A gift is a gift!

By contrast, the fruits of the spirit (Gal. 5) depend on our cultivation of godly character. There is some work involved. We develop fruit, but we receive gifts.

I say this to encourage you to believe that God can use you also in the gifts of the Spirit and especially the word of wisdom. Following are some examples of how the Lord uses this gift in the modern day. I know He wants to use you just as He has me, and so I share these examples from my ministry. I hope they are helpful and inspiring.

PERSONAL EXAMPLES OF THE WORD OF WISDOM

To Warn of Danger

When I served as youth director for the Louisiana Assemblies of God, I was on the road a lot because I ministered all over the state. The enemy tormented me with fears that something would happen to my wife and little children. Satan would ask, "What if something happens to your family?"

One evening, I was in Bossier City. Around one o'clock I was awakened with an intense burden to pray for my family's safety. I got out of bed, knelt, and prayed for almost an hour before the burden lifted. I wanted desperately to call my wife Virginia and see how everything was. However, I knew that they all must have been asleep, so I waited until around 7:00 a.m. to call.

"Yes," Virginia said, "we are all fine. But this morning around two o'clock there was a horrible accident. An 18-wheeler left the highway and was headed straight for the room where the babies and I were sleeping. But for some reason, about twenty feet from our window, the earth just opened up! The wheels of the truck sank into a hole, stopping the truck!"

I later found out that it had taken two big trucks with winches to lift that truck out of the hole. The police couldn't figure out why the ground had suddenly opened. It wasn't wet. The truck had left hardly any tire tracks in the grass as it rolled across the lawn toward our home. The two huge winch trucks were just as heavy. Yet they had no difficulty coming across that same ground in order to hook on to the 18-wheeler and lift it out of the hole.

The police said the driver of the truck had veered off the highway to avoid a crash. His truck headed straight for our house when the ground opened up and brought the speeding truck to a sudden halt.

My wife and babies, sleeping in the bedroom of our little wood-frame house, could not have escaped injury or death had it not been for the warning from God and the power of prayer. The results would have been disastrous. God's intervention that night put a stop to the enemy's tormenting about the safety of my family while I traveled. My wife and children were protected by God's mighty hands.

To Encourage Revealing the Future

A few years ago, I received a call from a young building contractor. He was bound by fear, depressed, and was in a hopeless situation financially. He wanted counseling because he saw no way out other than to file for bankruptcy.

When we met at a restaurant to talk, I encouraged him as best I could. But as I was praying with him before I left, the Holy Spirit spoke a word of wisdom to him through me:

> Within thirty days, so much business will be coming to you that you'll experience a breakthrough that will get you out of your financial difficulties. Within two months you will have more business than you have ever had, and within a year, you will have your debts paid off and will be put into the best financial position in your life."

That word seemed impossible to fulfill, but within thirty days, hurricane Katrina roared through the New Orleans area, leaving massive damage in its wake. The man couldn't keep up with all the demands for his services. The number of his employees quadrupled. He had more work than he could handle. Within a year's time he was totally debt free, and he had put over half a million dollars into savings, just as the Holy Spirit had foretold.

To Direct Church Leaders

First Assembly—the church I pastored in New Orleans—was the first church in that city to fully integrate with leaders from differing races. This drew a lot of criticism from old-line segregationists.

One day as I was praying, I received a word of wisdom about this: "Even some of the apostles who had been with Jesus struggled with racial prejudices. Yet God gave them divine love, wisdom, and revelation that enabled them to overcome and unite believers from differing backgrounds to build up His church."

Jews were so prejudiced they wouldn't even eat with Gentiles, whom they considered unclean (Acts 10 and 11). God taught Peter not to call any man unclean and to welcome Cornelius and other Spirit-baptized Gentiles into the body of Christ. God used that revelation in prayer to help us to lovingly work together to eliminate prejudice in our church.

To Avoid Trouble

As the youth director for Louisiana, it was my responsibility to conduct youth camps. In order to do that, of course, I had to rent facilities.

One year I secured an excellent campground near Minden. I had to follow the strict governmental rules regulating our camp, one of which forbade swimming in the lake nearby.

One afternoon I received a word of wisdom that a group was planning to go swimming after dark. The Lord told me to dress in black so I couldn't be seen and that I was to lie quietly on a lakeside picnic table, wait for the rule-breakers to arrive, and stop them.

So that is what I did. I took a large flashlight with me and quietly made my way through the woods to the lake. I climbed onto a picnic table and waited motionless.

Before long, I heard the whispers and giggles of the approaching counselors and campers. I then sprang to my feet on top of the table and yelled loudly, shining the blinding light into their faces. They screamed and scattered, heading back to their cabins as fast as they could go.

Moments later, as I stood unseen, a government official drove by, checking to see that everything was in order. How thankful I was that God had warned me in advance.

Sometimes Different Gifts Will Operate Together

More than one gift of the Spirit may be operating in manifestations of the supernatural. For example, the word of knowledge and the word of wisdom often work closely together, which can make it difficult to distinguish between the two. Like the word of wisdom, the word of knowledge can come in different forms: visions, dreams, or by an inward witness.

The differences between the gift of the word of wisdom and the gift of the word of knowledge are these:

1. The gift of the *word of knowledge* is the revealing of information of the present or past that can only be supernaturally revealed—not something that can be seen, heard, or known naturally. The gift of the *word of wisdom* is a revelation of the future.[19] In other words, the word of knowledge always refers to something in the present or past, while the word of wisdom deals with things that are still to come.[20]

2. The gift of the *word of knowledge* is a supernatural impartation of facts. The gift of the *word of wisdom* supernaturally imparts the wisdom to handle the facts. It also helps to remember that the gift of the word of wisdom is both predictive (foretelling future events) and directive (giving commands and instructions from God concerning those future events.)

SOME EXAMPLES OF GIFTS WORKING

The Word of Knowledge and the Word of Wisdom

A couple in my church was having marital problems. One morning the wife, her face wet with tears, came to the church office and asked my secretary if she could see me. Between sobs, the woman told me how mean her husband was and how he had no respect for her. Wiping tears, the woman made one negative accusation after another against her husband.

But even as the woman wept, the Lord gave me a word of knowledge that she was lying because she was making plans to leave her husband and wanted to set the stage so the church would respect her and not condemn her for leaving him and their two children. I tried to reason with her, but she would just counter with, "You don't know!" and then launch into another verbal attack on her husband.

The Lord showed me it was time to confront her. In a word of knowledge, the Holy Spirit revealed more of the facts and told me exactly what to say. "You've come here to lie to me and get me on your side," I said to her matter-of-factly. "You have your car packed, you're leaving your husband and children, and you have no intention of going back home."

The woman's eyes widened, and her face flushed with anger as I shared a word of wisdom from the Lord about what lay ahead: "The judgment of God will come on you for lying and for leaving your husband."

Furious, she jumped to her feet and sneered, "Yes, I'm packed, and I'm not going back!" Then she stormed out of my office, jumped into her car and drove away.

A policeman called me about 3:00 a.m. that night. He told me that a woman had been in an accident and said he was calling me because they'd found my business card in her pocket. He asked if I would please come to Charity Hospital and see her. He told me her name. It was the same woman who had blatantly refused to repent when God revealed her schemes and warned her of judgment!

I dressed and hurried to the hospital. The room to which they directed me was filled with patients on gurneys. I began walking about the room, trying to find the injured woman. Finally, I asked a nurse to help me, and she pointed the woman out to me. I realized that I had walked by her three times and never recognized her. I walked to the gurney and gazed in horror at the terribly swollen and disfigured face of the unconscious woman lying there. The woman survived, but her brain and body were so permanently damaged that she remained in a comatose state and had to be moved to a nursing home.

Word of Wisdom, Word of Knowledge, and Gift of Healing

At one point, we were having five services on Sundays at First Assembly in order to accommodate all the people. One Sunday the Lord awakened me with a word of wisdom (predictive) that a man would be in a service that day from another city, and that he was coming specifically to be healed. I looked for the man in the 7:00 a.m. service and again in the 9:00 a.m. service, but did not feel in my spirit that he was there.

In the 11:00 a.m. service, I had finished the altar service when a man burst through the front doors of the auditorium. Giving me a word of knowledge, the Holy Spirit said, "That's the man!" I called out the man, telling him to come forward for prayer. I laid hands on him and prayed for healing. The man had a blockage in his digestive system and had been in constant pain, but the Lord totally healed him that morning.

The Word of Wisdom and the Gift of Healing

The Lord gave me a word of wisdom through a dream. When the actual event took place, and I followed what I had seen in the dream, it resulted in a gift of healing to a blind woman.

In the dream, I saw a white man leading a black woman wearing dark glasses as they came into the church auditorium. Both the man and woman appeared to be in their early forties. In those days in New Orleans, you just didn't see a white man with a black woman. The auditorium was packed, and the only place for the ushers to seat them was in aisle seats about midway down. In the dream, I saw myself preach and then give the invitation. I watched as people surged forward, filling the altars to seek God. Just then in the dream, the Lord said to me, "Call the man and woman out and ask the man if the lady is blind."

I did as the Lord instructed, and the man replied, "Yes, sir. She is."

I asked him to bring her forward. Then, in the dream, I watched myself remove her dark glasses, place my thumbs over her eyes and pray for her two times. Nothing happened. But as I prayed for her a third time, she opened her eyes, smiled, and said, "You have pretty brown eyes." Then she touched my tie and said, "And you have a beautiful blue tie."

The dream ended, but I could not forget it. I sensed that it was only a matter of time until it would all come to pass just as the Lord had shown me.

About two weeks later, the auditorium doors opened, and a white man entered, leading a black woman wearing dark glasses. Just as in the dream, the only place available for the ushers to put them was midway down in aisle seats. My heart began to hammer in anticipation! I preached, gave the altar call, and the altar area filled with people. Exactly as in the dream, the Lord said to me, "Ask the man if the woman is blind."

"Yes, sir," the man answered. "She is."

I asked the man to bring the woman forward. Taking off her dark glasses, I placed my thumbs on her eyes and began to pray. Just as in the dream, nothing happened. I prayed again. Nothing happened. I could hardly wait to pray the third time because I knew she was about to be healed!

At that instant, I recalled the next "scene" in the dream. For a split second, sheer panic seized me! *Am I wearing a blue tie?* I glanced downward... *Yes!* To my enormous relief and amazement, I was!

Placing my thumbs on her eyes, I prayed the third time, knowing exactly what was coming. The woman's eyes opened. She smiled and said, "You have pretty brown eyes." Then she touched my tie and said, "And you have a beautiful blue tie!" The church erupted in praise!

I learned later that the woman had been blind about six years. The white man and this black woman were neighbors and had become good friends. The man had talked the woman into letting him take her to our church service.

Actually, *two* healings occurred that morning. God used that black woman's healing to bring about a wonderful healing in our church regarding the segregation issue.

The Word of Wisdom Leading to Healing

When I was twenty years old, I was invited to preach the first revival at Brother Cecil Janway's church plant in Des Allemands.

One afternoon while I was praying for the evening service, the Holy Spirit gave me a word of wisdom: "There will be a little woman in the service tonight who has a large goiter that comes out beyond her chin and lays on her chest. If you will call for her before you preach and will pray for her, I will heal her."

I'd never had anything like that happen before, but that night I went up on the low platform of the church and watched as the people came into the building. Although I looked carefully at the necks of various women as they entered, trying to find the woman God had told me about, I never did see anyone with a growth.

The service began and I said to myself, "I must have misunderstood." But when the time came for me to preach, and I started reading my text, in my spirit I heard the Lord command: "Obey Me!"

I stopped right then and said to the congregation, "This afternoon the Lord told me there would be a little, short woman with a goiter..."

Just then, way over to my left, a tiny French woman stood and made her way toward me. As she walked, the audience and I watched in joyous amazement as the huge goiter disappeared right before our eyes!

A WORD OF WISDOM, WORD OF KNOWLEDGE, DELIVERANCE, AND HEALING

When I pastored First Assembly in New Orleans, I taught a Wednesday morning Bible class. It grew to about 600 people. Many of those were from other church backgrounds, hungry to know about the Holy Spirit and His operations.

One morning I was awakened at 4:00 a.m., and the Holy Spirit gave me a word of wisdom:

> A demon-possessed girl with a spirit of suicide controlling her will be in the service this morning. First, teach the Bible class and minister to others. Then call for the suicidal woman. As the woman sees the others who receive from Me, it will increase her faith to believe and to receive from Me.

That morning I taught the Bible class and ministered to others first, just as I had been instructed. Then I was given a word of knowledge for the young woman I was to minister to, and I spoke it out for her to hear. "Yesterday you were going to commit suicide. A minister on television said, 'Stop! Don't do that!' You are here today."

A woman in her early thirties stood, trembling from head to foot. Under the power and anointing of the Holy Spirit, I prayed for her. She was totally delivered from the spirit of suicide.

Still trembling, the young woman shared what had happened the day before. She had been watching Pat Robertson on television. He had said, "Jesus is the answer. If you need help, call this number."

The woman told us that she dialed the number, but got our ministry's hot line instead. The person who answered her call was a medical doctor's wife. She told the young woman to come to our Bible study the next morning and promised to meet her and sit with her in the service.

We all rejoiced together with her that morning because of the powerful work our loving God had done in her life.

Because of her remarkable transformation, the woman's husband came with her that evening to our Wednesday night church service. In that service, I received a word of knowledge that a person was there whose eardrum had been destroyed.

I didn't know it, but that word of knowledge was for the woman's husband. He came forward for ministry. He told us that during the time he was a soldier in Vietnam, he'd had to lay a long time with the side of his head pressed against a generator, and the heat from the generator had destroyed his eardrum. After prayer, the man discovered that he had received a wonderful gift of healing, and his eardrum had been totally restored!

He told me later that when he went home and went to bed that night, he could hear sounds outside their house, even with a pillow over his good ear. He told me that the next morning, he had been awakened by sounds of horns and whistles from boats on the nearby river. He had never heard the horns and whistles before, although he and his wife had lived there for some time.

WORDS OF WISDOM, WORDS OF KNOWLEDGE, HEALING, AND DELIVERANCE

One day I was praying in the Spirit, and I received a word of wisdom about a married couple that would be in the service that evening. He also showed me that other manifestations of the Spirit would take place.

When I went to the church that evening, the Holy Spirit began to show me people in the audience who would be ministered to and helped. He began to reveal things to me that were wrong with them, things that only the Lord knew: sicknesses, marital problems, needs for direction, etc. Because the word of wisdom had given me faith, I was able to step out and follow the leadings of the Holy Spirit. As a result, person after person received answers to their needs.

As I looked out over the audience, the couple the Lord told me about just seemed to "light up" where they were seated. I did not say aloud those specific things the Lord had told me about the couple, but I did call them out for ministry that night and then asked them to come to my office later for counseling. (The Lord had told me that the husband had been caught up in homosexual activity and that in the loneliness and neglect the wife experienced, she had become unfaithful.) The wife repented and became faithful to her husband. I was able to help the couple for a season. Finally, however, the husband refused to pay the price to be freed.

IN CONCLUSION

Howard Carter puts this marvelous gift of the word of wisdom in perspective for us:

> There is nothing greater than the revelation of the mind and purpose of God. The word of wisdom transports one to the very council chamber of the Almighty and affords a participation, however infinitesimal, in the government of the universe. Since the Lord God will do nothing but He reveals His secret unto His servants the prophets, the smallest revelation of His purpose is more important than the greatest deliberations ever made in the councils of men, and such enlightenment becomes for us wisdom of the first magnitude. This therefore, is truly the word of God's wisdom, the first and greatest of the spiritual gifts, the most marvelous of all the manifestations of the Spirit of God.[21]

As Paul instructed, you and I should "covet earnestly the best gifts" (1 Cor. 12:31). In other words, we should *covet earnestly* (have warmth of feeling for; have desire for; be jealous over; be zealous for) the *best* (stronger; better; nobler) *gifts*. Are *you* zealously obeying that great apostle's counsel?

Chapter 5

THE GIFT OF THE WORD OF KNOWLEDGE

To another [is given] the word of knowledge by the same Spirit...
—1 CORINTHIANS 12:8

YOU WILL RECALL that there are nine supernatural gifts of the Spirit. We just completed our study of the word of wisdom. Now let's look at the word of knowledge. Here are some of the ways that various Pentecostal leaders through the years have defined it:

1. Lester Sumrall: "In the gift of the word of knowledge, God reveals to one of His servants something that now exists or did exist on the earth. This must be something that that servant could not know naturally—something his eyes have not seen and his ears have not heard."[1]

2. Ralph Riggs: "The word of knowledge is bits of knowledge concerning facts and happenings which are supernaturally revealed to the servant of God....Revelation of divine truth by the Spirit of truth is impartation of divine knowledge, a giving of the word of knowledge. A revelation of facts and happenings is also a part of this gift."[2]

3. Ray McCauley: "In the word of knowledge, God supernaturally reveals to one of His servants something that now exists or did exist on the earth. God reveals a piece of His knowledge concerning something that has taken place in the past or is taking place right now, in the present....Remember that the gifts operate as He wills. Don't ever try to conjure something up....Never be put under pressure to 'perform' by people. We are totally reliant upon the Holy Spirit for any of the gifts to flow. Sometimes the word of knowledge can help us find lost property."[3]

4. Ken and Lorraine Krivohlavek: "The word of knowledge is suddenly, miraculously knowing something by the Holy Spirit for which you have no natural or human explanation why or how you should know it. The word of knowledge is not a vocal gift, such as prophecy or the interpretation of tongues. It is not the ability to speak facts; it is miraculously knowing facts. The word of knowledge is a miracle of revelation that is over, above, and contrary to what we might have thought about the situation.... If the believer who receives a revelation of a word of knowledge speaks out that knowledge, he must do so by his own ability. On the other hand, there are occasions when a prophecy or an interpretation of tongues will contain supernatural information. Here we have the word of knowledge working together with the gift of prophecy or the interpretation of tongues."[4]

5. Howard Carter: "The word of knowledge is a gift of revelation. It has nothing to do with human knowledge. It is the communication by the Holy Spirit of the knowledge of the Lord. God's knowledge is so vast, shoreless, and fathomless that we call it omniscience—God's all-knowledge. He knows every star in the heavens, and they are innumerable.... millions and trillions of stars, great floating universes with billions of stars in each galaxy—and yet the Bible says God calls them all by names. He has named every star in the heavens.... What does God know of human affairs? God knows every nation, for the Bible says He works in the midst of the nations to set up and put down; but God not only knows every nation, He knows every person in every nation. Here is a verse to prove it: 'The man Moses was very meek, above all the men which were upon the face of the earth' (Num. 12:3).... The hearts of all men living at that time must have been examined individually by the Almighty before God could proclaim that the meekest man of that day was Moses. So God knows every man, and God knows more than that—He knows the footsteps of every person. The

Psalmist says, 'Thou knowest my downsitting and mine uprising.... and art acquainted with all my ways' (Ps. 139:2–3). God knows every step we take.... God knows every footstep; and if you would like to go further than that, God knows every hair on our heads.

Now, if God is pleased, for the fulfillment of His purpose, to communicate to us, by the Spirit, something of this amazing knowledge, and to let us partake, even though to an infinitesimal extent, of this amazing omniscience, then He gives to us a word of His knowledge.... It doesn't matter how small may be the knowledge communicated, it is miraculous if it is a word of knowledge by divine revelation.... If a child dips his little bucket into the ocean and fills it with water, he has a little of the ocean in his bucket—very little. What he has is infinitesimal in quantity, but in quality, it is precisely the same as the rest of the water in the ocean. There is nothing different in the quality of it, but only in the quantity. So, if God communicates to you one little drop of His amazing knowledge, you have a positive word of knowledge. In quality it is precisely the same as omniscience; in quantity, it is infinitesimal.

This gift of the word of knowledge is a communication from heaven by the Spirit of God of things that are on earth. It can be so clear that you know every detail. But it is a gift that is not appreciated by some because it can expose sin."[5]

WHAT THE WORD OF KNOWLEDGE IS NOT

Ken and Lorraine Krivohlavek carefully explain what the word of knowledge is *not*.

- It is not suspicion.

- It is not worrying.

- It is not knowledge of human character.

- It is not ESP.

- It is not psychology.

- It is not guessing.

- It is not great intelligence.

- It is not great Bible knowledge.

- It is not human insight.

- It is not knowing everything that God knows.

- It is not the ability to speak knowledge. It is supernatural knowing, only.[6]

SOME WAYS IN WHICH THE WORD OF KNOWLEDGE OPERATES

1. God may impart the word of knowledge by an audible voice as He did to Samuel (1 Sam. 3:11–14).

2. The word of knowledge may come through dreams or visions, as it did to Joseph (Gen. 41:25–36) or Daniel (Dan. 2:19).

3. The word of knowledge may come through prophecy.

4. It can come through the gift of interpretation. However, this gift is usually used in public for edification rather than imparting special revelation.

5. There are times during prayer or meditation when we are made aware of certain things though we have not had the information declared to us by actual words.[7]

A word of knowledge may also come as a direct, specific answer from God in answer to prayer. For example, when Samuel and Saul's family prayed, asking God where Saul was, the Lord replied: "Behold, he hath hid himself among the stuff" (1 Sam. 10:21–22).

Howard Carter shares an example of a word of knowledge that came as a direct answer to his prayer.

A friend of Carter's was a workingman, a devout man, who had a large family. He bought his boy a fountain pen, and the boy went to a cricket field and lost it. He came home and told his father.

He said, "Son, take me to the field." The father knelt in a corner of the field. He prayed, "O God, where is the fountain pen?" The Lord answered, "The fountain pen is under the tree at the other side of the field."

So the father said to his son, "Get up, your fountain pen is under that tree."

They found the fountain pen right under that tree.[8]

SOME EXAMPLES OF THE USE OF THE WORD OF KNOWLEDGE IN THE SCRIPTURES

1. To inform of imminent judgment (Gen. 18:1, 17–20).

2. To warn a king of an enemy's plan of destruction (2 Kings 6:9–12).

3. To enlighten and encourage a discouraged servant of the Lord (1 Kings 19:14–18).

4. To expose a hypocrite (2 Kings 5:20–27).

5. To convert a sinner and turn many to God (John 4:15–30; 39–42).

6. To discover a man in hiding (1 Sam. 10:22).

7. To indicate a man in need (Acts 9:11).

8. To indicate a suitable place for a meeting of God's people (Mark 14:13–15).

9. To know men's thoughts (John 2:24; 1 Sam. 9:19).

10. To reveal the secrets of men (1 Cor. 14:2, 5; John 1:47; 1 Sam. 8; 1 Sam. 9:19).

11. To encourage a prophet who was discouraged (1 Kings 19:14–18).

12. To recall knowledge that had been forgotten (Dan. 2:1–45).

SOME PURPOSES OF THE WORD OF KNOWLEDGE

1. To reveal medical conditions in people who are too weak in their faith or too shy or reserved to request prayer.

2. To bring inspiration to people and/or strengthen their faith by revealing facts that could be known only by a revelation from God.

3. To expose sin.

4. To reveal spiritual needs and bring deliverance.

5. To reveal unknown facts to Spirit-filled Christians to help them in their personal life, daily work, etc.

6. To show a need in another person so a Christian can help them by prayer, counsel, sharing finances or resources, etc.

7. To bring glory to God and cause Him to be honored through the manifestation of His Spirit.

8. To bring blessing to the church.[9]

PERSONAL EXAMPLES OF THE WORD OF KNOWLEDGE

A Word of Knowledge that Came During Prayer

One night after a time of ministry, I was sleeping soundly. Suddenly, late in the night, I was awakened. I knew in my spirit that Joe, one of my brothers, was in danger. I got up, knelt beside the bed and began to pray for him. Suddenly, a tremendous spirit of intercession came upon me in utterances and groanings in the Spirit that I couldn't understand. This went on for a little more than an hour.

Then a peace came over me, and I went back to bed, knowing that the Spirit of God had known that Joe urgently needed prayer, and had interceded through me on his behalf. This is what Rom. 8:26 promises: "Likewise the Spirit also helps in our weaknesses. For we do not know what we should pray for as we ought, but the Spirit Himself makes intercession for us with groanings which cannot be uttered" (NKJV).

Two weeks later, I was in Crowley, La., visiting with Joe and his family. Following the evening meal, we moved into the sitting room. I looked at Joe and said, "Friday night two weeks ago, where were you?" Joe turned very pale, stood, and walked out of the room. I looked at his wife Ella, and she had tears in her eyes. I asked if I had said something wrong.

"No, Bud," she answered. "Joe almost drowned two weeks ago tonight. He was loading some cement trucks—the type of cement used in oil well drilling. He was working for the Western Company. The barges they were loading the trucks on were in the Atchafalaya River, and the river was at flood stage. It's known as one of the most treacherous rivers in the United States..."

Ella paused, then continued: "Joe had gone around the back of a truck and was hooking chains into the wheels so they could buckle the truck on the barge to keep it from rolling off. Just then, they moved into the rough waters. His foot slipped and Joe fell into the water. The churning of the tugboat engines that moved the barges, along with the swift current of the river that was at flood stage, made the current extremely strong. Joe couldn't stay afloat, even though he's a good swimmer. After several minutes of him struggling in the water, someone missed him. They turned on the floodlights and saw Joe as he bobbed to the top. He had already gone under and come back up. They were able to rescue him, give him treatment, and save his life."

I was overjoyed with thanks to God! Although I was several hundred miles away, because of a word of knowledge and the power of intercessory prayer, my brother was saved.

Today, he is a dedicated Christian serving on the board of First Assembly of God in Longview, Texas. He is the father of five happily married children and enjoys spending time with his grandchildren. Joe is enjoying all of this today because God mercifully awakened me to give me a word of knowledge that was connected with intercessory prayer.

A Word of Knowledge Received While at Work and Praying

When I was around sixteen or seventeen years old, I was working in the field and praying as I worked. God spoke to me through a word of knowledge and said our country was about to go to war. I went into the house and told my mother what the Lord had said to me.

You must understand that this was before the time that lower-income farm people like my family owned a television set. We had no way of knowing that a problem was going on with Korea. Nevertheless, when North Korean troops invaded South Korea, our country went to war.

A Word of Knowledge Received in a Vision While Interceding

One day during my teen years I was praying, and received something like an open vision about my Uncle James, who was in the Navy. I could see a big ship and his face, and I knew he was in danger. This was the first time I was used with a spirit of intercession. As I prayed and sought God, the Holy Spirit interceded through me so intensely that my body was literally drawn into a fetal position. When my time of intercession had ended, I told my mother what I'd seen and the time it had occurred.

About three weeks later, we received a letter from my uncle telling us that, on that very day, his ship had moved in so close that they could shell a beach where the enemy was entrenched. Much of the enemy's heavy artillery fire came against them, but they had to continue shelling the beach. They couldn't move out into the sea to prevent heavy shelling onto their ship. Much damage had already been done to their ship when some smaller ships, called destroyers, moved in and began to shell the beach so their large battleship could move out of range of the enemy artillery.

When we checked the time and date, it was exactly when I was in great intercession before God for my uncle. Before Uncle James wrote us, the only person I told about this was my mother.

If I receive a word of knowledge concerning someone in the audience when I'm ministering, the victory that could come to that person is not likely to happen unless I speak the word. Once I have spoken the word, then it is up to the individual to receive and respond to the word or reject it. Sometimes, God will not let me say anything until the time He chooses. However, the blessing is not released until that word of knowledge is spoken.

A Word of Knowledge While Preaching on Television

One night as I was ministering on television, a strong word of knowledge was impressed upon my spirit. Rather than waiting until the end of my sermon as I usually did, I knew I had to stop my teaching at that moment and speak forth that word. So, I paused, looked directly into the eye of the camera and said: "There is a professional man in his early forties who is watching this program. You live in a high-rise apartment complex in the city of New Orleans. The unusual thing is that you live in an apartment across the hall from your mother—not in the same apartment. You are a Jew, and you are facing some major decisions. Drop on your knees now and pray this prayer after me." The Spirit directed me to pray a simple prayer; then I resumed my sermon, assured that I had obeyed God.

The following Sunday afternoon as I was entering the sanctuary to minister in the 3:00 p.m. service, a well-dressed, sharp-looking gentleman ran up to me. I had no idea what was happening until he blurted out, "I'm the man from television! You're going to have to help me!"

He was speaking with such urgency that the phrases tumbled out, one after another. "I'm forty years old! I'm Jewish! I live in an apartment across the hall from my mother in Claiborne Towers!"

Silent praise went up from my heart to God as I reached out to take his hand. After talking with him a few minutes, I invited him to stay for the service. He accepted the invitation.

The next Sunday, he came to the three o'clock service again. This time, the Jewish man had another gentleman with him. After I preached, he and the other man came forward to speak with me. The Jewish man turned to me, gestured toward his friend and said, "This is my friend. He is an Arab. We're not even supposed to be talking to one another since I'm a Jew, but we're friends. I am his legal counsel. He's going blind, and I want you to heal him."

Smiling, I explained, "Well, it doesn't work that way. Jesus is the healer—not me. I can pray for him, but that doesn't guarantee he will be healed."

Not discouraged in the least, the Jewish man replied, "I don't know all your terminology, but pray for him and heal him." I prayed for him in faith. Nothing happened in the natural, but I sensed God at work.

The next Sunday afternoon, the Jewish attorney returned with his friend, the Arab businessman who was going blind. This time, the Jewish man also brought his mother who was in her early eighties. I spoke with them briefly, then proceeded with the service as it began.

Just as I began to read the text for the sermon that afternoon, I heard a loud scream from the back of the church. Here came the Arab businessman running down the aisle, waving his glasses in his hand and screaming: "I can see! I can see! I'm healed! I'm healed!"

A move of God swept over the congregation. As they praised God, I approached the Jewish man and his mother, who was weeping. She and the Arab businessman both accepted the Lord as their Savior. I learned later that the Arab gentleman was a wealthy oilman. His family is related to the king of Saudi Arabia.

How thankful I am that the Holy Spirit loves each one of us and knows the key to every heart.

How to Use a Word of Knowledge

When You Receive a Word of Knowledge, You Must Do What God Directs

I have learned that almost always, when you receive a word of knowledge regarding some person or persons, there is some action that must follow. It may be to visit somebody, or to make a phone call, or to speak a word to an individual or group of people. Sometimes, an intense burden of intercession will come on you, and you intercede until the burden lifts. Your part and responsibility are not complete until you have obeyed God and done whatever His Spirit has directed you to do.

Sometimes a Word of Knowledge Can Come in a Dream

In his classic work, *The Gifts of the Spirit*, Harold Horton shares a story of an evangelist whom he knew personally. The evangelist told of how God used a dream to reveal some urgently needed information through this gift. This true story also illustrates how we must take action after a word of knowledge.

> I had an unsaved sister who was sick in Los Angeles, California. I dreamed one night that instead of my sister Mary being sick in Los Angeles, she was dying in Sapulpa, Oklahoma. It seemed as if she were in bed with a white sheet over her head, and on this sheet in orange letters were the words, "No smoking." The room filled with light. It made me afraid. All of a sudden I could hear my sister say, "I'm healed! I'm saved!" The white light vanished, and I could see her running back and forth, praising God. I awoke. The dream stayed with me. One morning I received a telegram saying that my sister Mary was dying in Sapulpa, Oklahoma. She had double pneumonia and was given up to die.

I rushed to the airport just in time to catch the plane to San Antonio. From there I took the bus to Sapulpa. I phoned the Sapulpa hospital and asked them if my sister Lucille was there. They replied, "Yes, she is here," and they called her to the phone. I asked her, "Lucille, how is Mary?" She answered, "She's just waiting for you to get here, to die. The doctors have given her up." I ran for a taxicab and said to the driver, "Take me to Sapulpa, Oklahoma, as fast as you can." I arrived. I jumped out of the cab and ran up the hospital steps. All my relatives were standing there. I hurried into the room where Mary was, took her hand, and began to pray. There she lay unconscious under an oxygen tent; it was white, with the words written on it in orange letters, "No Smoking." This was my dream! I prayed to God. He said, "Tell everyone you see that I am going to heal your sister." About four o'clock that afternoon, Mary awoke from her coma and said, "Mama, I'm so hungry. Won't you get me something to eat?" The doctor said they might give her anything she desired. She was dying in any case. "What do you want?" asked her mother. "I want some bacon, eggs, toast, and coffee!" She ate it ravenously. Ten minutes later the doctor examined her. "This is a miracle," he said. "The air is breaking under those lungs that have been packed full of pneumonia!" Mary went to sleep. The doctor asked if she had vomited what she had eaten. "No." More amazement! Mary slept till eight o'clock that night. She awoke and said, "Mama, I'm so hungry. Do get me something to eat." Mother phoned an inquiry to the doctor. He asked, "Has she vomited the other yet?" "No." He came and examined her and then with tears rolling down his cheeks, looked up and said, "These lungs are absolutely clear. Her heart is beating normally. Her pulse is normal. There is no reason for this woman to be in bed. Something has happened!" My sister was saved and was home in a few days, sweeping floors, singing, praising, and magnifying God.

Horton continues:

Someone might ask who showed the evangelist the white sheet with the orange letters. God did, by the word of His knowledge. Who led him, not to Los Angeles, but to Oklahoma? God, by a combination revelation of His knowledge and wisdom.[10]

EXAMPLES OF A WORD OF KNOWLEDGE
WORKING WITH OTHER GIFTS OF THE SPIRIT

The Gift of the Word of Knowledge Combined with a Word of Wisdom or Discerning of Spirits

One Sunday morning at First Assembly in New Orleans the service was already in progress when a thirty-year-old woman was brought into church. At that moment, a big commotion broke out in the back of the auditorium. Instantly, the Holy Spirit, through the gift of discerning of spirits, said to me: "There is a demon-possessed person."

I jumped off the platform. People scattered and pews emptied. The demons in the woman had thrown her under the pews. It took four men to get her out from under the pews. Through the gift of discerning of spirits, I already knew the woman was demon-possessed.

Then I was given a word of wisdom. I suddenly, miraculously, knew what to do in a situation where, in myself, I didn't know what to do. "Don't pray for her in here," said the Lord to my spirit. "Take her to a side room." So I told the men assisting with her to take her out of the auditorium to a side room. She weighed about 130 pounds, but it took four men to take her out of the auditorium as she fiercely kicked, fought, and scratched.

One of the men helping carry her out had a Bible. He felt he should put the Bible on her stomach. Even though the woman's eyes were closed, before he could place the Bible on her stomach and while his hand was still in the air, she spat on the Bible in his hand wherever he moved it.

The Lord spoke to me with a word of knowledge: "There's someone in this room giving strength to the spirits in her." The Holy Spirit then focused my attention on a strange man, exposing him. Just as I was walking out of the auditorium to minister to the woman, I pointed to the man and shouted: "You're a warlock!" The man ran out of the room and down the street. Ten minutes later, the woman had been totally set free from the demons that had held her in bondage.

That night, the woman who had been freed from the demons came back to the church. This time, she brought her husband, mother-in-law, sister-in-law, and a friend with her. All of them were saved in the evening service.

In that situation, the Lord used the gift of discerning of spirits, the gift of wisdom, and the gift of the word of knowledge—all three working together—to bring deliverance to that demon-possessed woman, to save her family, and to glorify His name.

The Gift of the Word of Knowledge Combined with the Gift of Healing

When preaching a revival in Harvey, LA, we saw great manifestations of the power of God. We were experiencing tremendous miracles and deliverances from demons.

One night as the Lord moved very powerfully, the Holy Spirit gave me a word of knowledge. Speaking into the microphone, I said: "Someone here has injured their hand and has no feeling in their fingers on that hand."

A young married man named Paul was helping at the altars by catching people as they fell under the power of the Holy Spirit. Paul heard the word I gave, but he had concluded long ago that he would never be healed.

When Paul was a child he was helping his dad, buckling down his dad's tugboats during a hurricane. His hand was caught in a chain and pulled through a roller. One finger came off, but he managed to hold the finger on during the three hours it took to get to the hospital because of the storm. The doctors had sewn the finger back, successfully reattaching it, but he had no feeling in his fingers since the injury.

After that night's service, Paul and his wife went home, and he took a shower. To Paul's utter amazement, when he reached for the towel to dry off, he could feel the towel! Paul excitedly shared with his wife that God had healed him and restored all feeling in his hand and fingers! After Paul was healed, he had lain beside his wife in bed, feeling her hair all through the night with that hand. He had little faith, but God healed him anyway!

The Gift of the Word of Knowledge Combined with the Gift of the Word of Wisdom and the Gift of Discerning of Spirits

A man began attending our church. The Lord showed me through a word of knowledge that he was a homosexual. I wasn't directed by the Spirit to confront him at that time, but I began interceding that he would be delivered.

After he had been attending church a few weeks, a Christian teenager came to me and told me that the man had tried to become involved with him. I thanked the teenager and cautioned him to stay totally away from the man. I told him to come to me immediately if he was approached again. Still, I sensed that I was to wait for God's timing before confronting the man. Although I wanted to deal with him immediately and sternly, I obeyed the Spirit's direction.

As I kept my eye upon the man, I noticed him surrounding himself with six teenage girls in the church. He was handsome and gentle in his demeanor, and he hadn't done anything wrong—yet. However, the Lord showed me he was attempting to lead them out of the church and into prostitution, so he could be their pimp. (As strange as that may sound, we had already had a young lady in the church that had had a homosexual pimp.)

I continued to pray that God would give me wisdom to know how to deal with the situation. And yet I didn't understand why God hadn't released me to confront him. The last thing I wanted was to lose those precious girls and their families.

Finally, the Lord gave me a word of wisdom on how to deal with the man. I called him into my office on a Sunday evening and told him I knew what he was, and I knew God could deliver homosexuals. I shared from my heart of former homosexuals in our church that had been totally freed. I shared about a young homosexual and a young lesbian woman who had been delivered while attending our church. They had met, fallen in love, and gotten married in the church. I shared other testimonies of God's grace and power in delivering homosexuals and lesbians, and I told him that I prayed he would let God deliver him, too.

It was God's moment for him—to be delivered and start a new life.

He sat there quietly listening, but when I told him I knew what he was trying to do with the girls, he exploded and yelled, "Do you realize you could be sued for saying I am a homosexual!"

Quietly and calmly, I replied, "Can you prove you are not?"

He jumped up and started to shout at me. I reached up to calm him, saying, "Don't talk to me that way."

But when I reached, he ducked away and his foot slipped. Off balance, he fell into a chair, and the chair turned over. Pulling himself upright, he jumped up and ran out of my office, yelling, "He's going to kill me! He's going to kill me! He's going to *kill* me...."

Startled board members standing in the area outside my office heard him yelling as he ran out of my office, down the stairs, and out of the church—never to return.

After the man's appointment, I met with the girls and their parents to explain, and we did not lose a single person from the church. Neither were any of our young people deceived and drawn into sin. God protected them.

I was so thankful that I waited for the Holy Spirit's timing. The man's plan to sue me and accuse me of intolerance toward homosexuals disappeared with him. God truly does all things well.

The Word of Knowledge Combined with the Gift of Healing in Evangelism

In 2000, the Lord directed me to accept an invitation from a church in Harvey, LA. The meeting had been scheduled to continue for four days; but God broke through, and I was there for ten months.

We had set aside a Monday night for a healing and miracle service. We announced it during our regularly scheduled services and on our daily television show. The young man who was the minister of music in the church had been trying to get his parents to come to the meeting, but they had refused. Finally, since this was going to be a healing service and they both needed healing, he got them to come.

During the service, God spoke to me and gave me the name *Crohn's disease.* I had never had the Holy Spirit name that particular disease in a word of knowledge during all the years of my ministry. So after the message, I prayed for several people, then said, "I've never had this word given to me before, and I don't know what it is, but is there anyone here who has Crohn's disease?" The minister of music came forward. He told me that Crohn's is an inflammatory bowel disease, and that he'd had it since he was seven (he was about thirty-five years old then.) His parents started weeping.

I prayed for him, and he felt the power of God on him. He said, "I feel I am healed, but I'll know by tomorrow." Sure enough, his body confirmed it! He is still healed today. As a result of his healing, his parents accepted Christ. Many times, God uses the supernatural to break down barriers to salvation.

The Word of Knowledge Combined with the Gift of Healing

Back in the 1960s, most hospitals had a desk you could go to as a clergyman. At that desk, on a Rolodex file card holder would be the names of all the people in the hospital and their room numbers. Pastors could go there, turn through the file, and see the rooms their church members were in. Pastors could find each patient's denominational affiliation.

As I walked down a hall to visit one of my church members, the Holy Spirit said: "Go in that room." I thought, "No, that's not one of the people I'm supposed to visit." I checked my list, and, sure enough, that number wasn't on it.

But a second time the Holy Spirit directed me to go into that room. I checked the nameplate on the door, and none of the names on my list were on the door. I hesitated. For the third time, the Spirit said, "Go in that room."

I knocked, and a faint voice answered: "Come in." So, I went in. As I entered, I saw two women. I said, "Hello, I'm Pastor Gorman. As I walked by, the Spirit spoke to me and said to go into this room."

The little lady about sixty-years-old, who was on the bed next to the wall near the window, exclaimed: "I have been lying here praying for two days that God would send somebody to pray with me! I'm not from here. I came here to visit a family, and while here I became very ill."

I talked to her a few moments, prayed with her, and she was instantly healed. She sat up and lifted her hands, praising the Lord with such joy because she knew her heart was healed. Then the elderly lady on the other bed asked: "Father, would you pray for me?"

"Sure I will," I said. I talked with her, and she told me she was from New Orleans. I shared a scripture about healing, and God miraculously healed her heart condition, too. The doctors confirmed their healings and dismissed them from the hospital.

About a week later, the lady from New Orleans visited our church with her son. Both accepted Christ and became faithful members of the congregation. I couldn't help wondering what would have happened if I hadn't obeyed the promptings of the Holy Spirit to go into that room?

Sometimes God will give me a word about an individual who is present in the audience or prayer line, yet the person's identity and location are unknown to me. I've learned that as I get nearer to the person and remain sensitive to what the Spirit is saying, the intensity and urgency I'm feeling in my spirit that I must speak the word and act on it will increase.

During a service in north Arkansas, I received a word of knowledge that someone was blind in their right eye. When the impression came, I felt an intensity that I must act on that impulse and speak the word right then.

A couple was entering the door just as I gave the word. They rushed forward to the altar, and I said simply, "Come, let's pray." As we prayed together, sight in the blind eye was instantly restored. Since that time, that individual has seen perfectly out of that eye.

The Word of Knowledge Combined with Feelings

Often, it seems as if I can feel people's hurts, depression, and pains. I can sometimes sense the part of the auditorium, the row, or even the seat where the person is sitting. Or I feel pain in my body in the same place as the person who needs healing.

For example, I remember feeling pain in my back in a service as I was ministering. Immediately I knew to say, "Someone sitting on this row is experiencing severe back pain." Then I said to a man, "Sir, do you have trouble with severe back pain?"

His wife began to cry, and he exclaimed: "Oh, yes!" He was instantly healed. I had no idea who the man was, but after his healing, I learned he was a former feather-weight boxing champion of the United States. After that, whenever he had extra time, he helped in the church's audio tape reproduction department. Even though that meant standing on his feet on a hard floor for hours at a time, he was never bothered with back pain.

Here's another example of the word of knowledge and gift of healing functioning together. During the nine o'clock service on a Sunday morning, I sensed I was to say: "Someone has just come from the hospital. You were rushed there after almost dying last night with a heart attack. You still have the hospital identification bracelet on your arm. You've been in severe pain."

A man in the congregation came forward for prayer and was slain in the Spirit for a long time. When he got up he had no pain. The man went back to his doctor in Indiana, who had written a letter stating that the man needed to receive early retirement. The doctor confirmed that the man was healed. The man moved to New Orleans and began helping in the church.

The Word of Knowledge Combined with Discerning of Spirits

One day, a couple came for counseling to my office in our church in New Orleans. The wife began accusing her husband of all kinds of things. He angrily denied it all and then retaliated, accusing her of similar actions. Several minutes of very heated verbal exchange took place.

I was praying inwardly as I listened, seeking God for direction. Then I sensed that the Lord was giving me a word of knowledge. The Holy Spirit said to me: "They are both lying." The moment they both stopped to catch a breath, I acted upon what the Holy Spirit had told me. "Both of you have a spirit of lying," I said quietly. "Both of you are guilty."

The Holy Spirit revealed their sins to me, and I told each of them what the Spirit had said. In the end, it boiled down to the fact that because of their previous lifestyles, each had begun distrusting and fighting the other. Each had become afraid that the other was cheating.

As they calmed down and talked, both realized that what the Spirit of God had revealed to me was true. As a result of the supernatural intervention of the Holy Spirit, their marriage was saved.

Learning to Hear the Spirit's Voice

A lot of times earlier in my walk with the Lord when I'd wonder if it was the Lord speaking to me or just my own imagination, I'd say, "Lord *confirm* this if it's You." I learned that I had to keep testing and listening time after time until I could recognize the voice of the Spirit. Over a period of time, I learned the Holy Spirit's voice just as I learned to recognize the voice of a human being on the phone.

However, even after we learn to recognize the Spirit's voice, we can become dull of hearing if He speaks and we don't obey. Each time He speaks and we disobey, His voice becomes more and more faint. Eventually, we get to the place where we don't hear or recognize the voice of the Holy Spirit anymore.

I wonder…How many opportunities do we miss because of our insensitivity and disobedience?

IN CONCLUSION

Lack of space prevents my sharing more examples of the present-day uses of this powerful gift of the Spirit. But every way in which the gift of the word of knowledge worked in scripture, will also work today.

Let me conclude with a quote from Harold Horton:

> As we pass to the consideration of the sister gift of the word of wisdom, we may say, as a guide to the identification of this gift in operation, that *the revelation the word of knowledge brings is never future.* Distance makes no difference to its operation. Age, education, nationality make no difference to its reception. Through its agency the whole realm of facts is at the disposal of the believer as the Spirit wills. Through its beneficent agency the Church may be purified, the distressed comforted, the saint gladdened, lost property rediscovered, the enemy defeated, and the Lord Jesus glorified in all.[11]

Chapter 6

THE GIFT OF DISCERNING OF SPIRITS

To another discerning of spirits.

—1 CORINTHIANS 12:10

BEFORE I GET into the details of the important revelation gift of discerning of spirits, I would like to lay a foundation that I think will be helpful to you in using this gift.

As you know, the great unseen spirit world is divided into *good* and *evil.* God and the devil are over these respective realms. However, this does not mean that God and Satan are equals. The eternal God who created all things is omnipresent *(present everywhere),* omniscient *(knows everything)* and omnipotent *(almighty).* Satan is none of these!

Cherubim, seraphim, archangels, and angels do the bidding of God, while Satan is the chief of fallen spirits (See Matt. 8:28; 9:34; 12:26; Luke 11:8, 19). Principalities, powers, rulers of the darkness of this world, wicked spirits in high places, and demons are all under the authority of Satan (See Eph. 6:12; 2:2, etc.).

Furthermore, God is love; He is light; He is holy; He is compassionate. He is just, kind, merciful, faithful, and true. God cannot lie. He cannot fail. His word is true, and it shall not pass away.

Lucifer or Satan (meaning "an adversary, an opponent"), on the other hand, is referred to in the Bible as the accuser of the brethren, the devil, the serpent, the dragon, father of lies, murderer, tempter, the wicked one, etc.

This is simplistic, but it helps to keep these attributes in mind as you use the gift of discerning of spirits.

THE ORIGIN AND FALL OF SATAN

The Bible tells us that angels are spiritual, immortal, superhuman, sinless beings, created by God and existing in great numbers. Originally, Lucifer ("light bringing") was a sinless, beautiful angel created by God.

However, his power and glory were corrupted, and he fell. Lucifer, later known as Satan, led a rebellion in heaven because he wanted to be like God. One-third of the angels followed him in the rebellion. Satan and those angels were defeated and forced out of heaven.

However, as I've already said, Satan and God are not equals. Satan's counterpart is not God. Satan's counterpart is the archangel Michael, one of the chief princes or archangels, the national guardian angel "prince of Israel", "the great prince which standeth in the time of conflict for the children of Thy people Israel" (Dan. 10:13, 21; 12:1; Jude 9; Jer. 30:5).

The archangel Gabriel represents the ministry of the angels toward men, while Michael typifies the angels' struggle against the power of Satan, especially as the guardian of the Jewish people. In Rev. 12:9, Michael fights in heaven against the dragon—"that old serpent called the Devil and Satan which deceiveth the whole world...", thus taking part in the struggle which is the church's work on earth.

It is important to understand that although Satan has his own special purposes and aims, he is still the servant of God for punishment or trial. He is the executor of the negative side of divine justice. God the Holy Spirit is the commander in chief of God's army.

Because some readers may not be familiar with the story of Satan's rebellion, let's pause for a quick review. In Ezekiel 28:12–16, 17 (NIV) we read:

> You were the seal of perfection, full of wisdom and perfect in beauty. You were in Eden, the garden of God; every precious stone adorned you: ruby, topaz and emerald, chrysolite, onyx and jasper, sapphire, turquoise and beryl. Your settings and mountings were made of gold; on the day you were created they were prepared. You were anointed as a guardian cherub, for so I ordained you. You were on the holy mount of God; you walked among the fiery stones, You were blameless in your ways from the day you were created till wickedness was found in you....So I drove you in disgrace from the mount of God, and I expelled you, O guardian cherub, from among the fiery stones. Your heart became proud on account of your beauty; and you corrupted your wisdom because of your splendor. So I threw you to the earth....[1]

Also look at Isaiah 14:12–15 (NIV):

> How you have fallen from heaven, O morning star, son of the
> dawn! You have been cast down to the earth, you who once
> laid low the nations! You said in your heart, "I will ascend to
> heaven; I will raise my throne above the stars of God; I will sit
> enthroned on the mount of assembly, on the utmost heights of
> the sacred mountain. I will ascend above the tops of the
> clouds; I will make myself like the Most High." But you are
> brought down to the grave, to the depths of the pit.

Satan infects the susceptible with demonic spirits to achieve his
plans, whether these people actually know it or not. He controls and
harms them spiritually, morally, mentally and physically. Satan also
uses his victims to oppose the gospel and to deceive God's people.
That is why the gift of discerning of spirits is so urgently needed today.
It enables a believer to look beyond the outward and know the source,
kind, and purpose of that spirit.

THE GIFT OF DISCERNING OF SPIRITS

> Discerning of Spirits is
> the power to:
> - Know what spirits are
>   present (angelic or demonic)
>   and their activities
> - Determine the purposes of
>   the enemy.
> - Perceive the source of a spir-
>   itual manifestation—whether
>   it is from God, of the devil,
>   or of man speaking out of
>   his own spirit.
>
>

When 1 Cor. 12:10 lists discerning of
spirits as one of the nine supernatural
gifts of the Spirit, the literal translation
is *plural*—discerning*s* of spirits. The
Greek word for discernment in verse
10 is *diakrisis*. According to *Vine's
Expository Dictionary*, diakrisis means
"a distinguishing, a clear discrimina-
tion, discerning, judging of spirits,
judging by evidence whether they are
evil or of God."

Accordingly, the gift of discerning of spirits is the ability to detect
spirits and their activities. It is the supernatural revelation of plans
and purposes of the enemy and his forces. It is the ability given by
the Holy Spirit to perceive the source of a spiritual manifestation and
determine whether it is from God (Acts 10:1–10, 17–20); of the devil
(Acts 16:16–18); or of man speaking out of his own spirit (Acts 8:18–23).

DISCERNING THE SOURCE OF A
SPIRITUAL MANIFESTATION

1. A Biblical Example of a Spiritual Manifestation from God

> At Caesarea there was a man named Cornelius, a centurion in what was known as the Italian Regiment He and all his family were devout and God-fearing; he gave generously to those in need and prayed to God regularly. One day at about three in the afternoon he had a vision. He distinctly saw an angel of God, who came to him and said, "Cornelius!" Cornelius stared at him in fear. "What is it, Lord?" he asked. The angel answered, "Your prayers and gifts to the poor have come up as a memorial offering before God. Now send men to Joppa to bring back a man named Simon who is called Peter. He is staying with Simon the tanner, whose house is by the sea." When the angel who spoke to him had gone, Cornelius called two of his servants and a devout soldier who was one of his attendants. He told them everything that had happened and sent them to Joppa. About noon the following day as they were on their journey and approaching the city, Peter went up on the roof to pray. He became hungry and wanted something to eat, and while the meal was being prepared, he fell into a trance….While Peter was wondering about the meaning of the vision, the men sent by Cornelius found out where Simon's house was and stopped at the gate. They called out, asking if Simon who was known as Peter was staying there. While Peter was still thinking about the vision, the Spirit said to him, "Simon, three[a] men are looking for you. So get up and go downstairs. Do not hesitate to go with them, for I have sent them."
>
> —ACTS 10:1–10; 17–20, NIV

2. Biblical Examples of Spiritual Manifestations from the Devil

The Bible speaks of *dumb* spirits (Matt. 9:32; Mark 9:17); *blind* spirits (Matt. 12:22); *deaf* spirits (Mark 9:25); spirits of *infirmity* (Luke 13:11, 16); and spirits of *lunacy/insanity* (Matt. 17:15, 18; Luke 8:26–36). Evidently, Satan uses various kinds of demonic spirits to torment and afflict his victims.

There are other cases where the type of spirit is not named, but the person is said to be "*possessed* with devils (demons)." (See Matt. 4:24; 8:16, 28; Acts 8:7; 16:16).

When praying for people with mental or physical sickness, the gift of discerning of spirits is essential in order to determine if you are dealing with a demonic spirit or with a problem that is physically based. (For more on this see the chapter on the gift of healing.)

But what about those times when we are dealing with spiritual manifestations that don't have anything to do with healing? The gift of discerning of spirits is needed in order to: (a) perceive the source of the manifestation and (b) to reveal the plans and purposes of the enemy.

The gift of discerning of spirits will also empower the Spirit-filled believer with supernatural knowledge and understanding to approach cases of demon possession so that:

1. The demonic spirit can be cast out (Mark 16:17; Acts 13:6) or

2. The individual can be dealt with.

That was exactly what happened with Paul and Barnabas on the island of Cyprus when Elymas, a Jewish false prophet and sorcerer (one who performs magic/witchcraft with the aid of evil spirits), opposed their ministry:

> They traveled through the whole island until they came to Paphos. There they met a Jewish sorcerer and false prophet named Bar-Jesus, who was an attendant of the proconsul, Sergius Paulus. The proconsul, an intelligent man, sent for Barnabas and Saul because he wanted to hear the word of God. But Elymas the sorcerer (for that is what his name means) opposed them and tried to turn the proconsul from the faith. Then Saul, who was also called Paul, filled with the Holy Spirit, looked straight at Elymas and said, "You are a child of the devil and an enemy of everything that is right! You are full of all kinds of deceit and trickery. Will you never stop perverting the right ways of the Lord? Now the hand of the Lord is against you. You are going to be blind, and for a time you will be unable to see the light of the sun." Immediately mist and darkness came over him, and he groped about, seeking someone to lead him by the hand. When the proconsul saw

what had happened, he believed, for he was amazed at the
teaching about the Lord.

—ACTS 13:6–12, NIV

Of course we may wonder why Paul, when he discerned that Elymas
was a child of Satan, didn't *cast out* the evil spirits working through
the man. Instead he struck Elymas temporarily blind. Were those
spirits too strong for Paul? Certainly not. However, God will not violate a person's will. Elymas was a proud, subtle false prophet and sorcerer who *welcomed* the evil spirits that helped him gain and maintain
his position of influence and prominence. He obviously *did not want*
to be delivered.

But God's servant Paul publicly exposed Elymas for what he was and
pronounced God's judgment upon that wicked, demon-possessed child
of the devil. In this way, Paul demonstrated that Satan is no match for a
servant of God equipped with the gifts of the Holy Spirit!

The valuable gift of discerning of spirits is not only an *offen-
sive* weapon for believers for discerning spiritual manifestations of
demonic spirits. It is also a valuable defensive weapon to help protect
and guard a believer's Christian life and testimony. For example, at
Philippi a girl was possessed with *a spirit of divination. Divination* is
the means of *imitating* the divine, or of *counterfeiting* the divine. The
spirit of divination that possessed this girl pretended to be from God:

> Once when we were going to the place of prayer, we were met by
> a slave girl who had a spirit by which she predicted the future.
> She earned a great deal of money for her owners by fortune-
> telling. This girl followed Paul and the rest of us, shouting,
> "These men are servants of the Most High God, who are telling
> you the way to be saved." She kept this up for many days. Finally
> Paul became so troubled that he turned around and said to the
> spirit, "In the name of Jesus Christ I command you to come out
> of her!" At that moment the spirit left her.
>
> —ACTS 16:16–18, NIV

The gift of discerning of spirits unmasked this demon, revealing
him as an enemy in disguise. The spirit had pretended to be a promoter of Paul and his company, but Paul discerned the true source of
this endorsement. The motive was to identify Paul's message with the
spirits of hell. Paul saw through this trick and cast out the evil spirit.

3. A biblical example of discerning of the human spirit

Some people question whether discerning of *the human spirit* is included in the scope of discerning of spirits.

I believe that discerning of the human spirit is definitely included in the gift of discerning of spirits. What is not clear is just where the operation of the word of knowledge ends and the discerning of spirits begins. The gifts are closely related. Generally speaking, when the revelation involves exposure for moral consideration, the gift in operation is the discerning of spirits.[2] We see an excellent example in Acts. This incident came about not long after a godly Levite whom the apostles called "Barnabas", meaning "son of encouragement", sold a field which belonged to him, brought the money, and laid it at the feet of the apostles.

> Now a man named Ananias, together with his wife Sapphira, also sold a piece of property. With his wife's full knowledge he kept back part of the money for himself, but brought the rest and put it at the apostles' feet. Then Peter said, "Ananias, how is it that Satan has so filled your heart that you have lied to the Holy Spirit and have kept for yourself some of the money you received for the land? Didn't it belong to you before it was sold? And after it was sold, wasn't the money at your disposal? What made you think of doing such a thing? You have not lied to men but to God." When Ananias heard this, he fell down and died. And great fear seized all who heard what had happened. Then the young men came forward, wrapped up his body, and carried him out and buried him. About three hours later his wife came in, not knowing what had happened. Peter asked her, "Tell me, is this the price you and Ananias got for the land?" "Yes," she said, "that is the price." Peter said to her, "How could you agree to test the Spirit of the Lord? Look! The feet of the men who buried your husband are at the door, and they will carry you out also." At that moment she fell down at his feet and died. Then the young men came in and, finding her dead, carried her out and buried her beside her husband. Great fear seized the whole church and all who heard about these events.
>
> —ACTS 5:1–11, NIV

In the case of Ananias the liar, there was not necessarily a lying demon involved, but Peter was able to see through the deceiving action of Ananias and the lying words of Sapphira and expose them publicly. As in this case, discerning of spirits is not mind reading, psychic phenomena, or the ability to criticize or find fault. It comes from the Holy Spirit. He bears witness with our spirit whether something or someone is—or is not—of God.

Let me share another example from the New Testament. It relates how Philip went down to a city in Samaria and proclaimed the Christ. It reveals the enormous value of this gift to preserve the purity of the church:

> When the crowds heard Philip and saw the miraculous signs he did, they all paid close attention to what he said. With shrieks, evil spirits came out of many, and many paralytics and cripples were healed. So there was great joy in that city. Now for some time a man named Simon had practiced sorcery in the city and amazed all the people of Samaria. He boasted that he was someone great, and all the people, both high and low, gave him their attention and exclaimed, "This man is the divine power known as the Great Power." They followed him because he had amazed them for a long time with his magic. But when they believed Philip as he preached the good news of the kingdom of God and the name of Jesus Christ, they were baptized, both men and women. Simon himself believed and was baptized. And he followed Philip everywhere, astonished by the great signs and miracles he saw. When the apostles in Jerusalem heard that Samaria had accepted the word of God, they sent Peter and John to them. When they arrived, they prayed for them that they might receive the Holy Spirit, because the Holy Spirit had not yet come upon any of them; they had simply been baptized into the name of the Lord Jesus. Then Peter and John placed their hands on them, and they received the Holy Spirit. When Simon saw that the Spirit was given at the laying on of the apostles' hands, he offered them money and said, "Give me also this ability so that everyone on whom I lay my hands may receive the Holy Spirit." Peter answered: "May your money perish with you, because you thought you could buy the gift of God with money! You have no part or share in this ministry, because

your heart is not right before God. Repent of this wickedness
and pray to the Lord. Perhaps he will forgive you for having
such a thought in your heart. For I see that you are full of bitterness and captive to sin." Then Simon answered, "Pray to the
Lord for me so that nothing you have said may happen to me."
—ACTS 8:5–24, NIV

An evil spirit could have lurked behind the former sorcerer's religious exterior, although no mention of that is recorded. Simon had
believed and been baptized, but he had not repented of his bitterness and conniving. He needed help. (Refer to the *Amplified Bible*, vs.
22–23.) Discerning of spirits enabled Peter to help him, even though
Simon's condition had been hidden from Philip (Acts 8:23). Then
Simon asked for Peter and John's prayers.

BIBLICAL WARNINGS AGAINST DECEPTION

A warning from the apostle Paul to Timothy, his son in the faith, reveals
a subtle trick of Satan, particularly in the latter times—using demons to
create false doctrines to turn people from the faith. You and I are living
in "the latter times" that Paul spoke about, and it would be wise for us
to heed his warning to pay no attention whatsoever to seducing spirits
and their false doctrines. Read this carefully:

> But the Holy Spirit distinctly and expressly declares that in
> latter times some will turn away from the faith, giving atten-
> tion to deluding and seducing spirits and doctrines that
> demons teach, Through the hypocrisy and pretensions of
> liars whose consciences are seared (cauterized)...But refuse
> and avoid irreverent legends—profane and impure and god-
> less fictions, mere grandmothers' tales—and silly myths, and
> express your disapproval of them. Train yourself toward god-
> liness (piety)—keeping yourself spiritually fit.
> —1 TIMOTHY 4:1–2, 7, AMP

Did you get it? Paul warned that demons will use and invent all
sorts of erroneous, impure, godless fictions and myths to spoil and
pollute sound doctrine. Furthermore, they'll use hypocritical, showy,
fake, hollow liars with seared consciences to preach and spread those
errors and godless myths. The errors and godless myths they teach

will be demonically designed to make solid, thoroughly biblical doctrine sound unconvincing or doubtful so that people will turn away from the faith.

Believers in these last days had better *know* what the Word of God teaches! We'd better have our spiritual ears tuned to heaven's frequency—not hell's—so we can train ourselves toward godliness and be able to recognize, refuse, and ignore Satan's lies!

You and I must know what the Word of God teaches so that we can immediately detect anyone denying the truths of the gospel, as shown in the following scriptures. Meditate on these verses, asking the Spirit to engrave them on your heart.

> But when the fullness of the time came, God sent forth His Son, born of a woman, born under the Law, in order that He might redeem those who were under the law, that we might receive the adoption as sons. And because you are sons, God has sent forth the Spirit of His Son into our hearts, crying, "Abba! Father!" Therefore you are no longer a slave, but a son; and if a son, then an heir through God,
> —GALATIANS 4:4–7, NASB

> For God so loved the world, that He gave His only begotten Son, that whosoever believes in Him should not perish, but have eternal life. For God did not send the Son into the world to judge the world, but that the world should be saved through Him,
> —JOHN 3:16–17, NASB

Why is it so vital that we believe, understand and forever cherish truths such as these? In his first epistle, the apostle John gives us a solemn warning. He declares that demons will seek to conceal and deny the truth that Jesus Christ was sent from God the Father to this earth to be born of a woman, to suffer on a cross, shed His sinless blood, and die for the sins of mankind as the one and only Savior. I've printed out John's warning so you can read, remember, and reverence it!

> Beloved, do not believe every spirit, but test the spirits to see whether they are from God; because many false prophets have gone out into the world. By this you know the Spirit of God: every spirit that confesses that Jesus Christ has come in the flesh is from God; and every spirit that does not confess Jesus

is not from God; and this is the spirit of the antichrist, of which you have heard that it is coming, and now it is already in the world.

—1 JOHN 4:1–3, NASB

Remember this! Any teaching or any person denying *any* or *all* of the following truths is *Not* from God!

- Jesus was sent by God His Father to this earth and was born of a virgin.

- He shed His sinless blood and died for the sins of mankind so we could be forgiven and have eternal life.

- He was resurrected from the dead.

- Jesus Christ now lives forever as the one and only Savior, Deliverer, and Redeemer of mankind.

Also remember that Pharaoh's magicians, Jannes and Jambres, withstood Moses and were able to replicate the first, but not all, of the miraculous signs that Moses performed. (See 2 Tim. 3:8–9 and Ex. 7:8–22; 8:1–19.) In the same way, Satan's servants and demonic powers may oppose the work of God in any age by producing lying miracles, signs, and wonders. Remember! If it takes the focus off Jesus—the sinless Son of God and mankind's one and only Savior—pay no attention to it. Instead, "Train yourself toward godliness (piety)—keeping yourself spiritually fit" (1 Tim. 4:7, AMP).

DO YOU WANT TO BE A VICTOR OR A VICTIM?

If you want to be a *victor* and not a *victim*, I solemnly declare that it is absolutely imperative that you:

- Personally, reverently study and come to know the Word of God and the character, nature, and ways of God that are revealed in the scriptures.

- Begin earnestly seeking God now for the three gifts of revelation to function in and through you:

(1) the gift of discerning of spirits

(2) the gift of the word of knowledge

(3) the gift of the word of wisdom.

Believe me when I say that in these coming days of increasing demonic deception, if these three supernatural gifts of revelation are not alive and functioning in your spiritual walk, you will be deceived!

ANOTHER WORD OF CAUTION

Do yourself a favor, take this spiritual "check-up", and truthfully answer the following questions.

- ___ Am I bored?

- ___ Am I empty?

- ___ Have I grown complacent?

- ___ Have I grown proud, self-sufficient, and overly confident?

- ___ Do I feel strong and invulnerable to attack?

- ___ Am I cold or lukewarm in my spirit?

- ___ Do I find myself drawn to darkness, to the wrong people, to wrong things? (Eph. 4:27)

- ___ Do I have an interest in the paranormal, the occult, the demonic, magic, witchcraft, etc.?

- ___ Are my passions ungoverned?

- ___ Do I have a taste for the pornographic and sensual or for terror and violence?

- ___ Am I feeding my flesh and starving my spirit?

- ___ Do I devote little or no time to reading the Bible and praying in the Spirit?

If you must truthfully answer "yes" to any of those things, you are in danger!

When sin is no longer grievous to your soul, when you consent to or you crave things that once pricked your conscience and distressed your spirit, or even if you have never been aware that these things are contrary to the Word of God, you are giving place to the devil! Such sin can give the enemy a way of entrance into the inner sanctum of your life. It can then allow him to produce whatever he wishes and make you his servant.

SUGGESTIONS FOR DEFEATING SATAN

1. Get rid of all habits, games, reading materials, emblems, or statues that suggest cooperation with Satan or his crowd (See Acts 19:19–20).

2. Stay away from questionable things. Stay on the safe side. Do not bring questionable or detestable things into your house (See Deut. 7:26).

3. Do not use demon-oppressed or possessed persons as a source of entertainment, amusement or presumptuous action (See Acts 19:11–20).

4. Remember that "those who practice magic arts" (witches, warlocks, mediums, fortune tellers, etc.) are going to hell, according to Rev. 21:8. Therefore, your intentional contact with such persons should be limited to witnessing about the power of Jesus. Even necessary business and working contacts should include a clear stand for the Savior and His blood.

5. Live for Jesus with sincere obedience. Strive to obey each Bible command and "submit yourselves therefore to God" (James 4:7).

6. Rest confidently in your God-given authority over Satan. (See Mark 16:17; Luke 9:1.)

7. Rebuke Satan boldly in Jesus' Name. "Resist the devil, and he will flee from you" (James 4:7).

8. Live in faith. Don't expect sickness! If a symptom comes, don't claim it. Rebuke it. Claim health. Don't talk failure. Speak of victory in Christ. Expect to be

a success for Jesus. "According to your faith will it be done to you," (Matt. 9:29).[3]

SOME PERSONAL ILLUSTRATIONS OF THE GIFT OF DISCERNING OF SPIRITS

Deliverance of a Man just Released from an Institution

As mentioned earlier I was asked to hold a four-day revival in a church in Harvey, Louisiana. However, we had such a move of God that I wound up staying ten months!

Many were saved, filled with the Holy Spirit, and healed. Several others had been delivered from demonic activity. Satan's territory was being threatened, so he went on the attack.

One night, just as a beautiful time of praise and worship had ended, a man in his early thirties suddenly strode into the back of the church and started yelling and cursing the pastor and me. I knew immediately that a demonic spirit was speaking through the man.

My son and a member of the church took the man into a room beside the auditorium and began ministering to him. After I finished preaching, they brought the man back to the altar area in the sanctuary. I helped them minister to him.

The demons controlling the man were so strong they would literally throw him several feet across the front of the church, and his body would go into various contortions. While the man was laying on his back, the demon powers would lift him until only his toes and head were touching the floor. Then they would slam his body back against the floor.

As we ministered to the man, several demons came out of him, but he did not receive total deliverance that night. Why? Because God will not violate a person's will. I knew that a master demonic spirit was at work, "holding together" the other spirits tormenting him. The man, however, was simply not willing to give up certain things at that time. He did continue attending the revival services, however, coming to the altar each night to commit himself in certain areas to the Lord. During those nights at the altar, the Spirit of God continued to deal with him. The man finally came to a place of willingness to surrender his life to Jesus. One evening as I was praying for him, through the gift of discerning of spirits I suddenly called the master demonic spirit by name. I commanded it to release the man and come out of him, and he was totally delivered!

After that, his sister shared some of his history. His family had been unable to control him, and they had to have him institutionalized. However, after she had seen several people in the revival who had been delivered from demons, she checked her brother out of the institution and brought him to the service for the first time. That was the night when he had cursed and disrupted the service.

I received a phone call from that same man a few years later. He shared that he was living in Indiana, attending church there, and teaching a Sunday school class. The man talked with me about his faith, his desire for the Word of God, and his involvement in the church. We rejoiced together that he was free from demons by the power of God!

A Young Man Enslaved by Fear, a Controlling Spirit, and a Familiar Spirit

A man about twenty-two years of age came to me for ministry. I'd been talking with him less than ten minutes when the Holy Spirit revealed to me that he was enslaved by fear and a controlling spirit. In many years of ministry I've come to believe that a *controlling spirit* works in conjunction with a *familiar spirit.*

A *familiar spirit* knows a person's weaknesses and strengths, as well as the weaknesses and strengths of that individual's relatives from previous generations. Experience has taught me that when a familiar spirit detects a weakness that is similar to a weakness in a relative, this spirit can call in other spirits in order to enslave the person.

I began asking the young man what he had been reading, whom he had been associating with, whom he had talked to, etc. He told me about a beautiful young woman in her early twenties he had met on the internet. He said that she had e-mailed him pictures of herself. She had promised several times to meet him, and he had made arrangements each time to fly to where she was. However, she had always phoned the night before he was supposed to leave, saying something had come up, preventing her from seeing him.

The Holy Spirit revealed to me that the young man was dealing with a psychic. Psychics use familiar spirits, and so they know the person they're dealing with. The Holy Spirit showed me that this psychic was not a young girl—as she had portrayed herself in a fake picture—but was actually an older woman.

When I shared this with the young man, he became very defensive. However, after several hours of counseling and prayer, the Holy Spirit Himself made the truth real to the young man's heart. When that happened, he immediately changed! Instead of me asking the young man questions, he was the one asking me questions.

We prayed together. By the authority of the name of Jesus, the controlling spirit was broken off, and he repented. Over the next several days, the psychic tried to weasel her way back into his life. However, I had the young man change his cell phone number, his mailing address, and his email address. He is now totally free.

The Word of Knowledge Working with Discerning of Spirits

One Sunday night, the First Assembly auditorium in New Orleans was almost completely filled. It was still about twenty minutes before time for service to start, when three people walked in and sat on the very back pew. The Holy Spirit spoke to my spirit: "They have come to deceive you, but trust *Me*." That's all I heard.

We went through the entire service. When I gave the invitation, I noticed that the two men and the woman, all in their early thirties, had come forward with the others. The woman was standing in the line at the altar, and the two men were among those along the wall.

I began ministering to the people, but when I got to the woman, the Holy Spirit would not let me pray for her. He said: "Skip her. She is here to deceive you."

I finished ministering to that first group, but the woman remained as a part of the second group that was brought forward. Again, when I reached her, the Spirit said: "Skip her. She is here to deceive you."

When the third group came forward, she was still there. Again, the Holy Spirit said to skip her, so I did. But as I walked past her, she grabbed my arm and protested angrily: "Three times you have bypassed me!"

I turned, looked her squarely in the eye and replied: "You came here to deceive me and make a fool of me, but the Holy Spirit has made a fool of you!"

The woman opened her mouth to protest, but I pointed toward the back and said: "Look behind you and see those two brave men who wanted to you to come down here. They're leaving the building! When you see them, you tell them never to set foot in this building again unless they're coming for spiritual purposes, or the judgment of God could fall on them, and they would find themselves in severe trouble!" The woman hurriedly left, and I never saw the three of them again.

When I dealt with that woman and her two accomplices that night, the three gifts of the Holy Spirit in operation were *the word of knowledge* (telling me the three had come to deceive me); the *discerning of spirits* (deception); and *the word of wisdom* (telling me what to do with the situation).

THROUGH THE GIFT OF DISCERNING OF SPIRITS AND OTHER GIFTS OF THE SPIRIT, GOD REVEALS THAT *HIS* POWER IS FAR GREATER THAN THE POWER OF THE ENEMY!

During the revival I mentioned earlier in Harvey, LA, the gifts of the Spirit moved in a powerful way. Many people came to know the Lord. Many were filled with the Holy Spirit, healed, and received words of knowledge and words of wisdom.

We also encountered many demoniacs and much demonic activity. Many of these people were not regular attendees of that church, but they came for the revival. There were so many manifestations of God's delivering power that the word went out to many parts of the U.S. regarding what God was doing through that revival.

About six months into the revival as I was ministering on a Friday night, I started feeling sick and began losing my strength. Saturday night I was weaker. I managed to minister Sunday morning, but by the Sunday night service I felt so tired and drained while ministering that I could hardly wait to get back to my room.

By Monday night I was very weak. At the end of the service, I had prayed for several sick people when a young man came forward who was demon-possessed. My son, Randy, who was a member of our ministry team, came and asked me to help them minister to the man. I went over, knelt beside the man, began ministering to him and, by God's grace and power, the demonic stronghold was broken and the man was set free.

However, when I tried to stand up from where I had been kneeling to pray with the young man, I didn't have the strength to rise to my feet. Randy and one of the other Christian men lifted me and sat me on a front pew in the church. When they realized that I was so nauseated and weak that I could hardly bear it, they took me to the hotel. Randy helped me put on my pajamas and get into bed. I was too sick to want anything to eat or drink that night.

The next morning I couldn't get out of bed, and I was still unable to eat or drink. Finally, late in the afternoon, my wife helped me get down a little soup. By then, since we were only having Friday through Monday services six months after the revival had started, my wife and I drove to our home that was only about twenty miles away. I asked her to get me a doctor's appointment or take me to the emergency room. However, after running a lot of tests, our doctor could not find anything wrong with me physically. Finally, although I was so weak I could hardly walk, he sent me home.

At 10:00 p.m. that night as I lay in bed, my wife came in to check on me. I told her I was going to pray that I would be able to sleep a little, and she slipped out so I could rest. Suddenly, surrounding the bed were thirteen demonic spirits! (I believe that the Lord opened my eyes to the spirit world so I could see them.) This was the only time in my Christian experience that I had ever seen or heard demons talking among themselves, though demons had tried to argue with me when I was casting them out of a person.

The demons were black, shadowy beings, but they moved around as if they were walking, not floating. They looked about three-and-a-half feet tall—not as tall as a man. I lay there and counted them as they were arguing and warring among themselves. I could hear what they were saying. They were discussing the revival and how they should have stopped it, but now it had gone so far that stopping it was impossible.

Their fussing and arguing with each other continued. Then one of the demons shoved me. Another demon protested: "Don't do that! If you hurt him, it will just rally the people behind him, and it will present a greater problem for us!"

The demons went into a football-type of huddle, and I could hear them arguing and blaming each other for not stopping the revival at the very beginning. Then one of the demons exclaimed: "I know how to stop it!"

Several asked, "How?"

He answered, "By bringing offense and disunity. Where there is offense, causing people to hurt and mistrust and turn against one another, we can operate! But where there is unity, we have no power or authority."

The demons began plotting to bring bickering and offenses between various members of the congregation in order to hinder the operation of the Holy Spirit. At that point, I began praying aloud in the Spirit and commanded the demons to leave. They obeyed, and I dropped into a peaceful, restful sleep.

When I awoke the next morning I was weak, but I felt great and was hungry. I had no nausea or other pains.

The revival continued to build in momentum. One morning the pastor called and excitedly exclaimed: "We really have the devil shook up! This morning around two o'clock a sheriff's deputy rang my doorbell to tell me that about thirty minutes before, there were nine witches chanting and walking around and around the large fountain at our church. The deputy ran them off."

Then the pastor said, "Brother Gorman, you'll have to come to the church and see what's written on the walls of our building!"

They had a beautiful church that had granite up about eight feet all around the outside of the building. I went to see what the pastor was talking about. There on the wall with black spray paint, they had scrawled: "The persecutions have begun!" On another wall they had sprayed "Subvert!" (e.g., to threaten, undermine, challenge; to weaken and destabilize).

That bold pastor refused to bend or back down. Instead, he asked if I would stay and continue the revival as long as the Spirit led. I agreed, but asked for a room where I and believers could pray for forty-five minutes before each service.

The pastor heartily approved. We averaged between sixty-five and eighty people each evening. The rule was that the people were to pray only in tongues, not in English, because the Holy Spirit knew who would be coming, and how we should minister.

The following Friday night about eighty prayer warriors had gone into the prayer room and were praying in the Spirit. I had a certain spot over in a corner where I prayed.

We had finished praying and all the people were leaving and going into the main service. Just then, the pastor's mother and sister entered the room to take care of something. I was the last to leave and had just walked out and turned to close the door when suddenly, I heard the pastor's mother and sister scream!

Rushing back into the room, I spied a cottonmouth moccasin coiled under the metal folding chair where I had been praying for forty-five minutes! I kept an eye on the snake, while the women ran to find someone with a hoe or shovel to kill the thing!

They returned very quickly with some men of the church and a shovel. The men struck the snake very hard several times, almost severing its head with the sharp blade. Then they took its body outside and tossed it on the ground beside the dumpster, relieved to have killed the thing and finally be rid of it.

The next day, Randy was taking some video shots around the property. He approached the dumpster, saw the semi-coiled body of the snake lying there, and kicked at it to get a look from a different angle. The instant the toe of Randy's boot hit it, the snake struck! Even though it was badly injured and couldn't crawl normally, the snake continued to try to attack anyone who approached it until its head was cut completely off, and it was dead for sure!

Thanking God for His power and protection, I reflected on the strange events of recent weeks: How I'd thought the lengthy, powerful revival would have to be closed due to my weakness and sickness, although the doctor had been unable to find anything wrong with me physically. How those thirteen demonic spirits had encircled my bed, arguing among themselves and conniving devious ways to close the revival. How I'd awakened refreshed and strengthened the next morning, able to continue the revival, after binding the demons the night before and commanding them to leave.

Was it just a coincidence that the witches had been at the church earlier that week? Was it just a coincidence that out of all the chairs in the room, that poisonous snake was coiled under the chair where *I* always sat to pray and intercede? How did it get there? Why hadn't the snake bitten me? Having been raised on a farm and being around snakes all those years, I knew that cottonmouths are poisonous and aggressive. I shook my head in gratitude and awe, unable to reach any conclusion except that the Holy Spirit had kept the snake from biting me, thwarting Satan's final desperate strategy to shut down the powerful ten month revival that was doing so much damage to his kingdom.

A series of coincidences? I know what I believe. You are free to make up your own mind.

A CONCLUDING CHALLENGE

Are evil spirits real? Are they still attacking, tormenting, oppressing, and possessing people? The very existence of the gift of discerning of spirits proves that Satan and his demons are still alive and well on planet Earth and, sadly, inside the church as well. They are still striving to steal, kill, dominate, destroy, devastate, and torture human beings just as cruelly today as they did when Jesus ministered among the desperate throngs and dusty streets of His day. At the very foot of the mountain of the Lord's glory today evil spirits are still throwing men into the water and fire, bullying and striving to stop any move of God, and boastfully attracting attention to themselves.

Are you already moving in the gift of discerning of spirits? Are you already experiencing the joy of seeing the oppressed go free and the enslaved liberated from the devil's destructive power? If not, dare to step away from the desire for comfort and selfish blessings and step away from the fear or unbelief that is holding you back.

Begin right now to earnestly seek the gift of discerning of spirits and the full equipment, enlightenment and protection of the Spirit's supernatural power. This gift will:

1. Help deliver the oppressed and tormented (Mark 5:5; Luke 9:39; Acts 5:16; Matt. 12:22; Mark 9:17, 25; Luke 13:11, 16; Mark 12:43–5; Acts 10:38; Luke 13:16).

2. Reveal a servant of the devil (Acts 13:9, 10).

3. Stop the plans of the adversary (Acts 16:16).

4. Expose lies, doctrines of devils, heresies, and demonic signs and wonders (1 Tim. 4:1; 2 Peter 2:1).

5. Help you avoid being deceived by the spirits of devils working miracles (2 Thess. 2:9; Rev. 16:14).

6. Show the source of a miracle and indicate inerrably its true character—whether true or false, heavenly or

hellish. It will reveal the kind of spirit motivating a
person.[4]

I gave a solemn warning earlier in the chapter, but it bears repeating.
Please believe me when I say that in these coming days of increasing
demonic deception, if these three supernatural gifts of revelation: *the
gift of the word of knowledge, the gift of the word of wisdom,* and *the
gift of discerning of spirits* are not alive and functioning in your spiritual walk, you *will* be deceived!

Part 3

THE THREE GIFTS OF POWER

The gift of faith
The gift of healing
The gift of miracles

THE THREE GIFTS OF POWER

N 1 CORINTHIANS 12:1–11, Paul lists nine different gifts of the Holy
Spirit. As we have learned, these nine gifts of the Spirit may be
divided into three categories—Revelation, Power, and Inspiration—
with three gifts of the Spirit in each category. In each of the three categories, God is doing a separate, distinct work.

We have studied the three gifts of Revelation, which *reveal* something. You will recall that they are the word of wisdom, the word of
knowledge, and discerning of spirits. These gifts are the vehicles God
uses to supernaturally reveal things to His people that they could not
know about in the natural or by way of their physical senses. They
come by divine revelation.

We will now study the three gifts of Power. They are faith, gifts of healing, and working of miracles. These gifts *do* something. They are the divine artillery God uses to endow His people with supernatural power and abilities to work His works and to destroy the works of the devil!

The three gifts of power "are second in appreciation and second in greatness, the revelation gifts being the greatest God can give."[1]

How are these three gifts of power defined? What are they? What do they do? In this next section, you and I will examine the gift of faith, the gifts of healing, and the gift of miracles. We'll start with the gift of faith. If you're ready, we'll begin!

Chapter 7

THE GIFT OF FAITH

I N THE OPERATION of all the gifts of the Spirit, faith must always be present. It is not always the *gift* of faith, but it is a faith like Paul described in Hebrews 11:6: "He that cometh to God must believe that He is…" My personal interpretation of that verse is: "He that cometh to God must believe that *God is whatever we need Him to be!*" I believe it's based on the same spiritual principle as when God told Moses: "Tell them that I Am That I Am: has sent you." (See Ex. 3:14, 15.) To me, this means, "I AM whatever you need."

This same kind of faith must be present as the gifts of the Holy Spirit operate in my life and yours. Whatever we need at that particular time—by faith, the gift that is needed is released. The Holy Spirit is faithful to show us what is needed. It is the Holy Spirit who works through us with His gifts to make us more than conquerors in Christ Jesus.

TWO KINDS OF FAITH: NATURAL AND SUPERNATURAL

If you look up the definition of "faith," you'll find this: belief, confidence, trust, assurance, conviction. If you have faith, you believe. You can believe in all kinds of things: a person, a product, an organization, etc. That's *natural* faith. But there are two principal kinds of faith—natural and supernatural. In this chapter we're talking about more than an ordinary, natural ability to believe in something or someone. We're talking about the *supernatural*, Bible kind of faith.

The Bible tells us that "God has dealt to each one a measure of faith" (Rom. 12:3). We could say that faith begins with recognizing that God is. The Bible says, "For he who comes to God must believe that He is, and that He is a rewarder of those who diligently seek Him" (Heb. 11:6, NKJV). Faith permits God to perform on your behalf![1]

When we have confidence that God will do what He has said He will do, that's *faith*: (Greek: pistis: persuasion; moral conviction of religious truth or the truthfulness of God, especially reliance upon Christ for salvation).

How does faith come? How does faith grow and become strong? The Bible answers those questions: "*Faith* comes by hearing, and hearing by the word of God" (Rom. 10:17).

Spiritual Christians strive to build their lives on the Bible because it is God's word. Although every Christian has a measure of faith, some have more than others, depending on how faithfully they study the Bible and then act upon what they read.

ALL FAITH IS NOT THE SAME

All faith is not the same. The Bible speaks of little faith, growing faith, and mustard seed faith, for example. In our study of the gift of faith, we want to look first at four different kinds of faith: (1) Natural Faith, (2) Saving Faith, (3) Faith, the fruit of the Spirit, and (4) Faith, the gift of the Spirit. Let's take a minute to understand each of them clearly.

FOUR DIFFERENT KINDS OF FAITH

1. Natural faith: Human beings have a natural kind of faith. This is the kind of faith a farmer has when, instead of eating his grains of corn, he plants them in the ground and expects them to sprout, grow to maturity, and produce more corn. It's the kind of faith a fisherman has that when he casts his hook or net into the water in the right place and the correct way, he will catch a fish.[2]

2. Saving faith: This special kind of faith is in the spiritual realm. "Believe on the Lord Jesus Christ, and thou shalt be saved" (Acts 16:31).

   The amount and type of faith can vary in the lives and ministries of different believers. For example, the scriptures speak of *little* faith, *growing* faith, and *mustard seed* faith.

   The Bible also speaks of faith that is a *fruit* of the Spirit (Gal. 5:22) and faith that is a *gift* of the Spirit

(1 Cor. 12:9). Fruit-of-the-Spirit faith and gift-of-the-Spirit faith are not the same.

3. Faith, the fruit of the Spirit: "But the fruit of the Spirit is love, joy, peace, longsuffering, gentleness, goodness, faith, meekness, temperance: against such there is no law" (Gal. 5:22–23).

   Fruit-of-the-Spirit faith refers to the faith of the Christian who has learned to confidently trust in the integrity, power, wisdom, goodness, and divine intervention of God. Paul expressed fruit-of-the-Spirit faith in Romans 11:33: "Oh, the depth of the riches both of the wisdom and knowledge of God! how unsearchable are His judgments and His ways past finding out!"

   Fruit-of-the-Spirit faith enables a believer to hold himself calm and undismayed in the face of the difficult and unexpected. Why? Fruit-of-the-Spirit faith believes that God will intervene and make him more than a conqueror in every situation.

4. Faith, the gift of the Spirit: Our focus in this chapter is the gift of faith that's mentioned in 1 Corinthians 12:8–10: "For to one is given by the Spirit the word of wisdom; to another the word of knowledge by the same Spirit; To another *faith* by the same Spirit; to another the gifts of healing by the same Spirit; To another the working of miracles; to another prophecy; to another discerning of spirits; to another divers kinds of tongues; to another the interpretation of tongues...."

The gift of faith is a *special* kind of faith ignited in a believer's heart by the Holy Spirit when an impossible situation exists. It's a special faith given at a special time for a special need. It supernaturally achieves what is impossible through human instruments. We observe the gift of faith in operation when God, through the power of the Holy Spirit, performs supernatural exploits that cannot be humanly explained. These exploits cannot be done ordinarily; otherwise, they would have no relation to the supernatural gifts of the Holy Spirit.[3]

The gift of faith is a direct impartation from God of a supernatural faith that reaches into the creative realm. It counts the things which are not as though they are.[4]

The gift of faith enables you to believe for God to undertake in a supernatural way.[5] God does the work *for* you. Therefore, when the supernatural solution comes for the impossible situation, God alone deserves the gratitude and the glory.

The gift of faith is suddenly knowing that a certain thing, for which you have been burdened, is going to be done. It is resting in the divine assurance which God has put into your heart.[6]

The gift of faith is that instantaneous assurance that something particular is going to happen, and—most of the time—that it's going to happen immediately. That is not always the case, however. Sometimes, after the Holy Spirit gives you that supernatural gift-of-faith assurance and you *know* that a certain thing for which you have been burdened is going to be done, a period of time may pass before faith becomes sight. It may be minutes, hours, days, weeks, months, or years, but that divine assurance remains. If that is the case, just continue to pray in faith as different situations arise concerning the person or thing. Bind the enemy, praise God, and confidently hold fast to that supernatural assurance that it will happen, just as God told you.

Remember! In a manifestation of the gift of faith, God brings to pass a supernatural change. *No human effort is involved.* In other words, the gift of faith enables you to believe God to undertake in a supernatural way. God does the work *for* you. We see an excellent example of the gift of faith in 1 Kings:

> And Elijah the Tishbite, who was of the inhabitants of Gilead, said unto Ahab, As the Lord God of Israel liveth, before whom I stand, there shall not be dew nor rain these years, but according to my word. And the word of the Lord came unto him, saying, Get thee hence, and turn thee eastward, and hide thyself by the brook Cherith, that is before Jordan. And it shall be, that thou shalt drink of the brook; and I have commanded the ravens to feed thee there. So he went and did according unto the word of the Lord: for he went and dwelt by the brook Cherith, that is before Jordan. And the ravens brought him bread and flesh in the morning, and bread and flesh in the evening; and he drank of the brook.
>
> —1 KINGS 17:1–6

What did Elijah do? He exercised the gift of faith! He simply obeyed God and sat calmly by the brook Cherith, confident that God would supply his need.

What did God do? He commanded the ravens to bring Elijah meat day after day until the brook dried up—and the ravens obeyed. They didn't follow their normal habits and eat the food themselves. They obeyed God and brought bread and meat to Elijah every morning and every evening.

Then things changed, "And it came to pass after a while, that the brook dried up, because there was no rain in the land" (1 Kings 17:7).

It's critical that you and I understand that just as we go through *earthly* times and seasons—days, weeks, months, years and winter, spring, summer, fall—we also go through *spiritual* times and seasons. Things change in the natural realm, and things change in the spiritual realm. But the God who orders the orbiting of the planets around the sun and guarantees that every sunrise and every sunset is right on time is the God who orders His own perfectly timed spiritual times and seasons in your life.

When things change, don't panic! God's hand isn't empty. His plans for you haven't suddenly swerved off course. God doesn't make mistakes. "We know that all things work together for good to those who love God, to those who are called according to His purpose" (Rom. 8:28, NKJV). Elijah knew that, and he trusted and obeyed when God's instructions and method of provision changed.

> And it came to pass after a while, that the brook dried up, because there was no rain in the land. And the word of the Lord came unto him, saying, Arise, get thee to Zarephath, which belongeth to Zidon, and dwell there: behold I have commanded a widow woman there to sustain thee. So he arose and went to Zarephath. And when he came to the gate of the city, behold, the widow woman was there gathering of sticks: and he called to her, and said, Fetch me, I pray thee, a little water in a vessel, that I may drink. And as she was going to fetch it, he called to her, and said, Bring me, I pray thee, a morsel of bread in thine hand. And she said, As the Lord God liveth, I have not a cake, but an handful of meal in a barrel, and a little oil in a cruse [jar]: and behold, I am gathering two sticks, that I may go in and dress it for me

and my son, that we may eat it, and die. And Elijah said
unto her, Fear not; go and do as thou hast said: but make
me thereof a little cake first, and bring it unto me, and after
make for thee and for thy son. For thus saith the Lord God
of Israel, The barrel of meal shall not waste, neither shall
the cruse of oil fail, until the day that the Lord sendeth
rain upon the earth. And she went and did according to
the saying of Elijah: and she, and he, and her house, did
eat many days. And the barrel of meal wasted not, neither
did the cruse of oil fail, according to the word of the Lord,
which he spake by Elijah.

—1 KINGS 17:7–16

Before we go on, I want to say something else that's very, very
important. Just like that little widow woman, when you and I choose
to trust, obey, and pay our tithes to God *first*, God will see to it that
our "barrel of flour and jar of oil" will not fail until He sends rain
upon our situation. Elijah, that widow woman, and her son were fed
supernaturally through three years of famine because of the word of
the Lord which He spoke by Elijah. That was a gift of faith to Elijah,
enabling Elijah to believe that God would undertake in a supernatural
way. God did the work *for* him.

The gift of faith *appears* to be passive—inactive; however, it sets
powerful forces in motion, and the results become apparent at a later
time. The gift of faith (like the gift of the working of miracles) obtains
supernatural results, but in a less spectacular way.

Look at Mark 11:14, for example: "When Jesus came to the fig tree
that bore no fruit but had only leaves, He said, 'Let no one eat fruit
from you ever again.'" Nothing *appeared* to happen in the natural, but
something actually *did* happen in the supernatural realm. The next
morning as Jesus and the disciples passed that way again, some very
shocked disciples saw that the fig tree had withered away!

The gift of faith works just the same for you and me—whatever the
need or circumstance. God works supernaturally on our behalf while
we watch with awe and gratitude. Remember: in the gift of faith, God
does the work *for* us.

REASONS WHY THE GIFT OF FAITH IS IMPARTED BY GOD

The gift of faith is imparted by God for divine protection, divine provision, divine health, supernatural transportation, deliverance, and divine discipline.[7] The gift of faith may also include the ability to impart blessing.[8]

The gift of faith is imparted by God for blessing.

In the days of the Old Testament patriarchs like Abraham, Isaac, Jacob, etc., the tribal blessing was imparted from father to son through a special dispensation of faith.[9] It was usually performed through the laying on of hands. However, laying on of hands in the Old Testament was not just for imparting the tribal blessing. Moses laid hands on Joshua, and he received the "spirit of wisdom" (Deut. 34:9).

The patriarchal sacrament of imparting the blessing foreshadowed special blessings that would be given to Christians through laying on hands in the New Testament dispensation.[10]

The gift of the Holy Spirit may be given through faith, by the laying on of hands.

1. During the revival in Samaria, the gift of the Holy Spirit was given through faith, by the laying on of hands when Peter and John came down to Samaria, prayed, and laid hands on the converts (See Acts 8:14–17).

2. In Acts 9:17, the Apostle Paul also received the Holy Spirit through laying on of hands.

3. In Acts 19:6, Paul laid hands on the disciples at Ephesus in order for them to receive the Holy Spirit.

4. In Galatians 3:5, when Paul infers that the Holy Spirit is ministered to Christians through faith, it's apparent that the gift of faith is involved.

5. Although the gift of the Holy Spirit may be given through faith, by the laying on of hands, God is not restricted to any particular method in giving the Holy Spirit. For example, the Holy Spirit may fall according

to the sovereign grace of God, as it did on the day of
Pentecost and as it did at Cornelius's house (Acts 2:1
–4; 10:44). Yet on other occasions, such as the revival in
Samaria, the gift was given through faith, by the laying
on of hands (Acts 8:14–17).[11]

*Gifts of healings may be received through the laying on of hands
and may also be received in other ways.*

1. The sick person can pray and receive healing.

2. Church members may pray for one another and be
   healed (James 5:16).

3. Sick people can be healed at a distance through the
   spoken word of faith (Ps. 107:20: "He sent His word and
   healed them.")

4. People may be healed through handkerchiefs or cloths
   that have touched the body of a person of faith (Acts
   19:11–12).

The gift of faith is imparted by God for divine protection.

*The apostle Paul's deliverance from a shipwreck and a poisonous
snake*

We see two tremendous examples of the gift of faith in Acts 28 and
29. When Paul was sailing to Rome, a powerful storm destroyed the
ship and all its cargo, just as God had warned Paul before they ever
set sail. But God had promised Paul that not one person would be lost.
Every person on board made it safely to land.

When Paul and the prisoners made it to shore, the people of the
island kindled a fire to warm Paul and his water-soaked companions
from the rain and cold. When Paul gathered a bundle of sticks and
laid them on the fire, a poisonous snake came out of the heat and fas-
tened its fangs on Paul's hand. The islanders said among themselves,
"No doubt this man is a murderer, whom, though he has escaped the
sea, yet justice does not allow him to live" (Acts 28:4). But Paul simply
shook the snake off into the fire, and suffered no ill effects.

The islanders watched, expecting him to swell or fall down dead suddenly. After they watched Paul a long time and saw that no harm came
to him, they changed their minds and said that he was a god.

As a result of this miraculous chain of events, the islanders asked Paul to pray for others in the island who had diseases, and they were healed and God was glorified.

The gift of faith is imparted by God for divine provision.

The gift of faith to provide for a missionary

Dr. John G. Lake's healing ministry in missionary fields was considered the greatest of his generation. In one of his faith-inspiring messages preached in the early 1900s, Dr. Lake related the following account:

> We left Indianapolis on the first day of April, 1908, my wife and self and seven children and four others. We had our tickets to Africa but no money for personal expenses en route except $1.50. (Dr. Lake then relates several remarkable provisions of God which supplied their needs.)
>
> Through my knowledge of the immigration laws of South Africa, I knew that before we would be permitted to land, I must show the immigration inspector that I was possessor of at least $125.00. We prayed earnestly over this matter, and about the time we reached the equator a rest came into my soul concerning it. I could pray no more.
>
> About 8 or 10 days later we arrived in Cape Town harbor, and our ship anchored. The immigration inspector came on board and the passengers lined up at the purser's office to present their money and receive their tickets to land. My wife said, "What are you going to do?" I said, "I am going to line up with the rest. We have obeyed God thus far. It is now up to the Lord. If they send us back we cannot help it."
>
> As I stood in line awaiting my turn, a fellow passenger touched me on the shoulder and indicated to me to step out of the line, and come over to the ship's rail to speak with him. He asked some questions, and then drew from his pocket a traveler's checkbook, and handed me two money orders aggregating $200.00. I stepped back into line, presented my orders to the inspector, and received our tickets to land.
>
> Johannesburg is 1,000 miles inland from Cape Town. Throughout the voyage and on the train we earnestly prayed about the subject of a home. We were faith missionaries. We

had neither a board nor friends behind us to furnish money. We were dependent on God. Many times during the trip to Johannesburg we bowed our heads and reminded God that when we arrived there, we would need a home. God blessed and wondrously answered our prayer.

Upon our arrival at Johannesburg I observed a little woman bustling up. She said, "You are an American missionary party?" The reply was, "Yes." Addressing me, she said, "How many are there in your family?" I answered, "My wife, myself and seven children." "O," she said, "you are the family. The Lord has sent me to meet you, and I want to give you a home."

That same afternoon we were living in a furnished cottage in the suburbs, the property of our beloved benefactor…of Johannesburg, who remains to this day our beloved friend and fellow worker in the Lord.[12]

The gift of faith for an urgent need

Dr. Sheba Koluthungan is a faith-filled woman who grew up in India, where she trained as a runner for the Olympics. Sheba, who earned two Ph.D. degrees and three master's degrees, shared the following story with her friend, Dr. Judy Doyle, a few years ago when the two women were professors at Southwestern Assemblies of God University in Waxahachie, Texas.

Sheba's mother-in-law was a woman of prayer and strong in faith. She was diabetic and did not have the money to buy insulin. There is a fruit in India that works like insulin to help control blood sugar levels, but she had no way of getting it. After prayer, an inner urging prompted her to go out and sit in her yard. She obeyed, waiting in faith. A bird flew over and dropped a piece of the fruit! But that was not all. In the days ahead as she continued to go out and wait expectantly in her yard, a bird dropped a piece of the fruit every day until God provided the money to get the insulin.

The gift of faith for healing.

From my late teens all the way into my early thirties, I suffered with horrible allergy problems. Almost without exception, whenever I preached I lost my voice. Then it would take me two to three days to regain it. If I preached on both Sunday morning and evening, it was certain that I would not be able to talk above a whisper until sometime on Wednesday. The first year or two that Virginia and I were married, she never heard me speak when I was not hoarse.

One day I was in my office in New Orleans, and I had been reading and praying. Suddenly, there was a release of faith in my spirit, and an inner voice said: "Claim your healing now!" So I threw my hands in the air and began to praise God for my healing. From that moment I started improving. I was not healed completely, but the process had begun.

I knew that healing is often stretched over a period of time before it is manifested fully, but one afternoon I was speaking to the Lord about why I was still struggling with this hoarseness if I was healed. The Spirit illuminated my mind concerning what the Lord had said to me that afternoon in my office in New Orleans. I realized He was saying: "Why don't you claim your healing?"

Prior to that time, I was on strong medication, and I gave myself two shots in the leg per week. But from that afternoon I never took the strong medication again, and I quit giving myself the shots. It took four to four-and-a-half years before the total healing was manifested, but I remained strong in faith. During the last twelve years I pastored First Assembly of God in New Orleans, I preached several times on Sunday, once on Monday night, and twice on Wednesday. I also preached many conferences across the nation and had a daily radio program and a daily telecast. I never suffered with my voice nor did I suffer with a sore throat or other allergy symptoms.

The divine promise was given to me that I would be healed, and with that promise came the gift of faith. I had to walk it out, but I walked in faith, *knowing* I would be healed.

The gift of faith, a word of knowledge, and a gift of healing.

The cameras were on, taping the program on which I was preaching for our telecast. As I was teaching, the Holy Spirit began speaking to me. Suddenly, I just knew in my spirit that there was a woman in Chicago who was in a wheelchair, and she had been in it for twelve years.

The Lord told me: "Tell her that she will begin to feel a tingling in her legs, and she is to stand up. So she will know for sure that she is the woman you are speaking to, tell her that she is in the room with her sister and her husband. Tell her that as this tingling sensation begins, she is to stand up, and God will enable her to walk."

As I was saying what the Lord had told me to say, it dawned on me that the program I was taping would not be shown in Chicago until two weeks from that date. I felt a surge of fear, but as the Lord helped me understand that He knew who would be watching two weeks down the road, the fear melted away. Calm, confident faith took its place.

Two weeks later while the program was being aired, one of the phone counselors ran into the office where I was and said: "Brother Gorman, come here quick! There's a lady on the phone from Chicago, and she's the lady you called out on the program about her legs being healed!" As I put the receiver to my ear, I could hear shouting in the background. The woman exclaimed: "the shouting is from my sister and husband who just saw me get up for the first time in twelve years! They're watching me walk around the room! I feel no pain!"

A few weeks after that, two women and a man walked into the service and headed straight for the platform. Two ushers tried to stop them, but one of the women said, "I'm the lady from Chicago!"

When I went down to her, she said, "I've come here today to give testimony of my healing! This is my sister and my husband who were in the room with me when I was healed!" I explained to the congregation how God had brought it all about, and the congregation erupted in praise as we all rejoiced together. I realized that several gifts of the Spirit had worked together in this situation: a word of knowledge, a gift of faith, and a gift of healing.

Healing and the gift of faith.

At Christ for the Nations Institute in Dallas, Texas, Dr. Eddie Hyatt shared a personal testimony regarding healing and a gift of faith:[13]

> I was three weeks old at the time, and my family lived on a farm in West Texas where my dad plowed large sections of land. One summer day, as he sat on his tractor plowing the miles of dry sod, he suddenly noticed a tractor going in circles in our yard.
>
> Previously, he had parked the tractor in the yard, but there was no one there who could operate it. Turning his tractor toward home, he arrived to find my mother sitting on the porch sobbing as she held my 7-year-old brother, Pete.

My dad said when he saw Pete, he looked as flat as a pancake. He was still alive, but as he labored to breathe, blood and water would bubble out of his eyes, nose, mouth, and ears. He and my 4-year-old brother had been playing like they were farming and somehow, they started the tractor. It ran directly over Pete, pulling the heavy plow discs across his body.

My parents rushed Pete to the nearest hospital where three doctors examined him. They all gave the same fatal prognosis: "He won't live more than 10 minutes." They explained that even without x-rays they knew a broken rib had punctured a lung. That was the reason for the blood and water coming out of his eyes, ears, nose, and mouth. It was obvious that there was other damage as well.

The doctors wheeled my brother away, and my parents were left alone. As my dad pondered what he had just heard, the one thing which occupied my dad's mind was the call of God to full-time ministry which he had ignored for five years. He had never told anyone of this call because it seemed impossible to him. Having only a fourth-grade education and a family to care for, the thought of becoming a pastor or minister seemed as impossible as going to the moon. Nonetheless, he stepped into a nearby restroom and offered up a simple, three-word prayer of consecration and dedication—a prayer of total surrender to God. Dad raised his right hand and said, "Lord, I'm ready." It was just three words, but at that very moment, the fire fell. Suddenly the gift of faith dropped into his heart and he knew that Pete was going to be fine. He didn't know how he knew, but he knew.

My parents waited another hour before anyone brought news of Pete's condition. Finally, one of the doctors came to the waiting room and said, "Mr. Hyatt, there has been a higher power here tonight." He went on to explain that all the bleeding had suddenly stopped. They had completed x-rays, and Pete did not have a broken bone anywhere in his body. A nurse in this hospital, who was assigned to Pete's room, attended the same church as my parents. She later told them that she had never experienced the presence and power of God as she did in Pete's room that day.

My dad kept the commitment he made to the Lord to fulfill

the call to the ministry that had been on his life. He went into full-time ministry and served God as a pastor for almost 40 years. My brother Pete is alive and well today, serving the Lord in music and singing and teaching auto mechanics at a high school in Honey Grove, Texas.

That one prayer of consecration and that gift of faith not only brought healing to my brother, it changed the entire destiny of my father and our family. Who knows how many other individuals and families have been changed by my father's dedication to God!

What a testimony! If you and I want to see incredible answers to prayer; if we want to see the fire of God fall and true revival break forth in the land, we need to reconsider the prayer of dedication and consecration and its place in the life of the church today. We, too, must rebuild the altars of consecration. As the old hymn says:

> I surrender all; I surrender all.
> All to Thee, my blessed Savior,
> I surrender all![14]

The gift of faith in Smith Wigglesworth.

Missionary-evangelist Dr. Lester Sumrall recounts an example of the gift of faith in the life of Smith Wigglesworth, who was known as "The Apostle of Faith":[15]

I was very well acquainted with Smith Wigglesworth, having visited in his home many times before he passed away. He was certainly a dynamic man of faith.

Smith Wigglesworth and his wife met and were married in the Salvation Army. Though a plumber by trade, he worked with his wife in a local mission. He was slow of speech, so he handed out songbooks and took up the offering while his wife did the preaching. But there was something big inside Smith Wigglesworth. When he prayed for people, things happened. He demonstrated some amazing feats of faith in his life.

One day, when he came home from work, he was met at the door with news that his wife had died—that she had been dead for two hours.

To that, Wigglesworth replied, "No, she's not dead." He

dropped his lunch bucket and tools, walked into the bedroom, pulled her out of bed, stood her against the wall, called her by her first name, and said, "I command you to come to me now!" Then he backed off, and here she came! She lived a number of years after that.

Faith was a primary strength in the life and ministry of Smith Wigglesworth. He knew what it was to have the gift of faith.

The gift of faith in the life of Howard Carter

When World War I broke out against England, Howard Carter, because he was a minister of the gospel, didn't feel he could take up arms against others. But England didn't recognize the Pentecostal faith as legitimate. As a result, he was imprisoned and his head was shaved. He was dressed in prison garb, placed in solitary confinement, and fed mostly bread and water through the remainder of the war years. While in prison he experienced a great demonstration of the gift of faith, as noted by Lester Sumrall:[16]

> He was placed in a cell so narrow that he could not move around. The concrete roof above him leaked, and the dripping of water on his head was extremely aggravating.
>
> Finally, one night he said, "Lord, stop that leak."
>
> The Lord answered, "No, I won't stop it. You stop it."
>
> "But, Lord, how can I stop it?"
>
> "Speak to it."
>
> That is when Howard Carter discovered his power with God. Lying on a cot in a prison cell, iron bars on each side, a concrete roof above him, water peppering down on his head, Rev. Carter spoke to the water. He commanded it to flow the other way.
>
> At that moment the leak stopped, and not another drop of water came through during the war! It was a dynamic act of the gift of faith. Howard Carter was a man of solid truth. I lived with him for many years and never knew him to exaggerate. Whatever he told was absolute truth.

I shared that story with you to build your faith and to remind you that there will be times when you're battling a mountain of your own. Yet you begin to sense that God doesn't want you to keep putting up with it or plead, "Lord, please remove that mountain!" Instead, a gift of faith will be imparted to your soul, and you will know *you* are to *speak out loud* to the mountain and *command* it to be removed!

In Mark 11:12, that's exactly what Jesus explained to His disciples that they were to do when faced with a mountain. This is how the verse reads if you look it up in the *King James Version with Strong's Numbers,* and study the Greek words used for the words *say* and *saith.*

> For verily I say unto you, That whosoever shall say [Gr: epo: *to speak or say (by word or writing): –answer, bid, bring word, call, command, say (on), speak, tell]* unto this mountain, Be thou removed, and be thou cast into the sea; and shall not doubt in his heart, but shall believe that those things which he saith [Gr: lego: *to "lay" forth, that is (figuratively) relate (in words) [usually of systematic or set discourse]* shall come to pass; he shall have whatsoever he saith [Gr: epo: *to speak or say (by word or writing):--answer, bid, bring word, call, command, say (on), speak, tell].*

That's exactly what Howard Carter did when he stopped the leak by speaking out loud to the water peppering down on his head, commanding it to flow the other way!

The Gift of Faith for Supernatural Transportation/

In the gift of faith imparted for supernatural transportation, the laws of nature such as gravity—as well as factors such as time and distance, are overruled. For example: Jesus walked on the water (Matt. 14:24–27). An iron axe-head—that had been lost in the water—rose to the surface and floated (2 Kings 6:5–6). The Spirit of the Lord transported Philip from Gaza to Azotus, a distance of forty to fifty miles (Acts 8:26–40).

A personal example of supernatural transportation

One Sunday night I was driving from New Orleans to Alexandria, LA. The day before as I'd been driving to New Orleans and was approaching the Mississippi River Bridge in Baton Rouge, I'd noticed they were working on the highway. A deep hole had been dug out. I'd supposed they were replacing a pipeline. The hole was so deep that I was barely able to see the shovels as the men down in that hole were working.

The next night, as I was returning home, I came over the same river bridge in Baton Rouge. At the foot of the bridge, there were several night-clubs with many cars parked beside them. As I passed them, a car pulled out from one of the night-clubs and started following me. As I watched the car behind me, swerving from one side of the road to the other, I assumed that the driver was extremely drunk. I grew increasingly concerned that he might rear-end me.

In the median strip, there was a cement wall, and there were two lanes of traffic on both sides of that median strip. Because the guy following me was driving so erratically, I sped up, hoping to get away from him. In the right lane beside me, there was an 18-wheeler. On my left side was the cement wall, and the person driving so erratically behind me was getting closer and closer, hemming me in. With all the activity, I completely forgot about the deep hole I was coming up to.

Suddenly, I remembered the gaping hole just ahead in my lane! Frantically, I sized up the situation. Here I was, driving a Volkswagen with nowhere to turn right or left. If I hit my brakes, the drunk driver would plow into me from behind. Fear gripped my heart that my little Volkswagen would plunge into the deep hole, and I'd be killed! Gripping the steering wheel, I braced myself and closed my eyes, awaiting the plunge.

Suddenly, I felt the presence of God so strong that I started speaking in tongues! I kept expecting to plunge into the hole, but nothing happened. Opening my eyes and staring into the rearview mirror, all I saw was the taillights of the drunk driver's car sticking up out of the yawning hole *behind* that *I* had been miraculously transported over and that *he* had nose-dived into! I was driving safely beyond, the 18-wheeler was still humming along on my right, and I was weeping and speaking in tongues, thanking God for His divine protection!

The Gift of Faith for Deliverance.

Once you and I make the commitment that we will live for God, be salt in the midst of corruption and bring the love and light of the gospel to every person and place to which He sends us, we will soon learn that the Christian life is a spiritual battle!

The Word of God reveals that powerful forces of darkness have always fought against God's people, seeking to attack them and hinder their spiritual progress. But as believers stand firm in faith and persevere, God will deliver them and bring victory. The prophet Daniel is an excellent example.

Daniel's faith that led to deliverance

In Daniel 10:5–7, we see that Daniel had been fasting for three weeks, seeking God for the future of his people. Suddenly, a powerful angelic being appeared before him in a vision:

> I lifted my eyes and looked, and behold, a certain man clothed in linen, whose waist was girded with gold of Uphaz: His body was like beryl, his face like the appearance of lightning, his eyes like torches of fire, his arms and feet like burnished bronze in color, and the sound of his words like the voice of a multitude. And I Daniel alone saw the vision, for the men who were with me did not see the vision; but a great quaking fell upon them, so that they fled to hide themselves.

In verses 12 through 14, Daniel relates what happened:

> Then said he unto me, Fear not, Daniel: for from the first day that thou didst set thine heart to understand, and to chasten thyself before thy God, thy words were heard, and I am come for thy words. But the prince of the kingdom of Persia withstood me one and twenty days: but, lo, Michael, one of the chief princes, came to help me; and I remained there with the kings of Persia. Now I am come to make thee understand what shall befall thy people in the latter days: for yet the vision is for many days.

These scriptures show us that from the first day Daniel set his heart to understand and fast and pray, his words had been heard in heaven. In answer, God had immediately dispatched an angel to Daniel to help him understand what was to happen to his people in the future. However, one of Satan's princes of darkness withstood the angel for twenty-one days, and the mighty archangel Michael had been sent to help the angel so he could deliver God's message to Daniel.

Remember those verses the next time you get discouraged and tired of waiting for an answer from God. Realize that unseen spiritual warfare is taking place all around you and that it's not time to quit. It's time to hold on in faith, like Daniel did, until your answer comes.

Paul recognized and overcame Satan's hindrances

Sometimes as we labor for God, striving to do His work and His will, Satan's forces try to thwart, block, oppose, defy, and frustrate every move we make for God. Paul was well-acquainted with the opposition of the enemy as he labored to win the lost and strengthen believers. In 1 Thess. 2:18, he writes, "Therefore we wanted to come to you—even I, Paul, time and again—but Satan hindered us" (NKJV).

After two years in prison, Paul was sent to Rome, where he spent two more years in confinement. Satan and his demons must have been making merry, thinking they had thwarted God's purposes for Paul and wasted years of valuable time that could never be recovered! But Paul's God overruled. During those lonely, solitary years Paul used the time to write many of his letters to the churches. Those epistles of Paul became an integral, valuable part of the New Testament. In 2 Tim. 4:18, Paul declares: "And the Lord will deliver me from every evil work and preserve me for His heavenly kingdom…" (NKJV). Checkmate, Satan! You lost *another* game, too. Outwitted and defeated again!

The gift of faith for deliverance from disease

In his book *The John G. Lake Sermons on Dominion Over Demons, Disease and Death,* Lake recorded a powerful testimony of the power of faith protecting and delivering him from disease in the midst of bubonic plague in Africa. I give it to you exactly as he wrote it:

> I was ministering one time where the bubonic plague was raging. You could not hire people for $1,000 to bury the dead. At such times the government has to take hold of the situation. But I never caught the disease.
>
> Now watch the action of the law of faith. Faith belongs to the law of life. Faith is the very opposite of fear. Faith has the opposite effect in spirit, and soul and body. Faith causes the spirit of man to become confident. It causes the mind of man to become restful and positive. A positive mind repels disease. Consequently, the emanation of the Spirit destroys disease germs.
>
> And because we were in contact with the Spirit of life, I and a little Dutch fellow with me went out and buried many of the people who had died from the bubonic plague. We went into the homes and carried them out, dug the graves and put them in. Sometimes we would put three or four in one grave.

We never caught the disease. Why? Because of the knowledge that the law of life in Christ Jesus protects us. That law was working. Because of the fact that a man by the action of his will, puts himself purposely in contact with God, faith takes possession of his heart, and the condition of his nature is changed. Instead of being fearful, he is full of faith. Instead of being absorbent and drawing everything to himself, his spirit repels sickness and disease. The Spirit of Christ Jesus flows through the whole being, and emanates through the hands, the heart and from every pore of the body.

You observe that we lay hands upon the sick for healing. What for? Simply that the Spirit of life in Christ Jesus that dwells in the Christian may flow through our hands into their body…"

During that great plague…, they sent a government ship with supplies and a corps of doctors. One of the doctors sent for me, and said, "What have you been using to protect yourself? Our corps has this preventative and that, which we use as protection, but we concluded that if a man could stay on the ground as you have and keep ministering to the sick and burying the dead, you must have a secret. What is it?"

I answered, "Brother, that is the 'law of the Spirit of life in Christ Jesus.' I believe that just as long as I keep my soul in contact with the living God so that His Spirit is flowing into my soul and body, that no germ will ever attach itself to me, for the Spirit of God will kill it." He asked, "Don't you think that you had better use our preventatives?" I replied, "No, but doctor, I think that you would like to experiment with me. If you will go over to one of those dead people and take the foam that comes out of their lungs after death, then put it under the microscope you will see masses of living germs. You will find they are alive until a reasonable time after a man is dead. You can fill my hand with them and I will keep it under the microscope, and instead of these germs remaining alive, they will die instantly." They tried it and found it was true. They questioned, "What is that?" I replied, "That is 'the law of the Spirit of life in Christ Jesus.' When a man's spirit and a man's body are filled with the blessed presence of God, it oozes out of the pores of your flesh and kills the germs."[17]

Throughout my ministry I've read and studied a lot about this spiritual gift. It would be hard to find a better example than that one of the gift of faith being imparted for deliverance from death and disease, wouldn't it! That's faith, my friend!

The Gift of Faith for Divine Discipline

The gift of faith is sometimes imparted for divine discipline, but God never intends for His power to be used with the wrong motives. For instance, do you remember that incident in Luke 9:51–56, when Jesus sent messengers before Him into a village of the Samaritans, but the villagers rudely turned them away? Indignant, James and John said, "Lord, do You want us to command fire to come down from heaven and consume them, just as Elijah did?" (NKJV). But Jesus rebuked James and John: "You do not know what manner of spirit you are of. For the Son of Man did not come to destroy men's lives but to save them" (NKJV).

Anger, wounded pride, and retaliation are of the flesh, not of the Spirit. The power of God is not to be used at the whim of misguided men. The integrity of the church is dependent upon whether we try to use God and His power for *our* purposes, or whether we humbly ask *God* to use and empower *us* for *His* purposes. We don't go around calling fire down from heaven on people who displease us. That's not what Jesus is like, and that's not what we're here for.

However, that doesn't mean that we are to look the other way. We must stand against the dishonesty, hypocrisy, and immorality used by Satan to weaken the church. These sins certainly were not tolerated in the New Testament church. The apostles foresaw the poisonous fruit they would produce if swift action were not taken.

Look at the way Peter was led to deal with Ananias and his wife Sapphira in Acts 5:3–14, NKJV. The two had sold property and hypocritically conspired to keep back some of the profit for themselves while pretending to give the whole amount to the church. Peter discerned what was going on and divine judgment fell:

> But Peter said, "Ananias, why has Satan filled your heart to lie
> to the Holy Spirit and keep back part of the price of the land
> for yourself? While it remained, was it not your own? And
> after it was sold, was it not in your own control? Why have you
> conceived this thing in your heart? You have not lied to men

but to God." Then Ananias, hearing these words, fell down and breathed his last. So great fear came upon all those who heard these things. And the young men arose and wrapped him up, carried him out, and buried him. Now it was about three hours later when his wife came in, not knowing what had happened. And Peter answered her, "Tell me whether you sold the land for so much?" She said, "Yes, for so much." Then Peter said to her, "How is it that you have agreed together to test the Spirit of the Lord? Look, the feet of those who have buried your husband are at the door, and they will carry you out." Then immediately she fell down at his feet and breathed her last. And the young men came in and found her dead, and carrying her out, buried her by her husband.

—ACTS 5:3–10, NKJV

Notice what resulted after the gift of faith had been imparted to Peter for divine discipline:

So great fear came upon all the church and upon all who heard these things. And through the hands of the apostles many signs and wonders were done among the people. And they were all with one accord in Solomon's Porch. Yet none of the rest dared join them, but the people esteemed them highly. And believers were increasingly added to the Lord, multitudes of both men and women.

—ACTS 5:11–14, NKJV

Great fear came upon the church and on all who heard these things—including other hypocrites and the insincere who had sought praise and acceptance through lies. On the other hand, multitudes of believers were increasingly added to the Lord.

A LAST WORD ABOUT THE GIFT OF FAITH AND PRAYER

Problems are different. Not every situation is an emergency. Problems can have to do with an unsaved person, with money or a different job or place to live, with the need for revival in a family or a church, etc. Some needs and situations must be battled in prayer time after time after time.

Many sincere believers, who have not been taught in the things of the Spirit, get weary of praying if they do not see the answer immediately. So, their faith wavers. They get discouraged. They stop asking, seeking, and knocking, as Jesus told us to do in Matthew 7:7. They *break down* before they *break through*. But we must keep on praying and persevering in prayer—even though the answer is nowhere to be seen in the natural—until the answer comes or until that supernatural assurance comes that God has heard and that He has answered!

That supernatural assurance—that gift of faith—may come to you in several different ways. It may come as a word spoken by the Holy Spirit to your spirit. It may come in the words of a song or a sermon or a friend. It may come as the Spirit of God illuminates and quickens a word or phrase or passage of scripture to you. In whatever way that word straight from God arrives, you will confidently *know* that the promise of God will surely come to pass. When that gift of faith has been released, you will have a peace concerning that person, problem, or situation. And this word will come before you actually see the answer taking place.

I feel very strongly in my spirit to encourage you to persevere. It is absolutely imperative. Pray as hard as it takes and as long as it takes until that gift of faith bursts in your spirit, and assurance floods your soul. You will *know* that you have prayed through!

Then hang on, refusing to let go. Continue to walk in faith. Praise God for His faithfulness. Rest in the knowledge that God cannot lie, and that He keeps His promises. Be alert and on guard in the Spirit. Battle the devil whenever he tries to hinder the working of God. Know that in God's perfect time, in His perfect way, when His divine purposes have been accomplished, it will surely come to pass just as God told you it would!

Chapter 8

THE GIFTS OF HEALINGS

To another the gifts of healings by the same Spirit....
—1 CORINTHIANS 12:9

GIFTS OF HEALINGS are manifestations of the power of God in the sphere of disease. They are for supernatural healing, without natural means of any sort. They are not to be confused with any human abilities or works, however praiseworthy. This composite gift is a manifestation of the Holy Ghost given to the church to remove sickness, disease, and infirmity.[1]

What the church has referred to as the "gift of healing" is literally "gifts of healings." It is mentioned three times in 1 Cor. 12 (verses 9, 28, 30) and each time the two nouns are in the plural.[2]

Some believe that the double plural may suggest different supernatural healing gifts operating through different people, in different ways, for different kinds of illnesses, or on different occasions. It definitely indicates a variety of forms of healings. To illustrate this, Howard Carter compared the different administrations and diversities in the gifts of healings to a bunch of grapes hanging from one stalk. Just as a bunch of grapes is not *one* grape, but a cluster of many grapes, many gifts of healings are clustered together in one composite manifestation. Just as there are *classes* of diseases—nervous diseases, muscular diseases, skin diseases, etc.—so each of the gifts of healing has a counteracting effect on some particular *class* of disease. Where *all* the gifts of healing are in operation, all classes of disease could be healed.[3] Gifts of healing can deal with every case of sickness, every disease that there is.[4]

Though there are different manifestations, they are all from the Holy Spirit and are operated "by the same Spirit." Paul explains that all the gifts of the Spirit listed in 1 Cor. 12:8–11 are the work of one and the same Spirit, and the Holy Spirit gives them to individual believers, just as He determines.

114

For example, some Christians are primarily used of God in opening blind eyes or in healing the paralyzed or crippled. Some are used of God more in the healing of people who have internal disorders and difficulties. Others seem particularly used in ministering to those with heart and lung problems. Some seem to deal more with mental or emotional disorders. The healing ministries of some individuals are used in remarkable deliverances from problems such as goiters, growths, cancers, etc.

This does not mean that these people cannot also be used of God to bring healing in other types of sickness. It simply means that some people are used more specifically in certain areas than in others.[5]

SOME NECESSARY CLARIFICATIONS

Supernatural or Natural?

Whatever the need, there is no disease, no infirmity, no sickness that God is not able to heal. However, these supernatural gifts of healing should not be confused with healings brought about through the practice of medicine. Some individuals, organizations, religions, and denominations establish hospitals and clinics. Some support medical doctors, nurses, dentists, and other medical personnel in many places around the globe. But practicing medicine to bring about healing through natural means is not a gift of healing.[6]

There have been times, of course, when a Christian in the medical profession has laid hands on a sick person, prayed in faith, and seen the person instantly, divinely healed. Thank God for Christians in the medical profession who have the wisdom and faith to ask God to intervene when they have come to the end of their own resources. But in the vast majority of cases, it cannot be said that medical personnel heal by gifts of healings. Many unconverted, even atheistic, individuals also practice medicine, don't they? Many of their patients also experience noteworthy recoveries. But those recoveries should not be attributed to gifts of healings.

Medical personnel—whether or not they are converted—help heal by means of abilities and skills they have acquired from arduous training and diligent study. A skillful surgery, a brilliant diagnosis, a new treatment, or the proper medication might be a critical component in the healing process. But no matter how successful the results, practicing medicine to bring about healing in sick persons through natural means should not be referred to as manifestations of the "gifts of healings." We must remember that the gifts of healings referred to in 1 Cor. 12:9 are supernatural manifestations of the power of God in the sphere of disease.[7]

UNLIMITED AND ABSOLUTE POWER TO HEAL?

Some people have the idea that if a person is moving in gifts of healings, that individual should be able to heal any sickness. Of course, a brief survey of the New Testament proves otherwise. Nonetheless, sometimes all diseases _were_ healed:

Matthew 9:35 tells us that "Jesus went through all the towns and villages, teaching in their synagogues, proclaiming the good news of the kingdom and healing every disease and sickness" (NIV).

Matthew 10:1 says, "Jesus called his twelve disciples to him and gave them authority to drive out impure spirits and to heal every disease and sickness" (NIV).

Matthew 10:7–8 states that Jesus sent out the twelve disciples with the following instructions: "As you go, proclaim this message: 'The kingdom of heaven has come near.' Heal the sick, raise the dead, cleanse those who have leprosy, drive out demons. Freely you have received; freely give" (NIV).

At other times, even the Lord Jesus' healing ministry was hindered by unbelief. Mark 6:4–6 notes: "But Jesus said unto them, A prophet is not without honour, but in his own country, and among his own kin, and in his own house. And he could there do no mighty work, save that he laid his hands upon a few sick folk, and healed them. And he marvelled because of their unbelief."

Similarly, John 5:2–9, tells us that many blind, lame, and paralyzed lay beside the pool of Bethesda, waiting for the waters to be miraculously stirred, then trying to be the first to get into the pool to be healed. But on this occasion, Jesus healed only one person—a man who had been an invalid for thirty-eight years. Then Jesus left.

So why is it that not all were healed in these cases? In the case of the man at the pool of Bethesda, we see one reason. Notice that before healing the man, Jesus asked him a very pointed question: "Do you want to get well?" Did you know that some people do not really want to be healed? You may be gifted in praying for the sick, but if someone does not want to get well, you are likely wasting your breath.

Also notice in verse 14, that when Jesus later found the man at the temple, He gave the man a stern warning. "See, you are well again. Stop sinning or something worse may happen to you" (NIV). Jesus' strict admonition reveals that it is possible for people to continue to sin and lose a blessing, such as healing, that God has bestowed on them.

If we earnestly pray for a person's healing, and they are not healed, we should stop and listen to God. He knows each person's history, and He knows each person's heart. Sometimes a person's most critical need is not physical healing.

First Cor. 11:28–32 sheds more light on this matter of why some people are not healed. Here, Paul warns that we must prayerfully examine our hearts before we partake of the Lord's Supper. Taking communion in an unworthy manner may cause sickness or even death.

> A man ought to examine himself before he eats of the bread
> and drinks of the cup. For anyone who eats and drinks without
> recognizing the body of the Lord eats and drinks judgment on
> himself. That is why many among you are weak and sick, and
> a number of you have fallen asleep. But if we judged ourselves,
> we would not come under judgment. When we are judged by
> the Lord, we are being disciplined so that we will not be con-
> demned with the world.
> —1 CORINTHIANS 11:28–32, NIV

We can pray all we want to, but if a person is under divine disciplinary judgment, our prayers for healing will go unheeded.

While many people were healed under the ministry of Paul, even that great apostle's prayers for the sick were not 100 percent successful. In 2 Tim. 4:20, Paul writes regretfully, "I left Trophimus sick in Miletus" (NIV).

Do we serve a God who heals? Absolutely. Does He heal everyone that His servants pray for? No. Should that dampen our faith or hinder our obedience to His command to lay hands on the sick? Absolutely not.

OUR GOD HEALS!

We serve a God who delights to heal His people. The Bible portrays Him as the God who heals. Consider these verses, for example.

- Exodus 15:26: If thou wilt diligently hearken to the voice of the Lord thy God, and wilt do that which is right in his sight, and wilt give ear to his commandments, and keep all his statutes, I will put none of these diseases upon thee, which I have brought upon the Egyptians: for I am the Lord that healeth thee.

- Psalm 103:2–3: "Bless the Lord, O my soul, and forget not all his benefits: Who forgiveth all thine iniquities; who healeth all thy diseases."

- Isaiah 53:5: "But he was wounded for our transgressions, he was bruised for our iniquities: the chastisement of our peace was upon him; and with his stripes we are healed."

- Malachi 4:2: "But unto you that fear my name shall the Sun of righteousness arise with healing in his wings…"

Some people object to a doctrine of divine healing. "Oh, those are just scriptures in the Old Testament," they say. All right then, let's look at some of the things the New Testament has to say about healing.

- Matthew 4:23–24: "And Jesus went about all Galilee, teaching in their synagogues, and preaching the gospel of the kingdom, and healing all manner of sickness and all manner of disease among the people. And his fame went throughout all Syria: and they brought unto him all sick people that were taken with divers diseases and torments, and those which were possessed with devils, and those which were lunatic, and those that had the palsy; and he healed them."

- Matthew 8:14–17: "And when Jesus was come into Peter's house, he saw his wife's mother laid, and sick of a fever. And he touched her hand, and the fever left her:

and she arose, and ministered unto them. When the even was come, they brought unto him many that were possessed with devils: and he cast out the spirits with his word, and healed all that were sick: That it might be fulfilled which was spoken by Esaias [Isaiah] the prophet, saying, Himself took our infirmities, and bare our sicknesses."

- Matthew. 9:35: "And Jesus went about all the cities and villages, teaching in their synagogues, and preaching the gospel of the kingdom, and healing every sickness and every disease among the people."

- Matthew 12:13–15: "Then saith he to the man, Stretch forth thine hand. And he stretched it forth; and it was restored whole, like as the other. Then the Pharisees went out, and held a council against him, how they might destroy him. But when Jesus knew it, he withdrew himself from thence: and great multitudes followed him, and he healed them all."

- Mark 16:17–18: "And these signs shall follow them that believe; In my name shall they cast out devils; they shall speak with new tongues; They shall take up serpents; and if they drink any deadly thing, it shall not hurt them; they shall lay hands on the sick, and they shall recover."

- Luke 6:19: "And the whole multitude sought to touch him: for there went virtue out of him, and healed them all."

"Sure," some people might argue, "but that was Jesus Himself healing people, proving that He was the divine Son of God. Those healings took place during Jesus' earthly ministry."

Yes, Jesus healed people during His earthly ministry. But was Jesus the only one who healed people? No. His disciples also were given power to heal the sick.

Then He called His twelve disciples together, and gave them power and authority over all devils, and to cure diseases.

> And he sent them to preach the kingdom of God, and to heal
> the sick…And they departed, and went through the towns,
> preaching the gospel, and healing everywhere.
> —LUKE 9:1–2, 6

Furthermore, his disciples continued to heal the sick even after
Jesus was crucified, raised to life, and had ascended to His Father in
heaven. The supernatural healing of the sick doesn't stop at the end
of the gospels. In the book of Acts we continue to see Jesus' disciples
healing the sick. Remember how Peter healed a beggar at a gate at the
temple, a man who had been lame from birth?

> Then Peter said, Silver and gold have I none; but such as I have
> give I thee: In the name of Jesus Christ of Nazareth rise up and
> walk. And he took him by the right hand, and lifted him up: and
> immediately his feet and ankle bones received strength. And he
> leaping up stood, and walked, and entered with them into the
> temple, walking, and leaping, and praising God….And as the
> lame man which was healed held Peter and John, all the people
> ran together unto them in the porch that is called Solomon's,
> greatly wondering. And when Peter saw it, he answered unto
> the people, Ye men of Israel, why marvel ye at this? or why look
> ye so earnestly on us, as though by our own power or holiness
> we had made this man to walk?…And his name through name
> through faith in his name hath made this man strong, whom
> ye see and know: yea, the faith which is by him hath given him
> this perfect soundness in the presence of you all.
> —ACTS 3:6–8, 11–12, 16

The religious establishment of the day became increasingly upset by
the miraculous signs and wonders. Many of Jesus' disciples healed the
sick. Acts 5:12 says, "The apostles performed many miraculous signs
and wonders among the people…" (NIV).

Ripples of the miraculous spread even wider than the ministry of
the apostles. Spirit-filled men chosen by the apostles to help care for
the needy also began ministering in the supernatural.

- Acts 6:8: "Now Stephen, a man full of God's grace and
  power, did great wonders and miraculous signs among
  the people" (NIV).

- Acts 8:5–7: "Philip went down to a city in Samaria
  and proclaimed the Messiah there. When the crowds
  heard Philip and saw the signs he performed, they all
  paid close attention to what he said. For with shrieks,
  impure spirits came out of many, and many who were
  paralyzed or lame were healed" (NIV).

The ripples of the miraculous spread still further after Saul of
Tarsus, who had held the robes of men as they stoned Stephen, was
apprehended and transformed by the Lord Jesus. As Saul (later known
as Paul) ministered the gospel, wonderful healings were performed.
Consider these passages, for example.

- Acts 14:8–10: "And there sat a certain man at Lystra,
  impotent in his feet, being a cripple from his mother's
  womb, who never had walked. The same heard Paul
  speak: who stedfastly beholding him, and perceiving that
  he had faith to be healed, Said with a loud voice, Stand
  upright on thy feet. And he leaped and walked."

- Acts 19:11–12: "And God wrought special miracles by
  the hands of Paul: So that from his body were brought
  unto the sick handkerchiefs or aprons, and the diseases
  departed from them, and the evil spirits went out of
  them."

It was Paul who wrote these words to the Christians at Corinth,
explaining the gifts of the Holy Spirit to the Church.

- 1 Corinthians 12:7–11: "But the manifestation of the
  Spirit is given to every man to profit withal. For to
  one is given by the Spirit the word of wisdom.... To
  another faith by the same Spirit; to another the gifts of
  healing by the same Spirit; To another the working of
  miracles...."

Divine healing was taught in the early church, as the following
scriptures show. James, writing between 45 to 50 AD, gives specific
instructions regarding praying for the sick.

- James 5:14–16: "Is any sick among you? Let him call for the elders of the church; and let them pray over him, anointing him with oil in the name of the Lord: And the prayer of faith shall save the sick, and the Lord shall raise him up; and if he have committed sins, they shall be forgiven him. Confess your faults one to another, and pray one for another, that ye may be healed. The effectual fervent prayer of a righteous man availeth much."

Peter also wrote about healing, about 63 AD:

- 1 Peter 2:21, 24: "For even hereunto were ye called: because Christ also suffered for us...by whose stripes ye were healed."

In the book of Revelation, written by John about 90 A.D., the aged apostle reveals the desire of God for healing.

- Revelation 22:1–2: "And He shewed me ... the tree of life...and the leaves of the tree were for the healing of the nations."

Furthermore, any honest study of historical examples from the end of New Testament times to the present day provides ample evidence that God's provision at Calvary for our sins and our sicknesses remains in effect.

Gifts of healings are for the healing of disease without natural means of any sort; they are totally supernatural. As we have already seen, the gift is termed the gift*s* of healing*s* because there are different administrations and diversities. Often the gift will operate differently through different people or on different occasions.

SOME DIFFERENT WAYS THE GIFTS OF HEALINGS OPERATED IN THE BIBLE:

- Matthew 8:3: "Jesus put out *His* hand and touched him (leper), saying, "I am willing; be cleansed" (NKJV).

- Mark 7:32–35: The deaf man with the speech impediment was healed as Jesus put His fingers into the man's ears, spat, touched his tongue, and said to him, "Be opened." Instantly, his ears were opened, and his tongue loosed so he could speak plainly.

- Acts 28:8–9: Paul prayed, laid his hands on a man lying sick of a fever and of a bloody flux, and healed him.

- Acts 3:1–11: Peter healed the lame man at the gate Beautiful.

- Matthew 8:8: Healing occurred at a distance without the Lord being there in person, in response to the faith of the centurion who said, "Lord, I am not worthy that You should come under my roof. But only speak a word, and my servant will be healed" (NKJV).

TEACHING FROM SMITH WIGGLESWORTH ON DIVINE HEALING

Wigglesworth said:

I have people continually coming to me and saying, "When you are preaching, I see a halo around you," or "When you are preaching, I have seen angels standing around you...."

The only vision I have had in a divine healing meeting is this: so often, when I have laid hands upon the people, I have seen two hands go before my hands. This has happened many, many times.

The person who has the gifts of healings does not look to see what is happening. You will notice that after I have finished ministering, many things are manifested, but they don't move me. I am not moved by anything I see.[8]

Regarding ministering healing, Wigglesworth said:

The gifts of healing are so varied. You may go to see 10 people, and every case will be different.... I have had more revelations of the Lord's presence when I have ministered to the sick at their bedside than at any other time. It is as your heart goes out to the needy ones in deep compassion that the Lord manifests His presence. You are able to discern their conditions. It is then that you know you must be filled with the Spirit to deal with the conditions before you.[9]

Wigglesworth continued:

When people are sick, you frequently find that they are ignorant about scripture. They usually know three scriptures, though. They know about Paul's "thorn in the flesh" (2 Cor. 12:7); they know that Paul told Timothy to take "a little wine" for his "stomach's sake" (1 Tim. 5:23); and they know that Paul left someone sick somewhere, but they don't remember his name or the place, and they don't know in what chapter of the Bible it is found (see 2 Timothy 4:20). Most people think they have a thorn in the flesh. The chief thing in dealing with a person who is sick is to discern his exact condition. As you are ministering under the Spirit's power, the Lord will let you see just what will be the most helpful and the most faith-inspiring to him....

> "The person who has the gifts of healings does not look to see what is happening. You will notice that after I have finished ministering, many things are manifested, but they don't move me. I am not moved by anything I see."
> —SMITH WIGGLESWORTH

A fruit of the Spirit that must accompany the gift of healing is long-suffering. The man who is persevering with God to be used in healing must be a man of long-suffering. He must always be ready with a word of comfort. If the sick one is in distress and helpless and does not see everything eye to eye with you, you must bear with him. Our Lord Jesus Christ was filled with compassion and lived and moved in a place of long-suffering, and we will have to get into this place if we are to help needy ones.

There are some times when you pray for the sick, and you seem to be rough with them. But you are not dealing with a person; you are dealing with satanic forces that are binding the person. Your heart is full of love and compassion toward all; however, you are moved to a holy anger as you see the place the devil has taken in the body of the sick one, and you deal with his position with a real forcefulness.

One day a pet dog followed a lady out of her house and ran all around her feet. She said to the dog, 'My dear, I cannot have you with me today.' The dog wagged its tail and made a big fuss. She said, 'Go home, my dear.' But the dog did not go. At last she shouted roughly, 'Go home,' and off it went. Some people deal with the devil like that. The devil can stand all the comfort you like to give him. Cast him out! You are not dealing with the person; you are dealing with the devil. Demon power must be dislodged in the name of the Lord.

You are always right when you dare to deal with sickness as with the devil. Much sickness is caused by some misconduct; there is something wrong, there is some neglect somewhere, and Satan has had a chance to get in. It is necessary to repent and confess where you have given place to the devil (Eph. 4:27), and then he can be dealt with.[10]

Regarding cancer, Wigglesworth said:

When you deal with a cancer case, recognize that a living spirit is destroying the body. I had to pray for a woman in Los Angeles one time who was suffering with cancer, and as soon as it was cursed, it stopped bleeding. It was dead. The next thing that happened was that the natural body pushed it out, because the natural body had no room for dead matter. It came out like a great big ball with tens of thousands of fibers. All these fibers had been pressing into the flesh. These evil powers move to get further hold of the body's system, but the moment they are destroyed, their hold is gone. Jesus told His disciples that He gave them power to loose and power to bind (Matt. 16:19). It is our privilege in the power of the Holy Spirit to loose the prisoners of Satan and to let the oppressed go free.

Take your position from the first epistle of John and declare, "He who is in [me] is greater than he who is in the world" (1 John 4:4, NKJV). Then recognize that it is not you who has to deal with the power of the devil, but the Greater One who is in you. Oh, what it means to be filled with Him! You can do nothing in yourself, but He who is in you will win the victory. Your being has become the temple of the Spirit. Your mouth, your mind, your whole being may be used and worked upon by the Spirit of God.[11]

I realize that I have already quoted extensively from Wigglesworth, but his teaching on the gifts of healings is so practical, so profound, and so powerful that I would be cheating you if I didn't include just a little more.

Said Wigglesworth:

> We need to wake up and strive to believe God. Before God could bring me to this place, He broke me a thousand times. I have wept; I have groaned. I have travailed many a night until God broke me. It seems to me that until God has mowed you down, you can never have this long-suffering for others. We will never have the gifts of healing and the working of miracles in operation unless we stand in the divine power that God gives us, unless we stand believing God and "having done all" (Eph. 6:13), we still stand believing.
>
> We have been seeing wonderful miracles during these last days, and they are only a little of what we are going to see. I believe that we are right on the threshold of wonderful things, but I want to emphasize that all these things will be only through the power of the Holy Spirit. You must not think that these gifts will fall upon you like ripe cherries. There is a sense in which you have to pay the price for everything you get. We must earnestly desire God's best gifts and say "Amen" to any preparation the Lord takes us through. In this way, we will be humble, useable vessels through whom He Himself can operate by means of the Spirit's power.[12]

ONE EXAMPLE OF THE GIFTS OF HEALINGS IN MY MINISTRY

Many supernatural manifestations happened at the revival at our church in New Orleans. However, the groundwork for one of the most outstanding of those miraculous manifestations was laid when three sisters with strong Roman Catholic backgrounds began attending a Bible study I was teaching at the church. Those three sisters were part of an ever growing group of people streaming into the church from all sorts of backgrounds and denominational affiliations. They were hungry to hear God's Word taught with anointing and to experience more of His presence and power. As the sisters attended, the Word of God and the power and demonstration of the Spirit in the services began fueling the flickering flame of faith in their hearts. It wasn't long before all three of them had accepted Jesus.

The sisters, who were marvelous cooks, sometimes invited my family and me to their home to eat with them. Wonderful opportunities arose to disciple them a little at a time as we all sat around their table, eating, laughing, and fellowshipping together.

At one Wednesday morning Bible study, Rose—the shortest and oldest of the three sisters looked to be in her mid-fifties—excitedly handed me an envelope. Overflowing with joy, Rose said, "This is some money I want to give to the church." It was a nice sum of money, and I accepted it, making a mental note to give it to our bookkeeper when I got back to the office.

Rose said, "Yesterday, I was watching the horse races, and they had a horse named Praying Hands. I told my sisters, 'I'm going to place my money on Praying Hands,' and he won!"

I started laughing at the sheer incongruity of the situation, but Rose stopped me. "Don't laugh," she scolded. "That's where the money came from."

I instantly felt a check in my spirit, and the Lord said: "Don't rebuke her! Don't make her feel bad. Receive it and use it in the kingdom." So I thanked Rose and took the money for the church, realizing that if I had rebuked her, we probably would have lost all three of them.

The faith of the three sisters just continued to grow. Early one morning a few months later, Rose came to my office crying. "Pastor," she said, "I just got a call from my husband Bill in Singapore. He's a captain on an ocean-going freight liner. Bill became sick during the night and when they arrived in Singapore, they took him to the hospital. He said the doctors discovered he has cancer, and they told him he has only a short time to live. They're flying him home. I'll meet Bill at the airport and drive him straight to the hospital."

After she checked Bill into the hospital, Rose called to let me know. I went by to see him, but the doctors were running tests. After visiting a while with Rose, I left.

Later that same day, Saturday afternoon, Rose called. "They have scheduled Bill for radical surgery on Monday to remove his vocal cords and a lot of glands and muscles in his neck and down into this arms," she told me. "They're giving him permission to go home, and we'll return to the hospital Sunday afternoon. The surgery will take place Monday."

I drove over to their home for a visit so Bill and I could get acquainted and I could minister to the family in their desperate time of need.

Bill was a tall, rugged-featured man with a gruff voice; brown, grey-streaked hair; and skin weathered by the sun and sea. As we chatted, I learned that his dad had been so physically and verbally abusive toward Bill as a child and toward his mom that Bill had run away when he was thirteen and later joined the merchant marines, lying to get in because he wasn't old enough.

After a while, Bill's wife and her sister left the living room where Bill and I were talking and went into another part of the house. It gave me an opportunity to speak with Bill privately. I said, "Bill, God can heal you if you'll turn your life over to Him and dare to believe Him."

He looked me straight in the face and replied matter-of-factly, "Rev, I'm a hard man. I've sailed the high seas over thirty years. I've been in storms where it looked like the ship would break in pieces. I've seen my crew grab whatever they could hold onto and lie on the floor, crying and praying for God to help. I never did that. I felt if I couldn't pray when the sun was shining, I would not pray when the storm came. The way I look at it, this cancer is just another major storm I have to ride out."

My heart went out to this proud, stubborn man. I could only imagine what it must be like not to know God and have to ride out the storm of my life without His comforting presence. Somehow, I had to reach this man! Somehow I had to throw him a lifeline of truth and hope! "Bill," I said softly, "Jesus loves you. In spite of all that may have happened He cares about you."

Bill sat there a moment, searching for words to explain himself and his dilemma. Then, meeting my gaze, he replied, "Rev, I haven't shed a tear since thirteen. Even when my father died I shed no tears. I'm a hard man."

Absolutely unwilling to leave him alone, helpless and hopeless in a sinking ship to ride out his storm, I threw him a lifeline again. "Bill, that may be true, but it doesn't change God's love toward you."

Feeling my deep concern, Bill listened intently as I spoke with him about the love of God. Then, sensing that I had said what God sent me there to say, I asked Bill if I could pray for him. I stretched out my hands to him across the coffee table, and he gripped them. It was spiritual life or death, and I knew it.

Refusing to pray just a "hope-so" prayer, I pled, "Lord, manifest your power to Bill in such a way that he will know you love him and will help him." Then I closed my prayer and stood to leave. But as I walked out the door, I followed the Spirit's prompting and said, "Bill, if you feel like it, I'd love to have you in church tomorrow."

"Well, Rev," he responded, making no commitment, "we'll see."

The next morning, a few minutes before 11:00 a.m., Bill Hill walked down the aisle of the church and was seated on the second pew. About ten minutes into my message, he took out his handkerchief and wiped his eyes. I saw his gaze focused on something right above the top of my head, not on my face as I continued to preach. When I gave the invitation, Bill was the first one who came to the altar. I went down and prayed with him. Then he left.

Rose had told me that the hospital had scheduled Bill to be admitted about three o'clock that afternoon. So I almost fell off my seat on the platform that Sunday evening when the door swung open as the service was beginning, and Bill, his wife, and two sisters-in-law walked in. I immediately went down to where they were seated on the second row from the front, greeted him, and I asked why he wasn't in the hospital.

He smiled warmly and replied, "I felt so good, we called and the doctor said I could go to church this evening and come to the hospital tonight at eleven o'clock."

After the sermon, Bill came to the altar again. After praying with him, I shook his hand, assuring him of our love and prayers. Then he left for the hospital.

The surgery was scheduled at 8:00 a.m. the next morning, so I was at the hospital early. Around 7:00 a.m., the nurse came in to take blood, and others came in to prep him for surgery. At 8:00 a.m. no one showed up. An hour passed, and still no one had come. Around 9:30 a.m., the doctor came in and said, "Mr. Hill, there has been a change in your blood, and we are going to delay the surgery until tomorrow morning and run some more tests."

Bill had been scheduled to go into surgery at 7:00 a.m. the next morning, so I got there about 6:15 a.m. to pray with Bill and Rose and encourage them. But 7:30 arrived, and they still hadn't come to get him. A little after 8:00 a.m., the doctor came into the room and said, "Mr. Hill, we've got to run some more tests because the blood is showing us some things we didn't see when you first came to the hospital." I left, and they ran tests on him all that day and the next.

Early Thursday morning I was in Bill's room when a very puzzled doctor entered the room with a startling announcement. "Mr. Hill," he said, "something has happened. Either we misread the tests when you first came in, or the whole thing has changed. We can find no trace of cancer in your body."

Bill, Rose, and I knew exactly what had happened. The hospital in Singapore and the hospital in New Orleans had found the same things and arrived at the same diagnosis, but God had miraculously healed Bill Hill!

One week later, Bill and I were seated in the same place we had sat in his living room before Jesus had forgiven his sins and performed a miracle of healing in his body. "Rev," he said, "who painted that beautiful picture of Jesus above the baptistery at the church? The eyes of Jesus literally move!"

Bill's question threw me for a loop. I had no idea what he was talking about. Puzzled, I replied, "There's no picture above the baptistery, Bill...just an eight-foot tall wooden cross mounted on highly varnished birch paneling. There's no picture of Jesus up there."

"Oh, yes," he insisted. "It's there every time I've gone. The first time, Jesus looked so disappointed in me, but when I came back from the altar, a smile was on His face. Every time I've gone into the church, He's been right there looking at me."

I was thrilled, but also perplexed. After leaving Bill's home, I went back to the church and looked at that cross over the baptistery from every position, direction, and angle I could think of. Lights on. Spotlights on. Lying on the floor. Standing. Sitting in the second pew in the place Bill had been seated. Gazing upward. Glancing sideways. Squinting sideways. Nothing! Nothing that even remotely resembled the face of Jesus.

Then I called in my associate pastor, my secretary, and others to look, but they couldn't see anything either. What was going on? I *knew* that Bill was absolutely, sincerely, unshakably convinced that he had seen the face of Jesus in sharp detail! But no face, of any description, was visible.

As I was walking back into my office, the Lord spoke to me, making it all plain. "This is how much I love mankind. Even though they have rejected My Son all their life, I will go to any extent like this to show them My love."

Then the Holy Spirit brought to my remembrance Paul's description of the limitless measure of God's love: "And I pray that you, being rooted and established in love, may have power, together with all the saints, to grasp how wide and long and high and deep is the love of Christ, and to know this love that surpasses knowledge…" (Eph. 3:17–19, NIV).

Following Bill's miraculous healing and conversion, another sister's husband, and Bill's daughter were saved, and God did a work in their whole family. It all started with a Bible study.

Bill Hill, his wife Rose, his daughter, a sister-in-law's husband, and the other sister-in-law are all in heaven today. But it was through a demonstration of the supernatural that this man was brought into the kingdom. It wasn't my sermon. It wasn't some powerful prayer I prayed. It was a divine work of the Holy Spirit, demonstrating the Lord's love and concern for one hard, stubborn, dying man standing on eternity's doorstep without God.

Chapter 9

THE GIFT OF THE WORKING OF MIRACLES

To another the working of miracles...

—1 CORINTHIANS 12:10

THE SPIRITUAL GIFT we are about to study is the gift of the working of miracles. It is one of the three power gifts: (1) the gift of faith, (2) the gifts of healings, and (3) the gift of the working of miracles. God uses the power gifts to channel His supernatural power through His church to destroy the works of the devil.[1]

WHAT IS THE GIFT OF THE WORKING OF MIRACLES?

This gift is mentioned in 1 Cor. 12:10: "To another the working of miracles." Now the wording there is extremely important. As Howard Carter so astutely pointed out: "It is not the praying for or hoping for miracles; it is the *working* of them."[2]

The literal Greek for the word "miracles" here in this passage is *dunamis,* meaning "operations of works of power." It is the power of God operating by the Spirit of God in and through His church.

> The gift of the working of miracles is a supernatural manifestation of the power of God that alters, suspends, or in some other way controls the laws of nature.
>
>

This spectacular gift of the working of miracles is full of signs and wonders. Carter observes:

It is a gift that was more in evidence in the Old Testament than in the New. In the New Testament God was showing His compassion; in the Old Testament He was demonstrating His power. Some people have erroneously supposed that the power of God is demonstrated only in the conversion of souls. It goes without saying that the conversion of souls is a supernatural experience; it is indeed a miracle. A person does not become converted by turning over a new leaf or living a better life; he is converted when the power of God gives him new life. However, the working of miracles is a supernatural manifestation of the power of God that alters, suspends, or in some other way controls the laws of nature.[3]

Lester Sumrall says: "The gift of the working of miracles means a supernatural intervention by God in the ordinary course of nature. It is God working through a person, an animal (for example, Balaam's donkey that spoke in Num. 12:22–23), or some other instrument (for example, Elijah's mantle in 2 Kings 2:8), to do something that could not be done normally."[4]

Harold Horton, in his book, The Gifts of the Spirit, says in regard to the working of miracles:

> A miracle is a supernatural intervention in the ordinary course of nature; a temporary suspension of the accustomed order; an interruption of the system of nature as we know it.
>
>

A miracle...is a supernatural intervention in the ordinary course of nature; a temporary suspension of the accustomed order; an interruption of the system of nature, as we know it. The gift of the working of miracles operates by the energy or dynamic force of the Spirit in reversals or suspensions of natural laws.

A miracle is a sovereign act of the Spirit of God, irrespective of the laws or systems. A miracle has no explanation other than the sovereign power of the Lord. God is not bound by His own laws. God acts as He will[s] either within or outside of what we understand to be laws, whether natural or supernatural. To speak of God as though He were circumscribed (limited) by the laws of His own making is to reduce Him to the creature plane and impair the very essence of His eternal attributes.

When in a sudden and sovereign act, God steps outside the circle by which His creatures or creation are boundaried, we call it a miracle. And so does God in the scriptures.[5]

And Lester Sumrall notes:

We are dealing with God, and it is a miracle only as far as
man is concerned. Since God is omnipotent—having all
power—He does not recognize a certain event as a miracle.
What we consider to be a miracle is only an act of God; it is
only the voice of God speaking, causing something to come
to pass. What might be a very small thing in God's sight is a
miracle to man because he is unable to perform it in his own
natural strength.[6]

The working of miracles involves different kinds of supernatural
marvels, and the scope of operation of the gift of the working of miracles is very broad:

At one end of the spectrum it merges with the gifts of healing.
Certain healings that involve creative action are true miracles.
At the other end of the spectrum are miraculous interventions
in the very course of nature—such as breaking droughts,
overruling gravity, rolling back the sea and making the sun
stand still.

The gift of working miracles involves various kinds of
supernatural phenomena, such as raising the dead, miracles
of supply, miraculously delivering God's people and invoking
special judgments against wicked people or nations.[7]

WHAT IS THE DIFFERENCE BETWEEN THE GIFT OF FAITH AND THE GIFT OF THE WORKING OF MIRACLES?

> The gift of the working of miracles produces instant, supernatural, spectacular results.
> The gift of faith obtains supernatural results, but in a less spectacular way. The results become apparent at a later time.
> In the gift of faith, God does the work *for* us.
> In the gift of the working of miracles, God does the work *through* us.
>
>

The gift of the working of miracles is
active and produces instant, supernatural, spectacular results. The gift of
faith *appears* to be inactive; however, it
sets powerful forces in motion, and the
results become apparent at a later time.
The gift of faith—like the gift of the
working of miracles—obtains supernatural results, but in a less spectacular way.

In *the gift of faith*, God does the work *for* us. In *the gift of the working of miracles,* the power of the Spirit of God surges into us, and God does the work *through* us. Through the supernatural power of the Spirit, God does a work through us that we are unable to perform in our own natural strength.

TWO REASONS GOD IMPARTS THE GIFT OF THE WORKING OF MIRACLES

Why should God impart the working of miracles to a person?

1. Miracles are Given as Credentials

When Moses fled from Egypt into the desert of Midian and became a shepherd, he saw a bush burning with fire without being consumed. He heard God speaking to him out of the midst of the fire: "Moses, put off thy shoes from off thy feet, for the place whereon thou standest is holy....I have seen the affliction of my people...and I will send thee unto Pharaoh" (Ex. 3:5).

Moses was afraid of the thought of obeying God and returning to Egypt where Pharaoh had sought to slay him after hearing that Moses had killed an Egyptian for beating a Hebrew slave (Ex. 2:11–15). So Moses protested: "Behold, when I come unto the children of Israel, and shall say unto them, The God of your fathers hath sent me unto you; and they shall say to me, What is his name? what shall I say unto them?" (Ex. 3:13).

As Howard Carter reminds us, God's reply was that Moses was to say, "I AM hath sent me unto you." (For God's name is, "I am that I am." He is the almighty; He is omnipresent; He is omniscient. He brings the eternal past and the eternal future into the present.)[8]

God told Moses He was sure that the king of Egypt would not let him go, but He would stretch out His hand, and smite Egypt with all His wonders which He would do in their midst, and after that Pharaoh would let Moses take the children of Israel out of Egypt (Ex. 4:19–20).

> And Moses answered and said, But, behold, they will not believe me, nor hearken unto my voice: for they will say, The Lord hath not appeared unto thee. And the Lord said unto him, What is that in thine hand? And he said, A rod. And he said, Cast it on the ground. And he cast it on the ground, and it became a serpent; and Moses fled from before it. And

the Lord said unto Moses, Put forth thine hand, and take it by the tail. And he put forth his hand, and caught it, and it became a rod in his hand: That they may believe that the Lord God of their fathers, the God of Abraham, the God of Isaac, and the God of Jacob, hath appeared unto thee. And the Lord said furthermore unto him, Put now thine hand into thy bosom. And he put his hand into his bosom: and when he took it out, behold, his hand was leprous as snow. And he said, Put thine hand into thy bosom again. And he put his hand into his bosom again; and plucked it out of his bosom, and, behold, it was turned again as his other flesh. And it shall come to pass, if they will not believe thee, neither hearken to the voice of the first sign, that they will believe the voice of the latter sign. And it shall come to pass, if they will not believe also these two signs, neither hearken unto thy voice, that thou shalt take of the water of the river, and pour it upon the dry land: and the water which thou takest out of the river shall become blood upon the dry land.

—EXODUS 4:1–9

When Moses obeyed God, went into the court of Pharaoh, and announced that I AM had sent him, Pharaoh said, "Who is I AM?" So Moses had his brother Aaron demonstrate by throwing down his rod in the king's palace, and it turned into a serpent.

You will recall how Pharaoh's magicians promptly threw down their magic wands, and they turned into serpents. But Aaron's snake swallowed the others.

> Miracles may be given as divine credentials.
> Miracles may be given as signs.

What does that tell us? The devil is mighty, but God is almighty! The powers of the devil may appear stupefying, but God's power is greater! God used all these signs as the credentials that He—the great I AM—had sent Moses. And believe me, in the days ahead—after God had used Moses to turn Egypt's waters into blood; caused frogs, lice, flies, and locusts to cover their land; killed all their livestock; sent boils on every Egyptian man and beast; and smote every firstborn in the land of Egypt, including the son of the Pharaoh himself—Pharaoh told them to go! All these miracles were divine credentials that God sent Moses. And God may choose to impart the gift of the working of miracles to His servants today as divine credentials.

2. Miracles are Given as Signs.

Sometimes, the working of miracles is used as a sign. For example, when the children of Israel demanded a king so that they might be like other nations, God told the prophet Samuel to give them a king (1 Sam. 8–12). Samuel said:

> Now therefore stand and see this great thing, which the Lord will do before your eyes. Is it not wheat harvest to day? I will call unto the Lord, and he shall send thunder and rain; that ye may perceive and see that your wickedness is great, which ye have done in the sight of the Lord, in asking you a king. So Samuel called unto the Lord; and the Lord sent thunder and rain that day: and all the people greatly feared the Lord and Samuel.
>
> —1 SAMUEL 12:16–18

Howard Carter points out that this miracle was a sign of God's displeasure and was an answer to Samuel's believing prayer, though prayer is not always essential to the functioning of the gift.[9]

Remember the time when Jesus and the disciples were in a boat in a storm, and the waves tossed the boat from side to side? (Mark 4:36–41). Jesus did not pray, "O Father, My disciples are afraid they are going to die. If it's according to Your will, would You please cause the storm to be stopped?" No, He didn't pray at all. Instead, He rebuked the wind and commanded, "Peace, be still!" The stormy winds subsided, and the sea became calm. He didn't *pray* for a miracle. He *worked* a miracle.

Jesus was hungry and came to a fig tree, looking for ripe figs to eat. After finding nothing but leaves, Jesus commanded: "Let no fruit grow on thee henceforward forever" (Matt. 21:19). Why? Because the one type of fig tree that retains its leaves through the winter usually also has figs. The tree showed promise, but it had no performance. (What a warning to us if we stand at the judgment with leaves of profession and no fruit! We will be reproved for unfruitfulness when fruit is expected.)

The next morning as they were passing along, the disciples—who had witnessed what happened the day before (Mark 11:14)—noticed that the fig tree was withered completely away to its roots.

> And Peter remembered and said to Him, Master, look! The fig tree which You doomed has withered away! And Jesus, replying, said to them, Have faith in God [constantly]. Truly I tell you, whoever says to this mountain, Be lifted up and thrown into the sea! and does not doubt at all in his heart but believes that what he says will take place, it will be done for him. For this reason I am telling you, whatever you ask for in prayer, believe (trust and be confident) that it is granted to you, and you will [get it].
>
> —MARK 11:21–24, AMP

Carter reminds us that Jesus *spoke* to the fig tree. "One might say, 'It has no ears.' Jesus went so far as to talk to the dead. Remember when they carried a man out of the gate of Nain, Jesus stopped the funeral? He said, "Young man, I say unto thee, arise," and the dead man heard His voice. Jesus did not pray for a miracle: He worked a miracle."[10]

Don't *worry* about your mountain. *Talk* to your mountain. Believe in your heart that what you say will come to pass: say it with substance, build it systematically, say it out loud. Command it! Don't just think it.

Prayer is not always absolutely necessary for the gift of the working of miracles to function. But, as with all things of the Spirit, we must be balanced. You and I are not to go around commanding everyone and everything all the time. But when God entrusts us with a strength and energy that we do not normally have, when we feel the anointing and empowerment and compassion of the Holy Spirit come upon us, we say what God tells us to say, we do what God tells us to do, we believe it is granted to us, and we will get it!

MIRACLES ARE NEVER GIVEN TO SHOW OFF OR ENTERTAIN

Gordan Lindsay states: "It is important to understand that miracles are never given for the purpose of amazing, astounding, amusing, or entertaining. They have a much more serious purpose that is compatible with God's dignity and majesty."[11]

Jesus refused cheap displays of supernatural phenomena:

- Jesus rejected the Pharisees' request that He show them a sign from heaven, and severely rebuked them (Matt. 16:4).

- After fasting forty days, Jesus refused Satan's temptation to turn stones into bread in order to prove He was the Son of God (Matt. 4:3–4). Jesus flatly refused to demonstrate His power to the devil. But later, when the multitudes were hungry, Jesus made bread enough to satisfy their need, and some was left over.

- Jesus refused to establish His claims by theatrical displays of power when Satan told Him to jump from the pinnacle of the temple to prove He was God's Son (Matt. 4:6–7). However, when Jesus' disciples were in a dangerous storm at sea, Jesus did not hesitate to overrule the forces of gravity and walk on the surface of the water to go to their aid (Matt. 14:24–25).

- King Herod was "exceedingly glad" when Jesus was arraigned before him because "he hoped to see some miracle done by Him" (Luke 23:8). This was Jesus' last opportunity to escape the cross, but He had come to do the will of His Father. Knowing that Herod's interest was rooted in curiosity and superstition, not a sincere desire to know or obey God, Jesus refused to even talk with him.[12]

It's interesting that Jesus began His ministry with a miracle: turning water into wine (John 2:3). On that occasion, He and His mother had been invited to a wedding feast. When they ran short of wine, Jesus' mother, who obviously believed He could do anything, said to Jesus: "They have no wine." He answered, "Woman what have I to do with thee? Mine hour is not yet come" (John 2:3–4).

Did you ever wonder why Jesus didn't want to make wine for the wedding crowd and why He responded to His mother in that way, calling her "Woman" instead of "Mother"? I agree with Howard Carter's explanation.[13] Carter reasons that Jesus did not normally take orders from human beings and that Mary was making a mistake when she suggested that He perform a miracle. Why? Only God, His Father, had that right. Only God the Father showed His Son what to do. Jesus hadn't come into the world to amaze and entertain or to make wine for people who had already had plenty to drink.

Why did Mary come to Jesus and say, "They have no wine?" Mary believed there was nothing impossible with Jesus, so she told Him.

Jesus said, "Woman, what have I to do with thee? Mine hour is not yet come." Why didn't Jesus say, "Mother"? Why did He say, "Woman"? Perhaps he was offended in His Spirit by Mary's suggestion that He should work a miracle. God, His Father, was the One who showed Him what to do. Jesus actually said that in His ministry later; but Mary presented the embarrassing need to Him, knowing He could do something about it.

Why did Jesus not want to make wine on this occasion? Think about it. Jesus had not come into the world to make wine for people who were not really thirsty, and He had not come to make bread for those who were full and satisfied. Jesus came to make food for the hungry.

But humanity was speaking to Deity—laying a need before the One who could do something about it. Mary's concern for the families and friends of the bride and bridegroom prevailed upon Him, and He granted her request. Mary's example tells us that we can prevail upon God so that He does what He otherwise would not do.

Note that Mary went even further: She said to the servants, "Whatsoever He saith unto you, do it."

Jesus was committed to action. He responded, "Fill the water pots with water."

Notice that the Bible says that they filled them *to the brim*—not just halfway. You and I must act in faith. If we do the *possible*, God will do the *impossible*.

The crowd watched attentively as the obedient servants tilted that first water pot. Then it happened. The tasteless, colorless water miraculously transformed, and sweet, succulent wine streamed over the lip of the pot! How? I like the interpretation of someone who said: "The water suddenly recognized the voice of its Creator...*and blushed*..."

The governor of the feast, the best man, sampled it and said, "You have kept the best wine until last."

WE NEED TO *EXPECT* THE MIRACULOUS AND *SEE* THE MIRACULOUS!

Jesus promised His disciples that they should perform the same miracles that He had performed, and that they would perform even greater miracles (John 14:12). It's not presumptuous or fanatical to expect that miracles may be worked in our day. All the current challenges of the occult and atheism and irreverence call for miraculous manifestations.

You and I both know that demonic supernatural power is at work today in the world. However, we should also know that just as God overwhelmed Pharaoh's magicians with his power, He is ready to do the same for you and me today.

Think about it. What could you and I see take place, if only we believed for the working of miracles? We have not yet seen all the things God is willing to do for us and through us for His glory. When we believe God, there will be a mighty demonstration of divine power. We must pray for these manifestations in the church, and in our *own* lives!

SOME EXAMPLES OF MIRACLES IN MODERN TIMES

I once laid hands on a sick woman named Eileen Lacoco, and she was instantly healed. Eileen began attending our church. After a time, I was able to lead her husband Kelly to the Lord.

Kelly and Eileen were in their late sixties when he became extremely ill and was admitted to Mercy Hospital in New Orleans. As Kelly's condition grew increasingly critical, he drifted into unconsciousness, and then sank into a coma. He had been in a coma between five and six hours when I entered the hospital to see him. A nurse met me downstairs as I was about to go up to his room and said, "They're looking for you." I got off the elevator on the second floor of the hospital and walked around the corner.

A Catholic nun smiled and said, "You must be the boss."

I grinned and said, "Yes, Ma'am, I am." (Kelly had always called me "Boss".)

The nun said, "Please go in and talk to his wife Eileen. She won't let them do anything to him except put an oxygen tent over his head until the boss is here, but the man is dying. He has severe heart problems, and such serious complications have developed that he's not expected to make it."

When I entered Kelly's room, I said to Eileen, "Mama, step out in the hallway and let me be alone with Kelly a few minutes."

As I walked over and stood beside his bed, Kelly turned his head toward me. It was his first movement in five hours. I lifted up the side of the oxygen tent and put my head under it.

In a weak voice, Kelly murmured: "Boss, if you'll put your hand on me like you did for Mama, I'll be healed."

I closed my eyes and prayed. Just as I was saying "Amen," I heard the oxygen tent make a noise. I looked, and Kelly had climbed out of the bed on the other side and was standing beside it!

The doctors insisted he get back into the bed, but Kelly refused. Instead, he demanded his clothes, dressed, and walked out of the hospital!

Two weeks later I received a call from the nun who was chief administrator of the hospital. She said, "Rev. Gorman, could you come to my office? I'd like to talk to you."

I went to her office, expecting them to reprimand me because of what Kelly had done. However, instead of lecturing me on hospital policy, the nun said: "Reverend, we know Kelly's healing was a miracle. We have contacted our headquarters, the Sisters of Mercy in St. Louis, MO, and have received approval for you to serve on the board of the hospital."

Surprised and grateful for their invitation, I thanked the nun and told her I would have to pray about it.

A couple of days later, I called and told her I would be honored to serve on their hospital board. Then I went to her office, where she informed me of my responsibilities as a board member, told me how often the board met, and gave me an overview of their routine. I learned that I was the first Protestant ever invited by the order of the Sisters of Mercy to serve on the hospital board.

A short time afterward she called and wanted to know if I would be the speaker for their awards banquet where they honor the doctors, nurses, and staff. The sister said, "We normally have the archbishop speak for this event, but this year we feel you are to speak."

At the banquet, everybody who was anybody in New Orleans—the leading bankers, doctors, lawyers, judges, and so forth—was there.

New Orleans was about eighty percent Catholic then, and even the mayor was present, so it was quite an event.

A short time after I spoke at the meeting, the sister asked my wife and me to attend a banquet for the hospital staff just before the Christmas season. As Virginia and I walked in for the banquet, a little nun walked up and introduced herself, explaining that she was to be our hostess for the event. Then, with a big smile and a twinkle in her eye, she said, "Stay close and I will show you which punch to drink!"

The evening was a very rewarding experience. I was able to meet and get acquainted with many people. I realized that God was opening up the city of New Orleans to us. Two weeks later an article with a photo of me standing between two Catholic sisters—the chief administrator and her assistant—appeared on the front page of *The Times Picayune*. The Lord used it to give me an incredible endorsement with the Catholic people.

Shortly after that, my wife Virginia and I were asked to come to the sisters' living quarters that occupied an entire upper wing of the hospital. Thirty women were present, and I was the only man! After a lovely dinner, we all moved into a huge, beautifully furnished sitting room. Virginia and I walked to the side and sat by ourselves.

The sister who served as the chief administrator of the hospital picked up a Bible and said, "Rev. Gorman, I know you can't stay long because you're busy, but please explain Acts, chapter two to us."

That night the chief administrator, her assistant, and five other sisters received the baptism of the Holy Spirit!

Following that experience, there were numerous times when I'd get a call from the chief administrator or her first assistant and they would say, "Rev. Gorman, the Father is administering the last rites to so and so in room so and so. The Father will be gone before you get here. You will be able to speak with and pray for the patient."

On several occasions I was able to lead patients to a personal relationship with Jesus. How I wish I could say that all the people I prayed for received healing, but not all did. However, several different people who, according to the doctors, were at death's door were miraculously healed.

I served on that board until our church grew to the point that I could no longer sacrifice the time, due to the growing demands of the church and its ministries.

CORRIE AND BETSIE TEN BOOM

We get the idea that ordinary people with their weaknesses can't be used by God to perform miracles. But very ordinary people have exercised some very extraordinary graces and gifts of the Spirit of God.

In her best-selling book, *The Hiding Place,* a Dutch watchmaker named Corrie Ten Boom tells the story of her family's involvement during World War II in the underground movement helping Jews escape from Germany. Corrie's sister, Nollie, was arrested along with a young Jewish woman staying in Nollie's home. After seven weeks, Nollie was released. But when the underground operation in their home was discovered, Corrie, her older sister Betsie, their brother Willem, and their elderly father were all arrested and taken to a Holland prison in February, 1944. Their eighty-four-year-old father died ten days after his arrest. Willem was soon released, but not before contracting a disease in prison.

But Betsie and Corrie were moved to Ravensbruck concentration camp in Germany. When the prisoners arrived, Corrie managed to smuggle in a small Dutch Bible and a bottle of vitamin oil without a guard seeing them. The 35,000 women in the crowded camp existed in deplorable conditions in cold barracks, sleeping on straw mattresses filled with choking dust and swarming with fleas. Though forced to do hard labor, the women were given only a potato and some thin soup for lunch and some turnip soup and a piece of black bread in the evening.

Most of the women reacted to the conditions with anger and selfishness and spent their time in arguments, fights, and looking out for their own interests. But soon after Betsie began to pray God would send peace into their barrack room, the atmosphere changed and women became more patient with each other.

After a hard day's work and their miserable supper each evening, Corrie and Betsie took out their little Dutch Bible and read to a growing group of women. The threat from the swarms of fleas kept the guards out, so the women didn't have to worry about being caught and punished. As she read, Corrie translated from the Dutch to German, reading slowly so various women could then translate to the Polish, French, Russian, and others.

Betsie gradually became weaker and weaker. Corrie gave her a few vitamin drops each day, but there were so many other needy fellow-prisoners that she began giving them drops, too. Day after day she shared the vitamin drops with more and more people. Corrie knew the bottle must soon be empty, but every day more drops came. Nobody could understand how such a thing could be until Betsie reminded them of the story in the Bible of the widow's jar of oil that did not run dry for many days.

Betsie weakened more and more until she died, but her face in death had changed from one of pain and suffering into one of beauty, like the face of an angel. Her face was full and young, joyful and healthy. Even her hair looked as if it had been graciously put into place by an angelic hand.

Not long after, Corrie was released and given a railway pass to Holland. Afterwards, she found out she had been released by mistake and that only a week later, all the women of her age in the camp had been killed.

Corrie's sister Nollie and her family were well. Her brother Willem died shortly after the war's end as a result of the disease he had contracted while in prison. His son Kik, once heavily involved in the underground movement aiding Jews, died as a German prisoner of war.

After the war ended, God gave Corrie a large, beautiful home where she could help former prisoners find peace and comfort through her loving care and the compassionate help of others. For over thirty years Corrie visited country after country—over sixty in all—telling sad, bitter people how God can heal and take away all feelings of hatred and bitterness. You can read many of her stirring, heartwarming experiences, including the story of the miraculously multiplying drops of vitamin oil, in her book called *The Hiding Place*.[14]

HOWARD CARTER

In his book, *Spiritual Gifts and Their Operation,* Howard Carter shares an interesting, enlightening story that further expands our understanding of the gift of the working of miracles and its operation. Carter says:

> It happened years ago when I was ministering in Wales. I was preaching in a different place every night, and it was hard going. One night was spent with a miner in one of the little

houses standing in a long, long line next to each other; and if any house was weak, the others on either side held it up. In this home, there were two bedrooms. I was given the better of the two, the front bedroom.

I tried to go to sleep, but outside my window was an oil lamp. There was evidently water in the pipe, for the light went up and down, alternating continually; it would go down until it was almost negligible and then up again. This worried me. If anyone has suffered from nerves, he will understand. Anything mechanical or regular in its alternation (the room now flooded with light and then with darkness) is unbearable.

I could not sleep. What could I do? I prayed fervently, "Oh, Lord, You know how bad my nerves are; please stop that thing outside." Nothing happened in spite of all my praying.

I sat up in bed and said, "It has got to stop!" There were beads of perspiration on my brow, for I felt the thing must stop. I decided that if it is all right to talk to the wind and waves, I could talk to the lamp. I waited until the unction of the Spirit was upon me; then I took a deep breath and cried out, "In the name of the Lord, stop!" It did! When I commanded, "In the name of the Lord," it stopped. I lay back in bed delighted, and had such a wonderful time with God. I had not been able to sleep when the flame went up and down, and now I could not sleep for sheer joy when it didn't go up and down!

I don't know how long it was before I actually did fall asleep, or how long I slept, but it was still dark when I awoke and I began another little praise service. Then something happened, as sometimes may have happened to you—the trouble returned. The light went up and down again.

People will sometimes get a remarkable healing from some horrible, malignant trouble, and it will be marvelous. They generally go about giving their testimony; then maybe nine months or a year after, the symptoms of the trouble return, and they will ask, "Brother Carter, what should I do?" I reply, "Refuse to doubt; you are healed; God's power has triumphed."

Now, let me finish the story of the lamp, which again began to fluctuate. I said in a loud voice, "No, you don't! You stop!" This time it stopped, and it gave me no more trouble. If you have had the victory, keep it; don't let the devil prevail.[15]

THE BEST IS YET TO COME!

In his stimulating book, *Smith Wigglesworth on Spiritual Gifts,* Smith utters this challenging word:

> We have been seeing wonderful miracles during these last days, and they are only a little of what we are going to see. I believe that we are right on the threshold of wonderful things, but I want to emphasize that all these things will be only through the power of the Holy Spirit. You must not think that these gifts will fall upon you like ripe cherries. There is a sense in which you have to pay the price for everything you get. We must earnestly desire God's best gifts and say "Amen" to any preparation the Lord takes us through. In this way, we will be humble, useable vessels through whom He Himself can operate by means of the Spirit's power.[16]

Amen and amen!

Part 4

THE THREE GIFTS OF INSPIRATION

- Gift of Prophecy

- Gift of Tongues

- Gift of Interpretation of Tongues

THESE GIFTS SAY something.

In 1 Cor. 12:1–11, Paul lists nine different gifts of the Holy Spirit. As we have learned, these nine gifts of the Spirit may be divided into three categories. We have studied the three revelation gifts and the three power gifts. The last of these are the three inspirational (or vocal) gifts (the gifts of prophecy, unknown tongues, and interpretation of tongues). God uses these gifts to supernaturally build up, strengthen, and encourage His people.

How are these three inspirational or vocal gifts defined? What are they? What do they do? We'll begin this study with the first of these gifts: the gift of prophecy.

Chapter 10

THE GIFT OF PROPHECY

And to another prophecy...

—1 CORINTHIANS 12:10, NASB

I wish you all spoke with tongues, but even more
that you prophesied; for he who prophesies is greater
than he who speaks with tongues, unless indeed he
interprets, that the church may receive edification.

—1 CORINTHIANS 14:5, NKJV

Do not quench the Spirit. Do not treat prophecies with contempt
but test them all; hold on to what is good, reject every kind of evil.

—1 THESSALONIANS 5:19–22, NIV

But he who prophesies speaks edification
and exhortation and comfort to men.

—1 CORINTHIANS 14:3, NKJV

OF THE THREE inspiration gifts, the gift of prophecy is really the most important. Note, for example, that some form of the word "prophecy" occurs twenty-two times in 1 Corinthians, chapters 11–14. As Harold Horton points out, "The unusual frequency of the word indicates not only the importance of the gift but the urgency of the need for its regulation. The sharper the tool, the more need for care in its employment."[1]

The gift of prophecy can be defined in its simplest form as an inspired utterance in a known language. It is

> The gift of prophecy is the simplest form of inspired utterance in a known language. It is entirely supernatural. As speaking with tongues is supernatural utterance in an unknown tongue, so prophecy is supernatural utterance in a known tongue. It is a manifestation of the Spirit of God, and not of the human mind.

entirely supernatural. As speaking with tongues is a supernatural utterance in an unknown tongue, so prophecy is a supernatural utterance in a known tongue. It is a manifestation of the Spirit of God, and not of the human mind.[2]

As Harold Horton so beautifully observes:

> It has no more to do with human powers of thought and reasoning than walking on water has to do with human powers of equilibrium. It is a miracle.
>
> It is an act straight from heaven, just as giving sight to blind eyes by a touch of human hands is an act from heaven. In its simplest form it may be possessed by all who have received the baptism in the Holy Ghost; "for ye may all prophesy one by one" (1 Cor. 14:31). The human will and faith are active in prophecy—but not the human intellect. Its pronouncements, therefore, come with the same divine authority and power from the lips of a peasant or a philosopher, for both are but "mouths" for the expression of divine words.[3]

Gordon Lindsay points out that in the Old Testament, the prophetic ministry was essentially *foretelling*, but in the New Testament, it shifts strongly to *forthtelling*. He says:

> The purpose of the New Testament gift, as exercised in the public assembly, was to edify, exhort, and comfort—in other words, make people better and more useful Christians. This is the usual manifestation of the gift which we see operating in the church today.
>
> When man was created and placed in the Garden of Eden, God talked with him directly. Sin broke the communion. Nevertheless, there still remains a deep longing in the human spirit for direct communication with the creator. This basic human need is supplied in a measure through the operation of the gift of prophecy, as manifested in the New Testament church. Congregations which do not have this gift operating are missing something vital to their worship.[4]

SOME SCRIPTURAL PURPOSES OF
THE GIFT OF PROPHECY

First Corinthians 14:22 tells us "prophecy is for a sign, not to unbelievers, but to those who believe" (NASB). What service does the gift
of prophecy render to believers? Paul answers that question when he
says to believers:

> Follow after charity, and desire spiritual gifts, but rather
> that ye may prophesy. For he that speaketh in an unknown
> tongue speaketh not unto men, but unto God: for no man
> understandeth him; howbeit, in the spirit he speaketh mys-
> teries. But he that prophesieth speaketh unto men to edifica-
> tion, and exhortation, and comfort. He that speaketh in an
> unknown tongue edifieth himself; but he that prophesieth
> edifieth the church. I would that ye all spake with tongues,
> but rather that ye prophesied: for greater is he that prophe-
> sieth than he that speaketh with tongues, except he interpret,
> that the church may receive edifying.
>
> —1 CORINTHIANS 14:1–5

LET'S REVIEW. WHAT DOES 1 COR.
14:1-5 TELL US PROPHECY IS FOR?

1. Verse 3 tells us that prophecy is for speaking unto
   men supernaturally. In prophecy, God speaks to men
   through the mouths of men, edifying, exhorting, and
   comforting.

2. Verse 4 tells us that prophecy is for *edifying* the church,
   the body of believers.

3. Verse 3 tells us that prophecy is for *exhorting*.

4. Verse 3 also tells us that prophecy is for *comforting*.
   1 Cor. 14:31 continues, "For ye may all prophesy one by
   one that all may learn, and all may be comforted."

What Does it Mean to Edify, Exhort, and Comfort?

Prophecy edifies the church.

In its root meaning, *to edify* signifies "to erect, to strengthen, to build up." When people speak in tongues, 1 Cor. 14:4 tells us that they edify themselves. However, when people prophesy, they edify the church. Prophecy is one of the Lord Jesus' major tools for building up His church. When believers with weak, trembling hearts hear a message in prophecy saying something like, "Fear not! Be bold and strong, for the Lord your God is with you. He knows your thoughts and hears your prayers," they can return to battle with renewed strength and determination. Many, many Christians today need to have their weak spiritual lives built up and strengthened. That is why the Holy Spirit gave the gifts of inspiration to the church.

Prophecy exhorts the church.

In the original language, *exhortation* signifies "a calling near."[5] Sometimes a group of believers can become so caught up in church business and organization, political happenings, social schedules, and a multitude of other things, they forget their most basic reason for existence. Their degree of spiritual fervency drops, and they begin to cool off. At times like this, the words of the Holy Ghost lead us away from the sin and cares of the world and "call us near" to God's encouraging, strengthening presence. This "calling near" can also be the means for a word of caution, warning, or reprimand. Below is an example:

> Nevertheless I have this against you, that you have left your first love. Remember therefore from where you have fallen; repent and do the first works, or else I will come to you quickly and remove your lampstand from its place—unless you repent.
>
> —REVELATION 2:4–5, NKJV

Obedience brings courage. As believers hear words of prophecy urging them to deeper consecration and holiness, and they obey, they gain wisdom and understanding in separating themselves from the world. The discouraged are encouraged. Thus, through the gift of prophecy, followers of Christ are built up spiritually.

Prophecy comforts the church.

To *comfort* means "to enable or empower." As Ken and Lorraine Krivohlavek explain:

> Our modern word *comfort* means something much different and has often confused our notion of the Holy Spirit's ministry, since He is called the Comforter. Comfort (or Comforter) originally came from two Latin words: *cum* (meaning with or alongside) and *forte* (which, as musicians know, means volume or power.) We think of comfort as ease or sympathy in trouble. But God's meaning here is *with power.* Prophecies stating, "I am with you" or "You are not alone" have given us a sense of power to return to our tasks. It is a consolation that makes us strong and secure.[6]

The Greek word for *comfort* can also mean *consolation,* which would include the healing of distress, sorrow, persecution, and suffering.[7] As Lester Sumrall reminds us:

> We live in a world of broken lives, broken homes, and broken ambitions. People today do not necessarily need sympathy or pity; they need comfort. The church needs divine comfort from the Holy Spirit to bring heaven's healing into their hearts. It is our duty and our privilege to come to church and say, "Lord, we want the tenderness of the gifts to function. We want prophecy to function...."
>
> Some people who come to our churches are so sad, they don't know what to do. Some of them are actually contemplating suicide. If there is anything we should give these people, it is comfort—healing of the inner person, healing of the memories, healing of sadness and depression....If prophecy is the most tender of all the gifts, how much should it function in all our lives![8]

Sumrall says:

> This gift is available not to just a few, but to the whole church. Begin now by saying, "Lord, I want these gifts to function in my life." If you are sincere, God will cause these gifts to

function in and through you. He wants you to be an instrument He can use to edify, exhort, and comfort His people.[9]

CONTROLLING THE GIFT OF PROPHECY

First Corinthians 14:32 plainly teaches that the possessor of the gift of prophecy can control that gift: "And the spirits of the prophets are subject to the prophets." Therefore, we can be certain that an alien spirit, not the Spirit of God, is involved if a person says regarding their utterances, "I cannot stop doing this." The devil binds and controls. God does not. We can stop God and grieve the Holy Spirit any time we choose. We are not under bondage to the Spirit of God. We work with Him and flow with Him because we want to. We have to keep flowing in the Spirit if we expect the gifts to operate in and through us.[10]

First Corinthians 14:29 teaches that there should be at the most only three messages of prophecy in one meeting: "Let the prophets speak two or three, and let the other judge." If God has already spoken three times, even if you feel a desire to prophesy, you should control it. The Bible plainly teaches that this is enough for one service.

Also, 1 Thess. 5:20 plainly commands: "Despise not prophesyings." Sadly, some church leaders do not want the gift of prophecy to function in their churches because they cannot personally control it. It is supernatural. If any gift of the Spirit is not functioning properly, it can be dangerous to the church. But anything worth very much involves some element of danger, just as flying an airplane or driving a vehicle— as valuable and helpful as those things are—can be dangerous.[11]

Sumrall also uses the example of a fire inside a furnace to illustrate the importance of the proper functioning of prophecy. Like a fire burning on the floor of a room instead of inside the furnace where the flames belong, the gift of prophecy not functioning properly can be dangerous to a church. Like every gift of the Spirit, the gift of prophecy has a proper place and a proper time. To function best, it should function at that place and time. This is why it is essential that church leaders know what God desires to accomplish in every service.

If leaders consider prophecies unnecessary—feeling that they are getting along just fine without them—they do their congregations a great disservice. How can we possibly not need what God has provided? We may be having good services, but we will have better services when we allow for the gift of prophecy, pay attention to what is said, and obey the instructions the Holy Spirit gives.[12]

Ken and Lorraine Krivohlavek are correct in saying that we treat prophecies with contempt (1 Thess. 5:20), by rushing frantically on in our services as though time were rationed. "Some ministers rarely leave room anywhere in a service for someone to minister a gift of prophecy, without interrupting someone or something."[13] Many leaders don't expect or pray for this gift to be manifested, and they don't encourage others to use this divine gift of utterance.

THE PROPHET

A lot of confusion exists in the minds of many people concerning the real nature of the office and ministry of a "prophet" in the church. Some believe that the "prophet" is simply another name for the preacher, that all true preachers are prophets and all their preaching is prophesying. But this completely fails to recognize the essential place in the New Testament of direct inspiration and immediate revelation. A "prophet", in the New Testament sense, is one who speaks from the impulse of a sudden inspiration, from the light of a sudden revelation at the moment (...1 Cor. 14:30).[14] ...Prophecy is not preaching. If it were, preparation for preaching would be unnecessary, since one might wait for the anointing of the Spirit without any premeditation. But the one who ministers should wait on his ministry. Scripture affirms that God saves men by the foolishness of preaching, not by the manifestation of prophecy.[15]

Prophets are also distinguished from "teachers" (Acts 13:1; 1 Cor. 12:28; Eph. 4:11) in that teachers exercise a more logical ministry in the Spirit, appealing principally to the reasoning faculties of the hearers. Prophets, on the other hand, appeal to the conscience more generally through the emotions. And prophets are also distinguished from "evangelists." While evangelists may be powerful emotional preachers, they do not necessarily minister from an immediate revelation at the moment.[16]

In the early church the prophets undoubtedly provided a large part of the preaching ministry and gave it a distinctive note of divine authority and power which must have been tremendously arresting to the hearer (1 Cor. 14:25). They were worthy successors of John the Baptist and the great prophet-preachers of the Old Testament. And today, we can recognize this ministry among preachers who speak very largely by inspiration as they go along. Often they bring real enlightenment to the understanding, but it's usually through the intuitive rather than the logical faculties. Such ministry is often a powerful agent to promote revival.[17]

Donald Gee reproves lazy preachers who rely on the Spirit's help to make up for their lack of preparation:

> A word of warning is required lest this truly God-given gift and ministry should be confused with the lazy, slipshod habits of some preachers who waste precious hours which should be spent in preparation, and then expect the Holy Spirit to help them out by a last-minute revelation. Such often quote, "Open thy mouth wide and I will fill it," but their messages are usually not such as to bring much glory to the supposed divine giver. A true prophet does need preparation, as much as any preacher, but his is the preparation particularly of the heart. He has to "prophesy according to the proportion of faith" (Rom. 12:6), and his faith must be kept living, strong, and enlightened by hours of communion with God.[18]

Lester Sumrall adds another dimension to Gee's interpretation of what it means to "prophesy according to the proportion of faith" (Romans 12:6). Sumrall says this means that if a person prophesies things that do not come to pass, the person should stop because he or she is speaking beyond his or her faith.[19]

HOW TO MINISTER THIS GIFT

Ken and Lorraine Krivohlavek share several very helpful and practical explanations regarding how to minister the gift of prophecy. I'd like to summarize and discuss them.

1. Like the other gifts of the Spirit, prophecy operates only in the lives of those who are saved and filled with the Spirit with the evidence of speaking in tongues. God intends that speaking, praying, praising, and interceding in tongues be a daily experience. [I know the Krivohlavek's will agree that it is not sufficient to have once been filled and spoken in tongues. Just as it is

not "once saved, always saved," neither is it "once filled, always filled."] A rich daily prayer life in tongues will be of great assistance in making one tender to what the Holy Spirit is doing and when to yield.

2. An understanding and use of the simpler gifts of messages in tongues and interpretation of tongues will usually be a great help in prophesying. It takes a little faith to give a message in tongues. It is a new experience, but the Spirit-baptized believer is accustomed to praying in tongues. A message in tongues is just one step forward from devotional tongues. It often takes a bit more faith to interpret a message in tongues because the interpretation is in your known language where people can understand and evaluate it. A message in tongues is usually understood only by God.

3. Prophecy usually demands a third and higher level of faith because one is not only speaking in the known language, but he has no message in tongues to tell him that now is the time to speak. He must rely entirely on the voice and urge of the Spirit.

4. Come to each service prayed up and expecting the Lord to urge you to minister a gift of prophecy. Stay in a spirit of worship throughout the service.

5. In this atmosphere of worship and expectancy, you will often have three or four words impressed upon your mind. These are not words that you have thought up or figured out, but words that are suddenly impressed upon you with an urge to be spoken. Those words are the beginning of a prophecy, and you should speak them out at the first appropriate moment.

6. A prophecy is received just the same as an interpretation of tongues except there is no message in tongues to precede it. As you obey, speaking the words God has impressed upon you, He will give you a few more words and then a few more and so on, until the prophecy is completed.

7. When you get the first words of the prophecy, feel free to use *The Ten Second Test*. First, ask God to verify that what you have received is indeed a prophecy by letting the words and urge remain with you while you wait for about ten seconds. Second, command the urge and words to disappear while you wait the same ten seconds if they are not a prophecy. Third, once you are sure you have a prophecy, ask God to give you a ten second quiet spot in the service so that you can minister without interrupting anyone. Wait quietly, and the service will become quiet for a few moments. Then speak what God has given.[20]

SHOULD A PROPHECY BE GIVEN IN THE FIRST, SECOND, OR THIRD PERSON?

The Krivohlaveks also have very helpful insights regarding whether a prophecy should be given in the first, second, or third person. They talk about some people who insist that interpretation of tongues be in the second person, such as "Oh, God we praise You" or "God, teach us to praise You," and who also insist that prophecy must be spoken in the first or third person, such as: "I am God. I will teach you to praise Me" (first person) or "God wants to teach us to praise Him" (third person). But the Kirvohlaveks rightly stress that the important thing in an utterance in the Spirit is the content of the message, not the person in which it is spoken. The statements are saying basically one thing: God wants us to praise Him.[21]

We see that the prophet Isaiah, under the anointing of the Holy Spirit, prophesies using first person (27:3) "I the Lord…," second person (25:1, NKJV) "O Lord, you are my God," and third person (25:6, NIV) "the Lord Almighty will prepare a feast." This would seem to verify that it does not make any real difference whether a prophecy or interpretation of tongues is given in the first, second, or third person.[22]

WHAT PROPHECY DOES AND DOES NOT INCLUDE

Does prophecy include foretelling the future? It has become common to link the word prophecy with predicting the future because so many of the prophetic books of the Bible contain predictions of the future.

I'd like to share some of the views held by various well-known writers and teachers from the past and present.

This is what Lester Sumrall believed regarding the gift of prophecy:

> The gift of prophecy is not foretelling the future. Prophecy in the New Testament is different from a prophet who foretells the future. God specifically limits this gift to three beautiful exercises—edification, exhortation, and comfort—and none of these have to do with the gifts of power or the gifts of revelation. According to Eph. 4:8–12, the prophet is one of the five ministry gifts given to the church. The prophet is a person, not a vocal gift. He holds the office of prophet. Acts 21:9 tells of Philip's four daughters "which did prophesy." They were not prophets, but they prophesied. They had a ministry of edifying the church, but they did not foretell the future. The prophetic *office* always predicts the future; the *gift* of prophecy never predicts the future."[23]

In reply to the question, "Is it not generally accepted that prophecy shows us things to come?" Howard Carter answered:

> Yes, but we use the term "prophecy" in a general sense when we mean "prediction." The general term "prophecy" can cover all the gifts of utterance, but the specific gift of prophecy is defined in 1 Cor. 14:3, "But he that prophesieth speaketh unto men to edification, and exhortation, and comfort." Revelation is not mentioned.

Carter then quoted other scripture to bear out this truth:

> In 1 Cor. 14:6, where the apostle is referring to the edification of the church, he says "What shall I profit you, except I shall speak to you either by revelation, or by knowledge, or by prophesying, or by doctrine?" Here revelation and prophecy are given as separate and distinct from each other, so that the simple gift of prophecy obviously does not contain revelation."[24]

Ken and Lorraine Krivohlavek state the following:

Prophecy, much less the gift of prophecy, is bigger than predicting the future. It also (perhaps more often) simply forth-
tells or speaks forth a message from God directly applicable
to us in our current circumstances....The gift of prophecy
forth-tells on all occasions except when the gift of the word of
knowledge blends its talents with it producing a Divine utterance that reveals the future.[25]

Harold Horton also wrote that it is a mistake to confuse the gift of
prophecy with prediction:

Careful examination will show that the gift does not in itself
convey the power to predict the future. The scripture definition in 1 Cor. 14:3 gives no hint of foretelling. As I have
said, the word "prophet" simply means "one who speaks for
another." It was only in medieval times that the word passed
into the English language in the sense of *prediction*, which
is its popular meaning today. "Etymologically," says William
Smith in his Bible Dictionary, "it is certain that neither pre-
science nor prediction is implied by the term in the Hebrew,
Greek, or English language."

To prophesy, then, does not mean to foretell, but simply
to speak for another. Prophecy may certainly be employed
as the medium of prediction, as a river may bear upon its
bosom a floating flower, or a wisp of moss or a branch or a
boat; but prophecy in itself is a simple stream flowing inde-
pendently and gracefully through happy Pentecost meadows.
If it uncovers or foretells, it is carrying something else not
native to it....If in prophesying a revelation is given of some
existing fact quite hidden from the senses, the word of knowledge is operating with the simple gift of prophecy. If an event
is predicted (an event, of course, that really comes to pass, like
the death foretold by Agabus in Acts 11:28), then the word of
wisdom is working in conjunction with prophecy. In 1 Cor.
14:6, we see this possibility of several gifts operating in asso-
ciation at the same time.[26]

DIFFERENT PROPHETIC GIFTS

As we've already studied, Paul lists nine different spiritual gifts in 1 Cor. 12:8–10 that are involved in receiving and giving a specific "word" to groups of people or a person. The word of knowledge, word of wisdom, and discerning of spirits *reveal* something. If we also add the gift of prophecy, we have the prophetic gifts involved in giving and receiving supernatural words for others.

WHAT ARE SOME WAYS GOD SPEAKS?

Why is it important to be able to recognize when God is speaking to us? Well, when we learn some of the ways God speaks and discern that He is speaking to *us*, we can hear what He is saying to us for *others*. Then we can share His words with them or follow that information so His purposes can be brought about.

God speaks to His children in all sorts of ways. We may hear His still, small voice speak in our spirits. He may speak to us through impressions or perceptions. Unfortunately, if we haven't learned this, we may think these are just stray thoughts. We may disregard them as nothing more than natural and unimportant, or just plain chance.

Sometimes He communicates with His children through gentle inner visions. At other times, God speaks to us through vivid, powerful visions. Sometimes He communicates with us in dreams. He may send angels to visit us. At other times, the Lord Himself may come to us, or people may be caught up in the Spirit in order to receive a message from God. Sometimes He speaks through a trance, where we seem to be in some sort of stupor or daze.

God uses many methods and chooses many ways to speak to us supernaturally. I am about to explain some of those ways in more detail. But before I do, three absolute essentials must be emphasized. (1) We must learn to recognize when it is *God* speaking to us. (2) We must learn to *correctly interpret* what God is saying or revealing to us. (3) We must learn to *wait for God* to show us exactly how, when, and where we are to act upon or share the revelation with the person or persons who are to receive the word from God.

Only when we heed those three critical guidelines will we truly know the joy of being used by God to edify, exhort, and comfort others. Only then can we experience the privilege of being an instrument through which His supernatural strength, wisdom, and healing can flow.

God Speaks to Us by His Voice

1) The still, small voice of God

Probably all Christians know what it is to hear the Lord speak to us inside in a gentle, soft voice. This is the "still small voice" of 1 Kings 19:12. As we wait in reflection, prayer, or meditation, He speaks. His still, small voice speaks, brings direction, instruction, or encouragement.

2) The loud, inaudible voice of God speaking inside us

This voice of God speaks very loudly within us. It's not really audible, but it resonates so loudly inside us that it seems to be.

3) The audible voice of God

If God speaks to you audibly, there will be no room for doubt! You will *know* that God Himself has spoken to you, even though at first you may not understand the exact meaning of what He has said. If that's the case, you must wait for Him to interpret and explain, revealing the meaning of His words.

You may be wondering just how loud the audible voice of God really is. Let me explain it like this. It's not how loud the voice is that makes such an impact when God speaks audibly. It is the vastness, the enormity of His voice! It shakes you to the core of your being, and its impact stays with you a long time.

Impressions Received in Our Mind, Spirit, or Body

God sometimes speaks through impressions we sense or feel in our mind, spirit, or body. For example, a lot of believers receive words of knowledge for another's healing as God allows them to feel a sensation or impression in their body that reveals the location or type of injury or sickness that the other person has.

You may begin feeling an unusual sensation in your body when you're ministering and someone touches you or you touch them—a feeling or sensation that was not there before. Through an unusual feeling or sensation like this in your body, God can help you identify a specific condition in the other person that needs healing. As you share through a word of knowledge what God has shown you, it strengthens the other person's faith, and you can minister healing to them.

Impressions in Our Emotions

Before we even get into this area of impressions received in our emotions, I feel compelled to issue a very strong word of caution. God-given impressions in our emotions have more to do with what we *feel* than they do with information and facts we *receive*. Therefore, what if you and I are all wrapped up in ourselves? What if we have been wounded inside and still haven't been healed? Could we trust our feelings and emotions to be reliable, safe, and accurate? How could we accurately discern what is coming *out* of our souls from what is coming *into* them from the Spirit of God? How could we ever accurately discern whether it is *God's* voice in our feelings and not *our own*?

You may be saying, "Well, Bro. Gorman, I guess that God can never use me in this area. I've been so broken and wounded in the past that my emotions have never been healed. How could I ever accurately discern God's voice in my feelings? I could never be trusted to minister accurately in this area. I'd just wind up doing a lot of damage."

No! That's not true. If your own feelings and emotions are damaged, unreliable, and inaccurate, the remedy has already been provided! It's found in Heb. 4:12, where God says that "the word of God is quick, and powerful, and sharper than any two edged sword, piercing even to the dividing asunder of soul and spirit, and of the joints and marrow, and is a discerner of the thoughts and intents of the heart." That means if you faithfully read and meditate on God's Word, the thoughts and emotions of your heart will be discerned. You will learn to compare your thoughts and feelings by the Word of God and tell whether they measure up or fall short. You will be enabled to accurately differentiate what is coming *out of your own soul* from what is coming *into your soul* from the Holy Spirit.

As you minister to someone, God may allow you to feel what they are feeling—grief, anxiety, sorrow, fear, shame, rejection, etc. When you begin to accurately recognize what is happening and what those impressions in your emotions mean, you learn how to minister so the individual can receive the healing or deliverance they need.

Another word of caution is needed here. Some feelings or impressions may be shared with people publically, and others should be shared quietly and privately with the person. For example, feelings that are surfacing in your emotions regarding another person's unconfessed sin should be shared with them privately, not in the microphone for all to hear. Quietly share your impressions regarding the feelings of hopelessness, shame, regret, longings for forgiveness, etc., that you sense the person is carrying over his or her sins. Share how God is longing for them to come to Him and receive His forgiveness. As they begin to comprehend God's love for them, they can accept His mercy, forgiveness, and restoration.

As you tell others that God has allowed you to feel the fears and insecurities that plague them, they will be comforted to know that God Himself feels what they feel. Then they can trust that such a loving God will protect them. They can rest and rejoice in the assurance that they do not have to be perfect to receive God's love and acceptance, and that *He* will never reject them!

Gods Speaks to Us Through Our Spiritual Senses

You've been taught that you have five *physical* senses: sight, hearing, smell, taste, and touch. But did you know that God has also given you five *spiritual* senses? Thinking back, you may be able to recall instances where God was using one or more of your spiritual senses to supernaturally communicate with you, even though you might not have understood what was taking place at the time.

1) Spiritual Sight

Believers need to be taught that God sometimes uses our *spiritual sense of sight* to communicate important information. For example, sometimes when you meet or look at someone, you *see* a similarity in that person to someone else you know or know about—even though the person may not even look like the person they are reminding you of. When that happens, be aware that the Lord may be using your spiritual sense of sight to reveal that the two people share something identical or similar. It may be that the two people have similar spiritual callings or are from the same area. It may be that they share the same kind of job, have the same name, or are both plagued by the same type of sin or problem, etc.

For example, the first time a godly woman of prayer saw a church's new minister of music ministering on the platform, two things happened. She immediately saw their former minister of music in her mind, and she felt the same sad, sickening feeling in the pit of her stomach she had felt when she had seen the former minister of music leading worship. The former minister of music had turned out to be homosexual, and the woman knew the Lord was revealing to her that the new minister of music also dealt with the same sin.

On the other hand, it may be that when we see a new individual, we find ourselves thinking of someone else and how God helped that other person overcome a certain thing. If so, God may be opening our spiritual eyes prophetically. He may be revealing something through our spiritual sense of sight that will enable us to encourage the new person in a similar area, or to bring healing, deliverance, or forgiveness for a similar thing. It may be that by opening our spiritual eyes, God desires to use the revelation to set the person free from the enemy's accusations, giving divine confirmation that they are not to blame. He may want them to receive some other word from Him that will help them overcome.

2) Spiritual Hearing

God also gives us revelation through our *spiritual sense of hearing*. We may receive a revelation from God when we hear someone's voice; when we hear a name spoken; when we hear someone talking about another person, etc. We may have never met the person who is talking. We may have never seen the other person whose name we heard spoken or who is being spoken about. However, as we sense something unusual and realize that we are receiving a revelation from God pertaining to these different circumstances, He will show us what to say. He will show us how to minister regarding needed confirmations, answers, encouragements, and so forth.

3) Spiritual Touch

Sometimes through impressions that come through *touching*, God speaks to us. For example, sometimes God will not speak to us until we lay hands on people as we're praying for them. This may be because God wants our ministry to that person to be more up close. Therefore, we will not receive revelation concerning a specific area of sickness, disease, etc., until we lay hands on the person while praying for them.

Our spiritual sense of touch may pertain to more than our touching people receiving a touch from God. It may be a feeling or revelation that comes to us as we touch a book, a CD or DVD, a piece of incoming mail, etc. For example, a book, DVD, CD, or tape may come to us with the giver's highest praises and recommendations. But when we reach out to receive it and our fingers touch it, suddenly we feel the Spirit of God recoil within us. We feel a warning, a revulsion, a "check" in our spirit, and we know that God does not want us to receive it, read it, view it, or even bring it into our home or office. Neither does He want us to recommend it to others.

Sometimes God reveals right then what the problem is. Sometimes we feel confused or condemn ourselves for being "holier than thou," yet we know we must be obedient to whatever it is that the Spirit is warning us about, which may include the following:

- Some damaging error in its teaching.

- Some prevailing, carefully concealed sin or sins in the life of the person for which there has been no repentance.

- Sin that will do great damage to others and bring shame upon the work of the Lord when it is eventually exposed.

- Sins such as financial greed and manipulation, homosexuality, alcoholism, or adultery, that will eventually be brought to light.

Or sometimes when we touch a fax or piece of incoming mail we "feel" a certain spirit on it:

- A spirit of manipulation.

- A spirit of control.

- A spirit of dishonesty.

- A spirit of rejection for the supernatural and the gifts of the Spirit, etc.

Also, as we shake a person's hand or touch them, God sometimes uses our *spiritual sense of touch* to give revelation about some sickness or disease. Other times, He uses it to reveal some problem and what should be done about it.

4) Spiritual Taste

We can sometimes receive a divine revelation through our spiritual *sense of taste.* For example, sometimes while looking at or praying for individuals or when meeting someone, you may suddenly have a very distinct taste in your mouth that was not there before. If that happens, stop a moment to pray. God may be showing you something. Then you will understand what is going on, and will know how to minister in that situation. You may experience this sometimes when making crucial decisions or while praying for the sick.

Here is an example. Dr. Judy Doyle, who is helping me write this book, was sent to Russia with her first adopted son in 2002 to adopt an orphan boy matching more than two dozen very specific details God had shown her youngest sister, Joy Davis, in visions and other supernatural ways we are discussing in this chapter. An overseas adoption official insisted that Dr. Doyle and her son go to an ancient, remote orphanage to see an orphan not exactly matching those details, but fairly close. The orphanage had a special lunch prepared for them when they arrived: hot tea; sliced, homemade bread; links of home-cured sausage; creamed potatoes; and dill pickles.

Dr. Doyle and her son were eating lunch with a few key workers at the orphanage. She had just put a bite of not-quite-fresh, smelly, smoked sausage into her mouth when the orphan boy was brought into the room. A wave of nausea washed over her, and she began rebuking herself for the weakness of her stomach. After all, the people had given them the very best food they had to offer! Just then, the voice of the Lord spoke to her from within: "It's not the sausage! This is My way of showing you that this is not the right boy!" Dr. Doyle leaned over and whispered into her son's ear: "Be kind, but don't get attached.... This is not the boy God sent us to adopt." The Lord used her spiritual sense of taste to answer her prayer and make His perfect will plain.

5) Spiritual Smell

God also speaks in an unusual way through the spiritual *sense of smell*. God will often cause us to smell something strange or unusual through our spiritual sense of smell that we could not smell or discern physically. That scent may actually be a message from God, pertaining to some good thing God is doing in that person's life. We need to share that for encouragement or confirmation.

Or God may use that smell to warn of some evil work of the enemy, such as sickness. If so, we will know to combat the work of the enemy by pleading the blood of Jesus, binding the enemy's work, and breaking his hold. As God's power and protection are manifested, we can declare in faith that God has triumphed over all!

Does the thought of being spoken to supernaturally through your five senses seem strange? If so, remember that Isaiah 55:8 says: "For my thoughts are not your thoughts, neither are your ways my ways, saith the LORD." If you and I want to hear God speak, we must be open to the different and unusual ways He chooses to communicate with us, including through our five spiritual senses!

Visions

Included under the general category of *visions* are many different ways in which God speaks to us. God spoke in visions to the Old Testament saints, to New Testament believers, and He continues to speak this way today.

1) Glimpses in the Spirit

These are brief, momentary, internal pictures given by God. They usually contain only a still picture instead of a scene or story line. Sometimes these glimpses in the Spirit are also symbolic. These pictures may seem meaningless at first. If so, we must pray for an interpretation to understand what God is saying to us.

2) Gentle Internal Visions and Strong Internal Visions

Although *gentle internal visions* are much stronger than simple *glimpses in the Spirit,* they are still "seen" internally. As a rule, these visions are more than just still pictures, but also include a "story line" of events as they transpire. Focus and concentration are needed to keep from missing these visions because they can be interrupted by distractions.

Strong internal visions are clearer and more pronounced than gentle internal visions and are a higher level of revelation.

3) Open Visions

Open visions are a significantly higher-level revelation than impressions, internal visions, or the internal voice of God. An internal vision could come from your own mind, like a daydream. However, your mind will not cause an open vision that is seen externally and cannot be stopped. Open visions are received when your eyes are open and are not stopped by distractions. They can start and continue even when you are involved in an activity that requires attention, such as watching a television program or driving a car. Having an open vision is similar to seeing a scene or scenes acted out physically on a movie or television screen. Open visions are obviously from the Lord, and they may be seen by more than one person at the same time.

Dreams

God gives several different types of dreams: *literal, symbolic, dreams of angels,* or *dreams of the Lord.*

1) Short, Literal Dreams

A literal dream is a brief picture that gradually fades away; a quick scene that shows us the future under certain circumstances. Many times these short dreams are easier to understand because they need little or no interpretation. Often you have a dream like this after a brief contact with a person whom you rarely meet.

2) Symbolic Dreams

Other dreams can be highly symbolic and have to be carefully interpreted over time. Joseph's dream about his father, mother, and brothers bowing before him, for instance, took many years to fully understand and come to pass (Gen. 37:9). Sometimes, a lot of prayer and meditation are necessary to understand the symbolism in these dreams and to interpret them correctly. Recognize that some symbolic dreams are very personal ways that God uses to speak to you about decisions you are confronting.

For example, a friend of my wife and mine was married to a strong-willed, outspoken, highly successful man. After she had confronted him and insisted he go with her for counseling, the Lord miraculously revealed her husband's sexual addiction and adulterous lifestyle. Now, she had confirmation that he had continued his lies and deception instead of repenting and forsaking his sin as he had promised her and the counselors they had seen. The woman began interceding for the strength and wisdom it would take to confront him, endure his wrath and threats, and bring their marriage to an end.

She dreamed of a beautiful, peaceful, small city filled with flower-lined brick walkways winding through wooded paths. The little city was encircled by a tall, thick, stone wall with strong, towering gates. She awakened with the assurance that the dream was symbolic and from God. She also knew she was to wait for its interpretation before proceeding any farther.

Just a short time later in her daily Bible reading and meditation, two verses suddenly stood out, filling her with divine peace and assurance:

> For I, behold, I have made you this day a fortified city, and an iron pillar... [giving you divine strength which no hostile power can overcome]. And they shall fight against you, but they shall not [finally] prevail against you, for I am with you, says the Lord, to deliver you.
>
> —JEREMIAH 1:18–19, AMP

With this confirmation of her dream, she was able to safely escape the control of this dangerous man and bring the marriage to an end.

3) Dreams of Angels or Dreams of the Lord

Some dreams are of an angel speaking to us. In other dreams, the Lord Himself may speak to us. These are dreams, not actual visitations, but they are a high level of revelation. (For some scriptural examples, see Gen. 20:3; 31:24, 1 Kings 3:5–15; Matt. 1:20; 2:12–13).

Trances

Trances are found in the New Testament (see Acts 10 for an example). Accounts of God speaking to people through trances continue to be found all through church history.

During a trance, your consciousness of the natural surroundings around you is hidden. Instead, your attention is riveted on the things taking place in the trance. It's not like an open vision where you're just *watching* something happening. In a trance, you actively *participate* in the scene. Trances can last from a few seconds to several hours. You cannot make yourself have a trance. Trances come from the Lord, and they do not stop until He stops them.

Being Caught Up in the Spirit

Satan may sometimes *counterfeit* this experience, but he did not *create* it. It is a biblical experience and is similar to a trance, except you seem to be transported somewhere. Paul, for example, was caught up in the Spirit into the third heaven. He said he was not sure if this happened with his spirit leaving his body or if he was actually caught up in his body (2 Cor. 12:23).

Angelic Visitations

We tend to think of angels as heavenly protectors or heavenly worshipers. Yes, they do those things, but the word *angel* means *messenger*. Several times the book of Acts shows angels bringing messages to the saints through dreams, visions, or visitations. Paul had angels speak to him (Acts 27:23–24), and Peter was released from prison by an angel who appeared to him and opened locked doors for him. God still speaks through angelic visitations today. Appearances of angels also often occur before some major development in the church.

Visitations of the Lord

Like angels, the Lord will often come in dreams, visions, or even reveal Himself visibly to people. Obviously, an actual visitation from the Lord Himself is the highest level of prophetic revelation possible. In Acts 9:37, Paul had a visitation from the Lord, and the apostle John received the book of Revelation from an actual visitation of Jesus.

All through the book of Acts, we find God speaking through all these ways to His people. You can read Acts 5:2–5, 19; 8:26–30; 10:10–20; 12:7; 13:2; 14:9; and 18:9 for just a few fascinating examples.

HOW TO HEAR GOD'S VOICE

1. Live in God's presence. As you cultivate the presence of the Lord in your life, you will become more aware of when God speaks. How do you cultivate His presence? Make it your prized, habitual practice to read and study the Word of God, meditating on the scriptures and on God's nature, character, and ways that are revealed there. As you worship the Lord and read and meditate on His Word day by day, you will begin to live in His presence.

2. Focus on God's purposes, not yours. Remember that you are here to serve God, not yourself. Seek to see His purposes fulfilled. Remember that ministry is about loving and serving God and loving and serving others, and that faith works by love. As you grow in your love for God and for others, you are putting yourself in position to receive prophetic revelation from the Lord. Then

you can minister His love, grace, and power to others through the supernatural gifts of the Spirit.

3. Ask persistently from pure motives. God will speak to you as you fervently, persistently ask Him for prophetic revelation so you can minister supernaturally to others and glorify His Name.

4. Learn to pay attention to what you're sensing or feeling. When you first come into a service or begin to speak with someone, be open and pay attention to what you sense or feel and to impressions in your spirit, soul, and body. God may be giving revelation. Then as you minister, continue to remain aware and open in your entire being to receiving sensations, feelings, and impressions as God speaks to you about people or situations.

5. Make all these disciplines a part of your life. As you habitually practice these principles and habits, building your whole life and ministry upon them, you will grow in your sensitivity to the Lord and His voice. You will be amazed at how clearly you receive revelation that you ignored or didn't recognize in the past.

IN CONCLUSION

In my experience, *prophecy* brings edification, inspiration, enablement, consolation, and—in many instances—a confirmation of that which God has spoken through others or in personal revelation.

The gift of prophecy enables us to hold on to the promises of God until we see their fulfillment. Many times the gift of prophecy prepares people for difficulties that are coming. Some prophetic words deal with judgment, but my experience has been that most prophetic words build up, urge, encourage, and give direction to believers.

The gift of prophecy is urgently needed in the body of Christ today. Many people have been misled by false prophets; however, a true gift of prophecy has been given to the body of Christ to help the Church equip itself for powerful present-day ministry!

Chapter 11

THE GIFT OF TONGUES

To another different kinds of tongues.
—1 CORINTHIANS 12:10, NKJV

THE REAL NATURE OF TONGUES

TO INTRODUCE THIS chapter, I'd like to open with a quote from Phil Taylor's book, *The Person and Work of the Holy Spirit:*[1]

> This gift is a supernatural utterance in a tongue unknown to the speaker. It may or may not be a known tongue or language. Depending upon the occasion, it is either a *sign for the unbeliever* (1 Cor. 14:22), *a personal edification for the one speaking and is not to be heard by everyone in a public gathering* (1 Cor. 14:28), or it is *a tongue that is to be interpreted for the edification of all present* (1 Cor. 14:5). (Italics added.)

Tongues May be a Sign for the Unbeliever

Isaiah 28:11–12 declares that in spite of the manifestation of this divine phenomenon, many will harden their hearts and reject it. In turn, they will be rejected by God. "For with stammering lips and another tongue will he speak to this people, To whom he said, This is the rest wherewith ye may cause the weary to rest; and this is the refreshing: yet they would not hear."

The New Testament tells us that speaking in tongues is a fulfillment of this Old Testament prophecy. In discussing different gifts of the Spirit with the Corinthians, Paul pointed out that the prophecy just quoted foretold the coming of the gift of tongues to the New Testament church. He also added that the prophecy mentioned one of the gift's great purposes—that it should be a sign to unbelievers, but there would be those who wouldn't hear or believe.

> In the law it is written, With men of other tongues and other lips I will speak to this people; and yet, for all that, they will

175

not hear Me, says the Lord. Therefore tongues are for a sign, not to those who believe but to unbelievers…"

—1 CORINTHIANS 14:21–22, NKJV

Tongues May be a Personal Edification for the One Speaking, Not to be Heard by Everyone in a Public Gathering

Read this verse very closely: "He who speaks in a tongue edifies himself…" (1 Cor. 14:4, NKJV). Did you notice that Paul did *not* say that speaking in other tongues is for the purpose of edifying the *listener*? No, Paul said that the believer who speaks in tongues edifies *himself.*"

Gordon Lindsay wrote:

> Most of the gifts are intended for the edification of the church and need to be exercised by people having certain qualifications. But no special qualification is needed for edifying oneself. Where an unlearned person might disturb the order of a religious service through lack of wisdom, there is no such difficulty presented when he/she edified themselves. If one feels like speaking in tongues for several hours, it is all right, and good is done rather than harm. Paul found the gift highly profitable in his devotions and prayer life. He said, "I will pray with the spirit, and I will also pray with the understanding.…I thank my God I speak with tongues more than you all"(1 Cor. 14:15, 18, NKJV).[2]

When we are baptized in the Holy Spirit, we are able to speak to God in His language. This is a language that only God understands. As Gordon Lindsay points out:

> If God chooses, He can give us a language that not even the devil can understand—a way of communicating with God that neither man nor devil can intercept. In time of war, nations have codes for secret communication. Sometimes the enemy is able to break that code, but we may be sure that not even the devil can break God's code![3]

People on the outside who overhear a believer speaking in tongues in a personal prayer language don't usually understand that the person is interceding, or that the individual is worshiping God and being edified and strengthened spiritually. Those listening may be curious, but they may have difficulty understanding the blessing or benefit of the supernatural experience they are witnessing. However, speaking in tongues is a part of the Great Commission to the church—Jesus' last words on earth before He was taken up into heaven:

> And He said to them, "Go into all the world and preach the gospel to all creation. He who has believed and has been baptized shall be saved; but he who has disbelieved shall be condemned. And these signs will accompany those who have believed: in My name they will cast out demons, *they will speak with new tongues*; They will pick up serpents, and if they drink any deadly poison, it shall not hurt them; they will lay hands on the sick and they will recover. So then, when the Lord Jesus had spoken to them, He was received up into heaven, and sat down at the right hand of God. And they went out and preached everywhere, while the Lord worked with them, and confirmed the word by the signs that followed. (Italics added)
>
> —Mark 16:15–20, NASB

After Christ's ascension, the 120 believers (including the apostles, the women, Mary the mother of Jesus, and Jesus' brothers) tarried in Jerusalem in the upper room in prayer and supplication (Acts 1:7–14). On the Day of Pentecost while they were in the upper room praising and blessing God, the Holy Spirit fell upon them. As you read, notice that in this original pattern for receiving and being filled with the Holy Spirit, each person spoke in tongues as the Spirit gave utterance.

> And when the day of Pentecost was fully come, they were all with one accord in one place. And suddenly there came a sound from heaven as of a rushing mighty wind, and it filled all the house where they were sitting. And there appeared unto them cloven tongues like as of fire, and it sat upon each of them. And they were all filled with the Holy Ghost, and began to speak with other tongues, as the Spirit gave them utterance.
>
> —Acts 2:1–4

Acts 2:5–8 tells us that devout Jews out of every nation under heaven were dwelling at Jerusalem. When this sound was heard, a multitude of people were drawn together to view this miraculous visitation. They were confounded because every man heard them speak in his own language. Amazed, they asked one another how it was that they were hearing these 120 believers speak the wonderful works of God in various languages, including the native languages of the visitors to Jerusalem!

Did you notice that these 120 believers were all speaking with tongues *before* any crowd gathered? It's apparent that what the crowd gathered to hear was not being directly preached to at that time. However, the phenomenon the people gathered to witness caused them to give serious attention when Peter preached to the crowd using the one common language they all could understand and explained what had happened. A revival broke out, and before night, 3,000 people had accepted Christ!

Acts 10 records the story of how the Gentile Cornelius and a large crowd of his relatives and intimate friends were saved, spoke in tongues, and magnified God after Cornelius obeyed an angel's urging and sent for Peter to visit his Gentile home and preach the gospel to them. Verses 44 through 48 tell us that while Peter was still preaching to them, the Holy Spirit fell on all those listening to his message, and they began talking in unknown languages, magnifying God. Then Peter baptized them in water.

The ninth chapter of Acts tells the story of Saul the Pharisee's miraculous transformation and conversion. And in 1 Cor. 14:2, this same man known as the apostle Paul and the outstanding figure of the early church, explained, "He that speaketh in an unknown tongue speaketh not unto men, but unto God: for no man understandeth him..." An equally supernatural gift of interpretation was necessary to make those utterances understandable to the assembly. Paul later wrote to the Corinthian church and testified, "I thank my God, I speak with tongues more than ye all" (1 Cor. 14:18). And in 1 Timothy 1:16, Paul said he obtained mercy, "That in me first Jesus Christ might show all longsuffering, as a pattern to those who are going to believe on Him for everlasting life" (NKJV). Paul said he was to be a pattern for all Christians who should afterward believe in Christ. This makes Paul's experience significant to us.

More than twenty-five years after the Holy Spirit was poured out on the Day of Pentecost, Paul was in Ephesus on another of his missionary journeys. Paul asked some of that city's disciples if they received the Holy Spirit when they believed (Acts 19:2). After Paul learned that they knew only about John's baptism of repentance, he explained that John had also spoken about One who would come after him, who would baptize with the Holy Spirit and fire (Matt. 3:11). After these disciples were baptized in the name of Jesus, Paul laid hands on them. They received the Holy Spirit and spoke in other tongues and prophesied (Acts 19:6). Notice that they weren't preaching the gospel to unbelievers. They were caught up in the Spirit, worshiping God, and prophesying.

I have just shared four different cases in the New Testament where people received the Holy Spirit. In every instance, the Word of God reports that the recipients spoke in other tongues.

In only one other place does the New Testament record that people received the Holy Spirit. In Acts 8:6–7 we read that a great move of God occurred in Samaria when Philip the evangelist conducted a healing revival there. Miracles were performed. Unclean spirits, crying with a loud voice, came out of many who were possessed, and many who were paralyzed and lame were healed.

However, when the apostles in Jerusalem received news of the revival in Samaria, they were concerned that no one had received the Holy Spirit. Acts 8:17 tells us that when Peter and John were sent to Samaria and laid hands on them, they received the Holy Spirit.

Notice that nothing is specifically recorded here about speaking in tongues as a result. As we continue reading, we learn that Simon the sorcerer had attended that revival and been impressed by the healings and miracles that took place, but not fascinated to the point that he considered parting with his money. However, Acts 8:18–19 records that when Simon saw that through laying on of the apostles' hands, the Holy Ghost was given, the amazed sorcerer offered them money, saying, "Give me also this power, that on whomsoever I lay hands, he may receive the Holy Ghost." Peter sternly rebuked Simon for thinking he could receive that supernatural gift of God through mere money!

Simon hadn't been willing to part with his money when he witnessed the healings and miracles. What did he see that moved him to make such a sacrifice? One logical answer is that Simon saw and heard those Samaritan believers speaking in tongues as they were filled with the Holy Spirit. Could *that* have been the startling phenomenon that astonished Simon the sorcerer, just as the people in Jerusalem had been amazed on the Day of Pentecost when they witnessed the supernatural results of the outpouring of the Holy Spirit upon those in the Upper Room?

The New Testament also teaches that the Holy Spirit helps us pray, making intercession for us as we pray in tongues:

> Likewise the Spirit also helpeth our infirmities: for we know not what we should pray for as we ought: but the Spirit itself maketh intercession for us with groanings which cannot be uttered. And he that searcheth the hearts knoweth what is the mind of the Spirit, because he maketh intercession for the saints according to the will of God"
>
> —ROM. 8:26–27

The Holy Spirit knows the mind of God. He always prays for us according to the will of God. In our personal prayer language when we don't know what to pray for, the Holy Spirit will pray through us in an unknown tongue, making intercession according to God's will.

Tongues to be Interpreted for the Edification of All Present

> I would that ye all spake with tongues, but rather that ye prophesied: for greater is he that prophesieth than he that speaketh with tongues, *except he interpret*, that the church may receive edifying." (Italics added)
>
> —1 CORINTHIANS 14:5

In the first part of this chapter, I dealt with tongues that are a sign for the unbeliever. In the second part, I discussed tongues that are a personal edification for the one speaking, not to be heard by everyone in a public gathering. Now we come to the third point—the subject of this chapter: tongues to be interpreted for the edification of all present.

WHAT IS THE GIFT OF TONGUES?

The gift of tongues is one of the three inspirational (or vocal) gifts: *the gift of prophecy, the gift of tongues,* and *the gift of interpretation of tongues.* The vocal gifts, designed as an inspiration in public worship, are the vehicles God uses to edify—supernaturally build up, strengthen, and encourage—the church and thus to glorify God (1 Cor. 14:12, 26).

Giving a message in tongues is a *sign gift* from God, a distinguishing gift that does something very particular. A message in tongues is for a *sign* (a miraculous token or wonder) to the unbeliever, to stir him or her up inside.

THIS GIFT ILLUSTRATED

Lester Sumrall shares a tremendous illustration of the fruit of this gift in the life of an unbeliever when Sumrall preached in Washington, DC:

> After my sermon, one brother gave a message and another interpreted.
>
> When they had finished, a young man walked to the front and spoke in a foreign language to the one who had given the message.
>
> The brother answered, "I'm sorry, sir, but I don't understand any other language."
>
> The man replied, "But you spoke my language beautifully. I am Persian. You spoke my language and told me that I must get right with God, that I must find God right now."
>
> The brother answered, "No, it was the Spirit who spoke to you. It was God talking to you, not me."
>
> Much to that young man's surprise, neither of the two men—the one who gave the message in tongues and the one who interpreted it—spoke or understood his language. He stood there, trembling, then knelt down and gave his heart to the Lord Jesus Christ.
>
> That night the gifts of tongues and interpretation were magnificently fulfilled. Just as the Bible says, it was a sign to the unbeliever. God spoke to that man in the Persian language through two men when neither of them understood a foreign tongue. One man was a real estate agent; the other was a car sales-man.[4]

DEFINITIONS

The public use of the gift of tongues is a supernatural utterance given by any Spirit-filled Christian, in a language unknown to the person giving it. It is always used in conjunction with the gift of interpretation.

The gift of tongues is a supernatural utterance that comes from God through the power of the Holy Spirit. This supernatural gift, directed through a believer's spirit, manifests as a divine and spiritual communication in a language that is unknown to and different from the believer's own language.

THOUGHTS TO PONDER

The gift of tongues is a miracle because the speaker does not have the ability in himself or herself to speak in the language being used. Howard Carter noted that speaking with other tongues is amazingly supernatural: "By the power of the Spirit of God (a person speaks in a language he has never learned; he uses a vocabulary that he has not committed to memory; he speaks clearly, not hesitantly, but fluently and positively. He speaks grammatically correct in a language he has never learned."[5]

> By the power of the Spirit of God (a person) speaks in a language he has never learned; he uses a vocabulary that he has not committed to memory; he speaks clearly, not hesitantly, but fluently; and he speaks grammatically correct in a language he has never learned."
> —HOWARD CARTER

"The baptism of the Holy Spirit is *evidenced* by speaking with other tongues (Acts 2:4). However, the evidence should not be confused with the *gift*. The gift is a *public* ministry by which one can utter a message in an assembly, and [that person or] another person, through the gift of interpretation, can give the meaning. He that speaks *privately* in an unknown tongue, as evidence of the baptism, speaks not unto men but unto God."[6]

In 1 Cor. 12:30, Paul asked: "Have all the gifts of healing? do all speak with tongues? do all interpret?" Not everyone in the church can give a message in tongues as a public ministry, but everyone should speak in tongues privately, communing with God in prayer. As Paul said, "I will pray with the Spirit, and I will pray with the understanding also" (1 Cor. 14:15).

The supernatural phenomenon of speaking in tongues began on the Day of Pentecost, the day when the New Testament church was born in Jerusalem. It was Jesus Himself who instituted the gift of tongues. But notice that Jesus didn't limit it only to believers of the early New Testament church and apostles. He said: "And these signs will follow those who believe: In My name they will cast out demons; they will speak with new tongues." (Mark 16:17, NKJV).

Does this mean that all those who neither speak nor seek to speak with new tongues are outside the group that Jesus in this verse calls believers? No. Jesus is not referring to those who have believed on Him for salvation. He is simply saying that only those who are equipped with supernatural powers and sign-gifts in apostate days can attest the authority of the word they are speaking.[7]

WHAT THE PUBLIC GIFT OF TONGUES IS NOT

- It has nothing to do with the mind, intellect, or linguistic ability of the person giving the utterance.

- It is not a language the person learned in school. (The gift of speaking a message in tongues doesn't have anything to do with the speaker's natural ability to learn and speak languages.)

- It is not the speaker's own personal prayer language given supernaturally when he or she received the infilling of the Holy Spirit as evidenced in Acts 2:4.[8]

- A message in tongues is not stuttering and it is not just "gibberish." On many occasions this has been made evident when people knowing a foreign language have been present and recognized and identified the language used in the message in tongues.[9]

- Giving a message in tongues is different from praising God in tongues, in that there is an urge to speak out in tongues a bit louder and with a different anointing than with ordinary praise or prayer to God in tongues.[10]

As Lester Sumrall points out, this means there is an element of faith and an element of courage related to this gift. You must be able to say in faith, "Lord, I believe this is You." You must be able to say with courage, "I don't care what men think; I'm going to let the blessing of God flow through me."[11]

THE DIFFERENCE BETWEEN SPEAKING IN TONGUES AND GIVING A MESSAGE IN TONGUES

Privately Speaking in Tongues (such as when we are baptized in the Holy Spirit or when we are praying or worshipping in our prayer language):

- May be spoken in public or in private.
- May be spoken quietly or loudly.
- Never needs interpretation.
- For personal edification.

Public Messages in Tongues:

- Are to be spoken in a group (preferably under the guidance of a Spirit-filled pastor or a wise, trustworthy spiritual leader).
- Must be spoken loudly enough for everyone present to hear.
- Are always intended to be interpreted.
- Are to *edify* the people present, strengthening and encouraging them, and building them up in their faith.[12]

WHO MAY MINISTER THIS GIFT?

Before a person can operate in this church gift of giving a message in tongues, he must first experience Acts 2:4; he must speak in tongues. As veteran Pentecostal missionary and healing evangelist Lester Sumrall explains:

> Only Spirit-filled, or Spirit-baptized, believers are candidates for this gift. The infilling of the Holy Spirit is the door to the operation of spiritual gifts in your life. You must pass through

that door to reach all the "goodies" on the inside. Many people want these mighty gifts of the Spirit to function in their lives, but are unwilling to step through that door."[13]

All Spirit-filled believers may give messages in tongues from time to time. Paul said in 1 Cor. 14:5: "Now I wish that you all spoke in tongues..." (NASB). We know that in this verse he is not referring to devotional tongues because in the chapter's first verse, he reinforces the fact that he is discussing spiritual gifts, and here in the fifth verse, Paul compares tongues with prophecy. Prophecy is a gift of the Spirit.

THE REGULATIONS FOR TONGUES-SPEAKING

The church at Corinth had the gift of tongues, but they didn't know how to make the best use of it. They needed more knowledge. Paul laid out some guidelines for them that are still valid today:

1. Speaking in tongues must not be given too much importance. (Read 1 Cor. 14:6 and 14:26). There must be a time and place for things other than tongues in the service—revelations, words of knowledge, prophecy, doctrine, psalms, interpretations.

2. Speaking in tongues is to be limited to two or three utterances in a service (1 Cor. 14:27).

3. Those who speak in tongues in the public service are to keep silent if no one is present to interpret (1 Cor. 14:28).

4. Those who speak in tongues in the public service are to pray that *they* may also interpret (1 Cor. 14:13).

5. Speaking in tongues is not to be forbidden (1 Cor. 14:39).

6. Speaking in tongues is not to create confusion (1 Cor. 14:40).[14]

Paul is revealing God's desire for all believers—everywhere, at all times—to be used in this needed gift. What God desires for us, He makes available to us.[15]

LET ALL THINGS BE DONE FOR EDIFICATION

The three vocal gifts of utterance—prophecy, tongues, and interpretation of tongues—are designed as an *inspiration* in public worship. As we have learned, this vocal gift of inspiration—the gift of tongues—is used publicly when the church meets together: "Whenever you come together, each of you has a psalm, has a teaching, *has a tongue*, has a revelation, has an interpretation. Let all things be done for edification" (1 Cor. 14:26, NKJV italics added).

When you use your own private prayer language, there is no need for anyone else. Spending time alone with the Lord is a beautiful experience between just the two of you. But giving a message from God in tongues is a gift that operates when we assemble ourselves together with other believers.

LESSONS TO LEARN

Ken and Lorraine Krivohlavek share several important lessons from 1 Corinthians. Please take a moment to examine them with me:

> If anyone speaks in a tongue, let there be two or at the most three, each in turn, and let one interpret. But if there is no interpreter, let him keep silent in church, and let him speak to himself and to God.
>
> —1 CORINTHIANS 14:27–28, NKJV

1. There are to be no more than three messages in tongues per service. "…At the most three" is God's command. Some may say, "But if God gives me a fourth message in tongues in a service, I should give it, shouldn't I?" The answer is, "No, they should not." Why? We are not robots when the Spirit of God is upon us. We are still in the position to choose whether or not we will obey and how.

   Also, many believers find that what they had supposed was a fourth "tongue" was actually the Spirit trying to give them a prophecy. Since they may be accustomed to messages in tongues, they may assume that is the gift the Holy Spirit is moving upon them to be used in.

   Furthermore, the Holy Spirit never prompts us to

do something that is contrary to the Word. We've been given three chapters of the Bible to instruct us in the use of the gifts of the Spirit. We are expected to know these chapters and use the gifts accordingly.

2. Messages in tongues are to come in orderly fashion. Each message is to wait for the former one to be interpreted before it is given. No message in tongues is to be given, either by the same speaker or a different speaker, until the preceding message has been interpreted. Many, who feel urged to give a second message in tongues while waiting for the first one to be interpreted, are possibly being anointed to interpret the first message and should open their heart to this gift of the Spirit.

3. How tragic that we are content to go service after service (in some cases even month after month) without these divine utterances. Instead, we should make it a matter of prayer and faith that we shall have at least two of these heavenly interventions that lift and bring needed life to our gatherings.[16]

How to Minister a Message in Tongues

1. Come to each service filled with the Spirit, prayerfully ready for God to use you in a message in tongues.

2. Participate and share in the service, but keep in a state of expectancy, ready to minister a message in tongues at any moment the Holy Spirit urges you.

3. In this atmosphere, there will be times when you will sense an urge to speak out in tongues more loudly than when you are normally just praising the Lord. The urge will often carry with it more anointing than when you are merely praising the Lord in your prayer language. The Lord is wanting you to give a message in tongues. Speak out loudly enough for the congregation to hear.

4. Some believers who may not be experienced in giving messages in tongues may want further assurance that

God is giving them a message in tongues before they
speak out....

(1) When you feel the urge to speak out a message in
tongues, pray, "Lord, if this is a message in tongues, let this
urge stay with me."

(2) When you know you are supposed to give a message
in tongues, do not be rude or interrupt someone who is
ministering in the service in some other way—making
announcements, singing, preaching, taking prayer requests,
giving the altar call, etc.

(3) When a short lull in the service comes, you can speak
out the message in tongues without interrupting or shouting
over someone else's voice.

(4) When God gives you a message in tongues, wait
patiently in the Spirit. The message will stay with you until
God provides the quiet break in the service that you need.

(5) A message in tongues may be spoken at any point or
time in the service where God gives the urge to give the
message and provides a quiet spot.

(6) Remember that the Bible says that one who gives the
message in tongues should also ask God for the privilege
of interpreting the message if no one else gives the
interpretation to the message (1 Cor. 14:13, NIV).

(7) If you start to give a message in tongues and someone
else starts at about the same time or immediately after you
start, this will cause confusion. First Cor. 14:33 says that
"God is not the author of confusion, but of peace."

Normally, the one who starts first should have the right to
proceed, while the other should stop speaking. However, we
are not concerned about our "rights." We are concerned about
everything being done decently and in order. Therefore, if the
second speaker continues his message in tongues, the first
speaker should stop.[17]

FORBID NOT

The supernatural gifts of the Spirit that God so graciously entrusts to us should not be neglected or allowed to lie dormant, but they can be. That's obviously why Paul the apostle wrote Timothy:

> Do not neglect the gift which is in you, [that special inward endowment] which was directly imparted to you [by the Holy Spirit] by prophetic utterance when the elders laid their hands upon you [at your ordination]. Practice and cultivate and meditate upon these duties; throw yourself wholly into them [as your ministry], so that your progress may be evident to everybody.
> —1 TIMOTHY 4:14–15, AMP

Leaders of churches must not hinder or forbid the use of this supernatural gift. We see this clearly in 1 Cor. 14:37–39 in the Amplified Bible where Paul wrote:

> If anyone thinks and claims that he is a prophet [filled with and governed by the Holy Spirit of God and inspired to interpret the divine will and purpose in preaching or teaching] or has any other spiritual endowment, let him understand (recognize and acknowledge) that what I am writing to you is a command of the Lord. But if anyone disregards or does not recognize [that it is a command of the Lord], he is disregarded and not recognized [he is one whom God knows not]. So [to conclude], my brethren, earnestly desire and set your hearts on prophesying (on being inspired to preach and teach and to interpret God's will and purpose), and *do not forbid* or hinder speaking in [unknown] tongues.

If the Word of God says, "forbid not," I think we had better be very careful about trying to prevent, hinder, or exclude this gift from our church services. How desperately the people of God need to hear inspiring messages from God!

Chapter 12

THE GIFT OF INTERPRETATION OF TONGUES

To another the interpretation of tongues...
—1 CORINTHIANS 12:10, NKJV

Wherefore let him that speaketh in an unknown tongue pray that he may interpret.
—1 CORINTHIANS 14:13

DEFINITIONS

THE THIRD GIFT of inspiration—the interpretation of tongues—is the supernatural verbalization of the meaning of a message just delivered to the church by a member of the body of Christ in a language he/she does not understand.[1] In other words, interpretation of tongues is the supernatural ability to interpret what has just been said in a message in tongues. The gift of interpretation goes into operation when a message in tongues has been given. The message that has been given in another language is interpreted supernaturally by the Holy Spirit through the person who gave the message or through another person, without the interpreter's mental faculties being involved.

In interpretation of tongues, God miraculously reveals to a Spirit-filled Christian the meaning of a public message in tongues (at a church service or prayer meeting), enabling him or her to "interpret" the message in tongues. The interpretation does not come from the mind of the interpreter. It comes from the mind of the Spirit of God. The interpreter never understands the tongue that he or she is interpreting. They are unknown words. Both the message in tongues and the interpretation are utterances from the mind of the Spirit of God, and both are supernatural.

When a person gives a message in tongues and it is interpreted, the presence of God is revealed in that place. God has brought to those people a very special message, and the church is encouraged and built up.

190

INTERPRETATION OF TONGUES AND PROPHECY

He who speaks in a tongue edifies himself, but he who prophesies edifies the church. I wish you all spoke with tongues,
but even more that you prophesied; for he who prophesies is
greater than he who speaks with tongues, unless indeed he
interprets, that the church may receive edification
—1 CORINTHIANS 14:4–5, NKJV

According to these verses, both prophecy and interpretation of a
message in tongues edify the church. Since the gift of prophecy and
the gift of interpretation are similar, interpretation is equal to prophecy,
except that a message in tongues must come before the interpretation.

REASONS FOR THE GIFT OF INTERPRETATION

The fact that prophecy and interpretation are equivalent gifts raises
some questions. What is the purpose of the gift of interpretation?
Why not use only prophecy in the assembly? Gordon Lindsay shares
several very important reasons for the manifestation of the gift of
interpretation.

First, Lindsay notes that without the gift of interpretation, there
would be no speaking in other tongues in a public congregation
because the speaker is instructed to be silent unless an interpreter is
present. Speaking in tongues is a sign "to unbelievers" (1 Cor. 14:22).
However, if speaking in tongues were never allowed, how could it be
a sign to unbelievers? Although some have rejected this sign in unbelief, as verse 21 declares will happen, others have been awakened to the
reality of the supernatural as a result of the gift's manifestation.

Another important reason for a public message in tongues is that it
alerts the congregation that the Holy Spirit is about to speak. Lindsay
points out that this gives the people time to get into a reverent attitude
of prayer before the interpretation is given. If the message was given in
prophecy without the introductory speaking in tongues, the audience
might not be prepared to receive it.

Lindsay explains that when a message is spoken in an unknown
tongue and then skillfully interpreted, the effect is greatly enhanced
upon the listener to whom this ministry is new. It's an excellent demonstration of members of the body of Christ working together.

Furthermore, when a message in an unknown tongue is given, it's not uncommon for someone present to recognize the language spoken as their own dialect. Naturally, this leaves a very deep impression upon that person, just as it did upon those in the crowd that gathered on the Day of Pentecost. They heard newly Spirit-baptized Galilean believers speaking the wonderful works of God in their own unique language (Acts 2:7–11). This was truly a sign of God's presence.

In summary, Lindsay emphasizes that the manifestation of the gift of tongues and the accompanying interpretation—given under a strong anointing—usually results in great blessing and edification to the listeners.[2]

WHAT THE GIFT OF INTERPRETATION OF TONGUES IS NOT:

Ken and Lorraine Krivohlavek have offered several helpful explanations regarding what the gift of interpretation of tongues is not. I've summarized some of them below.

1. Interpretation of tongues is not natural; it is supernatural. Therefore, if a person already knows the language used in a message in tongues and understands what was said, that is not the gift of interpretation of tongues.

2. Interpretation of tongues is not putting your own thoughts or ideas together to compose an interpretation to a message in tongues.

3. Although a scripture quotation may be a part of an interpretation, an actual interpretation of tongues is not just quoting scripture or stringing some scriptures together.[3]

TONGUES AND INTERPRETATION— RULES OF OPERATION

Do not forbid speaking in tongues—giving messages in tongues.

As mentioned in the preceding chapter, 1 Cor. 14:39 tells us not to *forbid* (prevent by word or act) those who would give messages in tongues: "Wherefore, brethren, covet to prophesy, and forbid not to speak with tongues."

If you give a message in tongues, you should pray that God will give you the ability to also interpret.

The person who operates in the gift of tongues should seek the gift of interpretation. "Wherefore let him that speaketh in an unknown tongue pray that he may interpret" (1 Cor. 14:13). If you possess the gift of tongues and happen to be in a gathering where there is no interpreter, you should be able to interpret.[4] Otherwise, you should keep silent

There should be a maximum of three messages given in a service, and each should be interpreted.

Paul instructs: "If anyone speaks in a tongue, let there be two or at the most three, each in turn, and let one interpret" (1 Cor. 14:27, NKJV). The apostle makes it clear that in any service there should be a maximum of three messages given in an unknown tongue, and there should be an interpretation each time. Why is this instruction given? Gordon Lindsay offers the following explanation:

> There is a limited amount of time available, and if it is all used for tongues and interpretation there is no time left for other important things in the service, such as prayer, worship, preaching, altar services, etc. There can be too much of anything.
>
> Even if each message is only two minutes long, the tongues and interpretation for three messages would take twelve minutes. Paul said not to permit more than three messages.[5]

Lester Sumrall observes: "I have always thought that, since heaven does things so precisely, surely the Holy Spirit can say all that needs to be said in three messages."[6] What is the reason for this limitation? "For God is not the author of confusion, but of peace, as in all churches of the saints" (1 Cor. 14:33).

Notice that 1 Cor. 14:27 states: "If any man speak in an unknown tongue, let it be by two, or at the most by three, and that by course; and let one interpret." Does this mean that in a service only one person should interpret?

Howard Carter was asked the question: "If three persons gave

messages in tongues would it be right for the same person to interpret them?" Carter answered: "If there are other interpreters present
he should not monopolize the meeting to the exclusion of other persons with their gifts."[7]

Lester Sumrall relates that in Great Britain, at the opening session
of a conference, it will be announced who will interpret during the
conference. No matter who gives a message in tongues, that same
person will interpret each time, even though there may be many interpreters in the meeting.[8]

Gordon Lindsay also offers helpful comments on this subject:

> While several people may speak in the unknown tongue, only
> one should interpret. Otherwise, there might be the spectacle
> of two people attempting to interpret at the same time. That
> would be very confusing.
>
> We might state here, however, that often when the Spirit
> is moving mightily in a service, and a message in tongues is
> given, several people may begin to feel the quickening of the
> Spirit for the interpretation. It is then very necessary to wait
> quietly for a specific "go ahead" to interpret. Sometimes, it is
> best "in honor preferring one another" to let another give it. If
> prophecy is to represent God speaking, people would rightly
> wonder why He would interrupt Himself by attempting to
> speak through two people at the same time.
>
> Paul recognized that this was possible, because of the
> nature of the gift. It is God speaking, but the directing comes
> from man. God is infallible; mankind is fallible. In prophecy
> and interpretation, we have the merging of the fallible with
> the infallible, the blending of God's conscious mind with
> man's subconscious mind.
>
> For this reason, Paul said, "The spirits of the prophets are
> subject to the prophets" (1 Cor. 14:32). If prophecy and interpre-
> tation did not come through the vehicle of a human, no instruc-
> tion would ever be needed, and the manifestation would be
> perfect at all times. But since these utterance gifts represent the
> fusing of the human mind with the divine mind, the human will
> is involved and becomes an active factor in the manifestation of
> the gift. Therefore, it is important that those who manifest these
> gifts receive teaching and instruction concerning their use.

In light of this, Paul's instructions make sense. As an example, a fourth person might feel that they ought to give a message, but the scripture says three messages are sufficient, so they should refrain from giving it. Some ignore this instruction and give six or seven messages. This not only takes more time than is available, but makes the things of God appear common.

Again, one might feel an anointing to give a message while another is still speaking. However, if they are instructed, they will wait until the other is through. The scripture says to do it in turn. Common sense also would dictate this procedure."[9] (See 1 Cor. 14:31, 33.)

IF THERE IS NO INTERPRETER, THE SPEAKER SHOULD KEEP SILENCE.

First Cor. 14:28 declares: "If there be no interpreter, let [the speaker] keep silence in the church; and let him speak to himself, and to God." This is a very clear principle for maintaining church order. If there is no interpreter and the speaker who gives the message does not possess the gift of interpretation, then the speaker should keep silent.

Lester Sumrall makes a very important observation regarding Paul's command that the speaker keep quiet.

"This proves that when we are operating in spiritual gifts, we have control over the situation. We are not controlled by an extraneous power. According to the Bible, the Holy Spirit is a true gentleman. He will never force a person to do anything. He offers the opportunity; whether or not we take it is our choice."[10]

> Let two or three prophets speak, and let the others judge. But if anything is revealed to another who sits by, let the first keep silent. For you can all prophesy one by one, that all may learn and all may be encouraged. And the spirits of the prophets are subject to the prophets.
> —1 CORINTHIANS 14:29–32, NKJV

As to keeping silence if there is no interpreter, Lester Sumrall says regarding the gifts of the Spirit:

God will not force them on you. When you do receive them, have respect for them. Learn what God has said about them; then you will have great wisdom in the operation of these gifts, and they will remain with you. There is no reason for the gifts to ever leave your life."[11]

Sumrall clearly explains why it is so vitally important that tongues and interpretation of tongues be regulated by the scriptures:

If a fellowship of believers does not function properly in the gifts of the Spirit, those gifts will cease to function. If believers try to operate the gifts outside the bounds of the Word, the gifts will cease. There are literally thousands of churches in our generation that at one time possessed the gifts of the Spirit to some extent; but because the people did not understand them correctly, the gifts ceased."[12]

HOW TO MINISTER THE GIFT OF INTERPRETATION OF TONGUES

Ken and Lorraine Krivohlavek share the following specific, helpful guidelines for an individual desiring to be used in the ministry of the gift of interpretation of tongues.

1. Be saved and baptized in the Holy Spirit.

2. Have a consistent, fluent, and free prayer life and pray daily in tongues, praising God and interceding for your own needs and the needs of others.

3. Be in a spirit of worship and expectancy in each service. Be yielded to the Holy Spirit.

4. Fervently lift your heart to God when there is a message in tongues, asking Him for the privilege of interpreting. Don't always be content for someone else to interpret. Seek to be used of God yourself.

5. Speak what God gives you, and He will give you the rest. In an atmosphere of worship and expectancy, *a few words* may be impressed upon your mind—words that are the beginning of an interpretation of tongues.

When you speak those words in obedience to the Spirit, He will give you more words until the entire message is interpreted.

How many words can you say at one time? Only one. If God gave you the entire interpretation at once, you might not remember it all and you might lose a valuable part of it. In wisdom, God gives us the interpretation in bite-size words, phrases, or sentences that we can handle.

6. Use the Ten Second Test if you want to be very sure that the few words in your spirit are really the interpretation as described in previous chapters.

7. Speak boldly, clearly, and distinctly. You do not need to wait for a quiet spot, because the entire congregation should always be quiet from the time the message in tongues is spoken until the interpretation of tongues is given.[13]

Sometimes the person with the interpretation may be hesitant to speak out at first. Therefore, the person in charge of the service at that time should not rush on to something else, but should wait—reverently, prayerfully, and expectantly—for the Lord to speak to His people.

There is to be only one interpretation for each individual message in tongues, and the interpretation must follow the particular message for which it was given.

Sometimes if we have a message in tongues, and what would appear to be two interpretations of tongues following it, we actually had an interpretation of tongues, followed by a prophecy. Prophecy is for edification, exhortation, and/or comfort.

REASONS WHY SOME MESSAGES IN TONGUES ARE NOT INTERPRETED

1. Sometimes, the one giving the message in tongues did not speak loudly enough for the leader of the meeting and the congregation to be able to recognize it as an utterance from the Spirit.

   Any time we suspect someone is giving a message

in tongues, we should be totally quiet. Ask the Lord
to show you if the person is only *praising* the Lord in
tongues instead of *giving a message* in tongues.

2. Messages in tongues are often quickly dismissed as
   just being praise to God. People have become fearful
   to speak messages in tongues due to this practice. This
   has hampered the use of the valuable gift among us,
   causing messages in tongues to become scarce or absent
   in many Pentecostal congregations.

   The following instructions will help us in this matter.
   Anytime one person in the group is clearly lifting their
   voice above all others while speaking in tongues, the
   utterance should be considered a message in tongues,
   and an interpretation is to be expected. If there is still
   a doubt, the person in charge of the service should ask
   the Lord.

3. Sometimes a message in tongues is ignored and not
   interpreted because the people or the leader of the service did not feel some certain emotion, or "anointing"
   on the utterance. Emotions are a poor basis for evalu-
   ating the work of God. Elijah's emotions told him that
   he was the only God-fearing man left in Israel, but
   the Word of the Lord told him that there were 7,000
   (1 Kings 19:1–18). Emotions can be unreliable.

4. Messages in tongues have been disqualified as being
   from God when the interpretation was not spoken
   immediately. Some have stated, "I like to have the interpretation come right after the message in tongues with
   little or no break." I might say to them that I like a certain kind of singing or preaching, but I am willing to
   be blessed with whatever sort of singing or preaching
   they are able to offer. What we happen to like or dis-
   like does not determine the authenticity of an utterance
   in tongues. Let us set all else aside and wait until that
   message in tongues is interpreted.[14]

CLARIFYING OTHER CONFUSING CONCERNS

It is the gift of interpretation—not translation—of tongues.

Harold Horton explains:

> Most of the obstacles to our clear understanding of the gift
> vanish when we consider the exact title of the gift. It is the
> gift of interpretation—not translation—of tongues. A trans-
> lation is a rendering from one language to another in equiv-
> alent words or grammatical terms. An interpretation is a
> declaration of the meaning, and may be very differently
> stated from the precise form of the original. It may be picto-
> rial, parabolic, descriptive, or literal, according to the urge of
> the Spirit or the character of the one interpreting. The Greek
> word in the original means "to explain thoroughly"—not to
> translate. It is more of a transposition than a translation—
> as when Joseph showed the meaning of the baker's and the
> butler's dreams....And in Matthew 6:26–34, the words that
> Jesus spoke, presumably in Aramaic, are of course appro-
> priately *translated* in our authorized version as: "Behold the
> fowls of the air...Consider the lilies of the field..." and fol-
> lowing; another suitable *translation* is given by Weymouth as
> "Look at the birds which fly in the air... Learn a lesson from
> the wild lilies." A perfectly legitimate if prosaic *interpretation*
> might have been: "The heavenly Father is a universal provider
> for those who look up to Him. He will find you clothing and
> renew it as He gives new feathers to the molted birds. He will
> even take care moreover that the garments are beautiful, if
> need be, as is His custom with the wild flowers. He will give
> you food when you are hungry, just as He finds berries and
> insects for the wild birds. You need therefore never have any
> undue anxieties about daily provision."
> Many varieties of expression might be employed and many
> details added without materially altering the sense of the words
> so far as the simple message is concerned. Of course, I do not
> mean that my awkward paraphrase would be equally inspired
> with the exact scripture words. I am just using an illustra-
> tion to show how an interpretation differs from a translation,

or transliteration, and how much more liberty of expression there is in an interpretation than in a translation....

The interpretation can be, however, a literal translation of the message in tongues; for of course the Spirit is at liberty to dictate what words He will. Many an instance might be cited of an utterance in tongues receiving an exact literal translation in the hearing of one familiar with the language spoken, and therefore in a position to verify it....

Why should a God who spake with His own naked voice in Hebrew from the fiery top of Sinai; who spake by a cherub in Chaldean to the presumptuous Babylonish monarch "flourishing" in his palace; who commanded His "anointed shepherd" Cyrus concerning His beloved Israel in Persian—why can He not in tongue of any tribe or people or nation, living or dead, either by His own awful voice or through the lips of whomsoever He will, supernaturally communicate with His people today?...Since God can think in Chinese, speak in Polish, and hear your thinking in English, all at the same time, and since He can make a donkey speak Hebrew, can He not make me His mouthpiece in whatsoever language He pleases, and you His interpreter in whatsoever other tongue He will, if you yield to His plan?[15]

The Lengths of a Message in Tongues and its Interpretation May be Very Different.

The lengths of a message in tongues and its interpretation may differ. Ken and Lorraine Krivohlavek explain why:

Some people are troubled when they hear a message in tongues that is fairly long, and then the interpretation of the message is relatively short. Others are troubled when the message in tongues is not too long, but the interpretation becomes lengthy. Most of this problem is solved by the fact that this is the gift of *interpretation* of tongues, not the gift of *word-for-word translation* of tongues.

We need to understand that there is a difference between interpretation and translation. In *translation*, one attempts to give each word in one language its nearest word equivalent in another language. So in translation, one usually ends up with nearly the same, if not the same, number of words.

But this is not the method or the result of *interpretation*. The interpretation is concerned with the general meaning of what has been said in another language. The result may be many more or many less words than the original message. The length or total number of words is of no special consideration in interpretation.

We have an example of this in Daniel 5:25, where *the message* supernaturally written on the wall contained only four words. Yet, look at *the interpretation* in verses 26–28. Count the words in the interpretation that Daniel gave. (Since the word "mene" occurs twice in the message, its interpretation should be counted twice.)

There are only four words in the message, yet there are thirty-three words in the interpretation. The interpretation is almost nine times longer than the message, and the Word of God certifies that the interpretation is correct.

Also, those who know more than one language will testify that often there is not just one word in a certain language that will properly express that word in another language. Often, two or more words must be used to give the meaning of a certain word in another language.

And so to avoid confusion, we should understand that the *lengths* of the utterances in tongues and interpretation may be different, but our main concern should not be the lengths of the utterances, but that what is said is *scriptural*.[16]

MESSAGES IN TONGUES AND PROPHECIES OFTEN OCCUR IMMEDIATELY FOLLOWING A TIME OF PRAISE AND WORSHIP. WHY?

- People often feel a refreshing, refilling, or stirring in their spirit after a time of praise and worship. They may have come to expect the Spirit to move at this time because that has been the pattern in the past.

- Too many believers come into service in an unprepared attitude. They have not prepared for the service with prayer and praise in daily prayer times. As a result, if God urges them to minister a gift early in the service, they remain unresponsive. But after a time of praise, their hearts are more receptive to the move of the Spirit.

- This does not mean that God's choice time for a message in tongues is always following a time of praise and worship, though that may be the way He moves in a particular service. God may have wanted to move earlier in the service, but the leader of the service may not have been sensitive to the Spirit and did not allow time for the gifts to operate. Also, due to a lack of teaching or due to believers' spiritual immaturity, a time of praise and worship is the only time God can get the attention of some. It is not wrong to have utterance gifts immediately following praise. They are perfectly in order at that time, but we must recognize that they may also be perfectly in order at many other times in the service.[17]

SOME OF THE WAYS THE GIFT OF INTERPRETATION MAY COME

The Lord may choose to use many different ways to introduce a person to the gift of interpretation. For example, when Dr. Judy Doyle and I were working on this book that you are now reading, Judy told me the following true story that her mother-in-law, Helen Doyle, had shared with her years before.

When Helen was newly saved and baptized in the Spirit, a woman gave a message in tongues, but there was no interpretation. After the service, Helen exclaimed to her pastor's wife, "Wasn't that *wonderful* what the Lord said to us today!"

Not sure what the young convert meant, the pastor's wife asked, "Are you referring to the sermon that pastor preached this morning, Helen?"

"Oh, that was very good, too," Helen assured her. "But I was speaking about what the Lord said to us when the lady spoke in that language."

"You mean you could *understand* her, Helen?"

"Of course," Helen answered. "Couldn't everybody?"

"No, Helen," explained the pastor's wife. "When that woman gave a message in tongues, God gave you the interpretation to the message.

The Lord wants to use you in the gift of interpretation of tongues. Next time that happens and you understand what is being said, wait until the person finishes speaking. Then, loudly and clearly so everyone can hear, tell the congregation what was said."

"Oh! Okay. Thanks for explaining that to me," Helen said. "I will."

Not long after that, another message in tongues was given. Helen did exactly as her pastor's wife had instructed, and the congregation was wonderfully blessed.

As time went on and her faith and understanding increased, Helen began to be used in other gifts of the Spirit, as well. But the way that interpretations came to her began to change. Instead of being given the entire interpretation in advance, she was given a few sentences. As she spoke them, the remainder of the interpretation would come.

As more time passed, Helen began receiving just a few words in advance, such as: "The Lord would say unto this people…" As she obeyed and spoke those words, the remainder of the interpretation would come, phrase by phrase. At other times, she might see some scene or something transpiring in the Spirit, and she would simply allow the Spirit of God to speak through her, describing the meaning of what was taking place before her eyes.

Helen said that the Lord taught her the importance of faithfully spending her daily time with Him in the Word and prayer if she desired to be used by Him. "I began noticing that if I let myself get too busy to spend my usual time with the Lord during a week, the Lord would have to pass me by and use someone else. I realized that if I wanted to be anointed and used by the Spirit of God to minister to His people in various gifts, there was a price to pay in faithful communion with Him in order to be entrusted with the privilege and responsibility of hearing His voice and having Him speak through me."

Here is another helpful example. When asked how the gift of interpretation comes, Howard Carter answered:

> Well, I will give a personal experience. When I first began to interpret I saw everything in the most graphic way; the Lord was pleased to give me a picture, and all I had to do was to describe it in the Spirit. Then that passed away, and I had interpretation by words. Words would come and I would just speak them out. Later came the most difficult time of all,

which I am experiencing at the present time. When a message in tongues is ended I generally have nothing in my mind at all; I have to set out in the dark, as it were; or, to use a Bible figure, I have to start out in faith like Abraham, not knowing whither I am going."

Carter then recounted the case of a woman in his church in London who had a good gift of interpretation but developed an idiosyncrasy of screaming just before she gave the interpretation. Because I have also known of those in congregations who were untaught and made the same mistake, I'd like to share the wise, gentle way Carter used to correct the error without doing permanent damage. First of all, he did not rebuke the lady publicly. Instead, he asked to speak with her privately about her gift of interpretation. Carter explains it this way:

I thought, *How can I tell her about this scream without offending her?* Then a happy thought came. I said, "Sister, what I want to say can be expressed very briefly. It is this: we want the train to start without the whistle blowing."

It was the shriek of the whistle that got on our nerves. For about three weeks after this we had no interpretations. Then the dear sister got over it and began to interpret again, and there was no struggle, no scream, but beautiful interpretations—the train without the whistle.[18]

OTHER ILLUSTRATIONS OF THE GIFT OF INTERPRETATION

Lester Sumrall shared the following:

I have been in foreign countries and heard a person speak. Though I did not know the language, I knew supernaturally that it was a message in tongues, so I stood up and interpreted it in English. Since no one present understood English, my interpreter had to interpret what I said into their native language. If I had not interpreted the message, it would have been lost.[19]

In his classic work, *Spiritual Gifts and Their Operation*, Howard Carter related the following story about tongues and interpretation:

In 1914, I was in a convention in England. Alexander Boddy was the chairman and there were numerous speakers on the platform. There were several from Germany, some from Holland, and others from America, including a missionary named Miss Alma Doering. There were also a number of English speakers, including Smith Wigglesworth. Behind me in the congregation, a Scotsman spoke in other tongues; it was a clear resounding message. Mrs. Crisp, the lady principal of the Women's Bible School in London, was sitting in the front row and she gave the interpretation. The Scotsman spoke again in this tongue, and Mrs. Crisp interpreted a second time. It happened a third time. Then Miss Alma Doering, the American missionary from Africa, spoke to the chairman, and he said, "Miss Alma Doering wishes to address the convention respecting the message that has just been given." We were all very much interested to hear what she had to say. She said: "Friends, the language that has just been spoken is the language of the Kifiote tribe in Africa; it is next to the tribe of people among whom I am working. Just as one native will call aloud to a native on another hill, and get his attention, and then give him a message, so the Lord has spoken through the message and called us to attention, and given us the word that He would have us receive.

"Regarding the interpretation," she continued, "the sister who interpreted has given us a faithful interpretation of the message." She said, "If I had sat down with pen and paper and had translated what I heard, I should have put it in plain language; but the lady who interpreted has not only given us the sense of the message, she has given it to us in the most ornate language; it has been most beautifully expressed."

So there was a double miracle—a Scotsman who knew only English was speaking clearly and fluently in the language of the Kifiote tribe. A lady who did not even know what language it was, gave a most wonderful interpretation by the Spirit. So you see, God is doing a most amazing thing in the midst of His people.[20]

Jackie Pullinger was only twenty-years-old when God called her to minister to the prostitutes, pornographers, gangs, and drug addicts in the infamous Walled City of Hong Kong. Strangers were not welcome there, and police hesitated to enter. Jackie learned to pray in the Spirit as she walked the dangerous, filthy streets. She spoke of Jesus to the poor, the lost, and the forgotten with amazing results. Hundreds found new life in Christ. Prostitutes were saved and left their trade, brutal hoodlums and gangs were converted, and junkies were freed from the bondage and pain of drug addiction as they were baptized in the Holy Spirit—usually within moments or minutes of giving their hearts to Jesus and becoming Christians.

In her book, *Chasing the Dragon,* Jackie tells of the conversion, infilling, and empowerment of the Spirit and remarkable spiritual growth in the life of convert after convert. One such boy was Christopher. After God changed his life, Christopher bravely refused to carry on with his initiation into one of Hong Kong's two main gangs operating in the Walled City, the powerful 14K, which controlled all opium, gambling, pornography, child brothels, illegal dog restaurants, and protection rackets on the west side of the city.

> The change in Christopher was remarkable. He worked so well at his factory that he was promoted to the rank of supervisor. Instead of gambling sessions with the Triads, he now spent his time at the Youth Club, and on Sundays he came to the evening service in the little Oiwah church.
>
> As I continued praying in the Spirit in private, the results became apparent when more boys like Christopher made decisions to become Christians; we met together for Bible study and prayer anywhere we could—in the Youth Club room, in teahouses, in the streets or in my home. One day when we were praying one of them had a message in tongues. We waited, and then Christopher began to sing the interpretation. Astonishingly this beautiful song came in English, which he hardly spoke. This is what he sang:
>
> Oh God, who saves me in the darkness,
> Give me strength and the power
> So I can walk in the Holy Spirit,
> Fight against the devil with the Bible,
> Talk to the sinners in the world,
> Make them belong to Christ.

Another boy, Bobby, had the same interpretation, but in Chinese. He did not understand Christopher's English song, and so he did not know that what he spoke was a confirmation of God's message.[21]

Jackie also shares how she learned that God would often use very young believers to encourage the others and to encourage her when she became exhausted or deeply worried about the pressures and demands of the ministry.

> All those who became Christians received the power of the Spirit at the same time they believed....We encouraged them to share spiritual gifts when meeting together, so they knew clearly that having these gifts was no cause for pride but a way of helping one another....
>
> I was...much heartened by the boys...when I arrived home exhausted and deeply worried about the situation in the house....I was feeling quite unable to manage the many converts plus a succession of boys referred by prison workers....
>
> "Please find me a nice, encouraging Bible verse," I asked the boys, feeling too tired to give them a teaching lesson. After thumbing through the Bible for some minutes, the most encouraging thing any one of them could find was a very depressing text from Revelation. "Enough of that," I decided. "Let's pray instead."
>
> As we were praying, I had a message in tongues, and one of the boys interpreted it immediately. He had only been to school for a couple of years in his life. He could not read the Bible, and he had only believed in Jesus for a few days before this event. But his interpretation was a clear, direct quotation from the psalms: "Those who sow in tears will reap with songs of joy. He who goes out weeping, carrying seed to sow, will return with songs of joy, carrying sheaves with him. Unless the Lord builds the house, Its builders labor in vain...In vain you rise early And stay up late, toiling for food to eat—For He grants sleep to those he loves. (See Psalms 126:5–6; 127:1–2)
>
> These spiritual babes through the working of the Holy Spirit were able to say exactly the right words to me at that time. Thus ministered to, I could not agree with those who considered spiritual gifts merely an optional extra. It was no

wonder that St. Paul exhorted us to desire these gifts, for their purpose is to edify one another and thus glorify God. (1 Cor. 14:12, 26).[22]

In Conclusion

Let me share one final quote from Howard Carter:

> It is wonderful to have a message in tongues with interpretation—not that all messages are striking and remarkable, but the fact that God is in manifestation in the church is so encouraging. It is an assurance to us that we are in the line of His will, and that we have no need to write *Ichabod* [the glory hath departed] over our meetings. I trust that we shall never lose the manifestation of the Spirit of God from our Pentecostal churches.[23]

And to that, I add my own heartfelt, Amen!

Part 5

LIVING ON THE CUTTING EDGE

Chapter 13

FASTING: FUELING THE FIRE

*And whenever you fast, do not put on a gloomy face as the
hypocrites do, for they neglect their appearance in order to be seen
fasting by men. Truly I say to you, they have their reward in full.
But you, when you fast, anoint your head, and wash your face. So
that you may not be seen fasting by men, but by your Father who
is in secret; and your Father who sees in secret will repay you.*

—MATTHEW 6:16–18, NASB

INTRODUCTION

I WAS A TEENAGE boy spending a lot of time in prayer and reading
the Word of God when He first spoke to me about fasting. However,
I didn't understand what that meant and no one had explained it to
me. The word had not been part of my vocabulary. I had to go to the
dictionary and look it up. It wasn't a word often heard in the environ-
ment I grew up in. However, as my hunger for a relationship with the
Lord and the manifestation of the Holy Spirit's gifts in my life continued to grow, I began spending much time in prayer and fasting, in
addition to studying His Word.

During my early pastorates I fasted often. When pastoring the
church in New Orleans, I fasted several days at a time and repeated
that several times a year. One year I recall going on five 21-day fasts
and several 2 or 3-day fasts in between the longer fasts.

So in addition to the practice of daily study of the Word and times
spent in prayer, for many years now I have added fasting whenever I
encounter one or more of the following situations:

SIX REASONS FOR FASTING

1. When I need direction.

2. When I face situations where I must be more sensitive to hear the Holy Spirit.

3. When my spiritual senses need to be sharpened, and I need to be more attuned to the Spirit.

I don't fast in order to "make" God do something. Fasting is not a hunger strike.

4. When the Spirit of God alerts me that I need to prepare myself for a difficult situation that is coming.

I don't fast *after* I face a demonic stronghold. Fasting gets me ready, just as a ballplayer practices *before* he plays a game; or just as the boxer works out, stays in shape, and prepares *before* a fight. It's not that we *can't* fast in the midst of a storm. It's more effective if we fast *in preparation for* a storm. We shouldn't wait until the storm hits.

5. When my faith must be increased and divine power must be brought to my assistance. "This kind goeth not out but by prayer and fasting" (Matt. 17:21).

The extraordinary power of Satan must not discourage our faith, but quicken us to a greater intenseness in the acting of it, and more earnestness in praying to God for the increase of it. Fasting and prayer are proper means for attaining divine power for assistance. Fasting sharpens our prayers; it brings the humility that is necessary in prayer.

6. When I need to deny and crucify self.

PRAYER AND FASTING IN SCRIPTURE

When I study the scripture and see a city like Nineveh protected from the judgment of God that had already been spoken—and that protection coming about through fasting and prayer, it challenges my spirit. The great victories of Esther had behind them the power of fasting and prayer. It's the same with Nehemiah, Joel, and Daniel.

Then we step into the New Testament where Jesus said, "And *when* ye stand praying," not "*if* ye stand praying" (Mark 11:25). To our Lord, it was a foregone conclusion that believers would pray and that they would fast as He did. We find Paul, for example, urging believers to "give yourselves to fasting and prayer" and beseeching that they approve themselves as the ministers of God in many things, such as fasting (1 Cor. 7:5:2 Cor. 6:5).

Now, before we go any further, I'd like you to look back with me at these challenging words from the Old Testament prophet Isaiah.

> Shout it aloud, do not hold back. Raise your voice like a trumpet. Declare to my people their rebellion and to the descendants of Jacob their sins. For day after day they seek me out; they seem eager to know my ways, as if they were a nation that does what is right and has not forsaken the commands of its God. They ask me for just decisions and seem eager for God to come near them. "Why have we fasted," they say, "and you have not seen it? Why have we humbled ourselves, and you have not noticed?" Yet on the day of your fasting, you do as you please and exploit all your workers. Your fasting ends in quarreling and strife, and in striking each other with wicked fists. You cannot fast as you do today and expect your voice to be heard on high. Is this the kind of fast I have chosen, only a day for people to humble themselves? Is it only for bowing one's head like a reed and for lying in sackcloth and ashes? Is that what you call a fast, a day acceptable to the Lord? Is not this the kind of fasting I have chosen: to loose the chains of injustice and untie the cords of the yoke, to set the oppressed free and break every yoke? Is it not to share your food with the hungry and to provide the poor wanderer with shelter—when you see the naked, to clothe them, and not to turn away from your own flesh and blood? Then your light will break forth like the dawn, and your healing will quickly appear; then your righteousness will go before you, and the glory of the Lord will be your rear guard. Then you will call, and the Lord will answer; you will cry for help, and he will say: Here am I.
>
> —Isaiah 58:1–9, niv

GETTING YOUR LIFE IN ORDER

Notice that in Isaiah 58:1, God commanded that prophet to cry aloud, lift up his voice like a trumpet, and declare to God's people their transgressions and sins. Why? As the Lord explained to Isaiah, outwardly, it *appeared* that the house of Jacob was doing everything right. They sought Him daily and delighted externally to know His ways as if they were really a nation that did righteousness and refused to forsake His ordinances. They asked Him for righteous judgments and delighted to draw near to God in visible ways. Their "form of godliness" appeared to be in order, but God ignored it all. Now, as God explained in Isaiah 58:3–5 to His prophet, Israel wanted to know why. "'Why have we fasted,' they say, 'and you have not seen it? Why have we humbled ourselves, and you have not noticed?'"

Their complaint was that they fasted and prayed, yet they did not get an answer. (You and I would have to admit that many Christians today have done that same thing.) Notice here that God didn't argue with His people. They *had* fasted and done without food. They *had* prayed. Yet He had not answered. Why? As God explained, one reason was because their attitude toward people around them was wrong.

> Yet on the day of your fasting, you do as you please and exploit all your workers. Your fasting ends in quarreling and strife, and in striking each other with wicked fists. You cannot fast as you do today and expect your voice to be heard on high. Is this the kind of fast I have chosen, Only a day for a man to humble himself? Is it only for bowing one's head like a reed and for lying on sackcloth and ashes? Is that what you call a fast, a day acceptable to the Lord?
>
> —ISAIAH 58:3–5, NIV

There are many Christians today who do that same thing. However, God makes it plain right here that He is big on attitude. Maybe it would be good to ask right now: "Do *I* need an attitude adjustment?
Isaiah 58:6–7 describes the fast that God has chosen.

> Is not this the kind of fasting I have chosen: to loose the chains of injustice and untie the cords of the yoke, to set the oppressed free and break every yoke? Is it not to share your food with the hungry and to provide the poor wanderer with shelter—when you see the naked, to clothe them, and not to turn away from your own flesh and blood?

People usually fast because they're in trouble. But God wants to bring us to where we are walking humbly before Him, loving others who are hurting.

Do I really want to fast? Then I must get the structure right. I must do it right, and I must do it in order. I must repent of what's wrong in my life—attitudes, the past, etc. I must allow the Holy Spirit to make me a fruit producer, not a gift user. God says that when I get things right, I can seek Him, and He will answer. You can read His words right here for yourself.

> Then your light will break forth like the dawn, and your healing will quickly appear; then your righteousness will go before you, and the glory of the Lord will be your rear guard. Then you will call, and the Lord will answer; you will cry for help, and he will say: Here am I. If you do away with the yoke of oppression, with the pointing finger and malicious talk.
>
> —Isaiah 58:8–9, NIV

Notice here that God is warning us not to become slanderous and shut off our prayer life. You and I must keep our opinions to ourselves. Our opinions can turn to slander. Remember: Pharisees point fingers. Work on *you* and what God wants *you* to be. Don't bring up others' pasts. Stay out of the garbage heap and anything that puts other people into bondage. That means you and I had better watch our tongues. Sometimes we want to be the Holy Ghost and tell people what to do and how to live, but that's not our job. We must let the Holy Spirit teach others!

> And if you spend yourselves in behalf of the hungry and satisfy the needs of the oppressed, then your light will rise in the darkness, and your night will become like the noonday.
>
> —Isaiah 58:10, AMP

To help the hungry and afflicted we must love them. You and I must feel the neglect, pain, and shame of the hungry. We must reach out to those not really living fully for God, whose souls are not at peace with Him. Then people will be drawn to us. Our gloom and doom will be gone! Our confusion about where to go and what to do will disappear!

The past will be left behind, and we will experience His love, peace, and rest.

Did you notice that after we do those things, *then* when we fast and pray, it's different? Fasting and prayer bring us through stress and into right relationship, peace, and rest. Fasting and prayer clear our hearts, minds, and spirits, and put us in His presence. *Then* our own light will rise in the darkness and our night will become like noon.

Now, see what He promises next through Isaiah 58:11, AMP:

> The Lord will guide you always; he will satisfy your needs in a
> sun-scorched land and will strengthen your frame. You will be
> like a well-watered garden, like a spring whose waters never fail.

All you and I have to do is follow His Holy Spirit. He provides and guides and makes the way. He satisfies the soul in sun-scorched drought. He strengthens our frame, or as the King James promises, He will make fat our bones. We will be refreshed, in place and in order. All that hell brings against us cannot push us out of place. Why? Our spiritual structure is right!

When we have plenty, the thirsty and hungry will come to us. His living water will flow through us, and we will have enough to share with others in need. We will be like a spring, continually bubbling up, whose source cannot be depleted and whose waters never fail!

FORGIVENESS AND MERCY

Listen to me very closely. You will recall from our reading of the first four verses of Isaiah 58 that the Lord brought strong accusation against Israel—not because they didn't fast, but because they didn't fast the right way. You see, a lot of people fast, but they never change what they're doing. They go right on with their routines. If anything, they get *busier*.

God said to Israel: "When you fast, you don't do it *that* way. You don't fast by going along and saying to yourself, 'Well, I'm going to fast and bow my head like I'm in deep meditation.'" God said, "No! That's mechanical. You have to do this thing from your heart. It's got to come out of your spirit. You've got to start out this thing by repenting of anything in your life that should not be there."

Let me speak to you frankly. I don't care who you are or what you're doing. You may be locking yourself in your bedroom, but even then you're feeling sorry for yourself and you have to repent of *that*. So we must face the fact that there are things we have to repent of... things that are done to us, things that are said to us. There are actions taken against us and people that get on our nerves. There are people that misunderstand you and speak accusations against you. On and on and on it goes until every day, if you're not repenting and purging out of your mind and spirit the things that accumulate there, those things will build up and block you in your prayer life and when you fast.

You know what? There's no need for Bertha to fast if she doesn't like Shelley. There's no need to go through all this deal of fasting and praying and doing without food. You can sit in the church all day long. You can sit there day and night. But if you have unforgiveness in your heart, it's all in vain. If there's someone you're holding a grudge against, it's in vain. If there's someone who has hurt you, forgive them in your heart and go on serving the Lord.

You say, "Oh, but Brother Gorman, *they* are the one who hurt *me*!" You must forgive them and earnestly pray for God's blessings on them.

See, we cannot keep holding on to these things. It doesn't matter if it's your parents, your brother, or your sister. It doesn't matter if it's a step-mother, step-dad, step-brother, or step-sister. It doesn't matter what they've done to you. They could have cheated you out of your inheritance or beat you out of this or that. It doesn't matter. If you want God's favor, you can get it one way and one way only. Forgive! Unconditionally forgive! You can't get anywhere until you do.

You have to forgive. That's the first step you have to take. It has to be done from your heart. None of this, "Well, I'll forgive, but I won't forget" business. That means you haven't forgiven. Aren't you glad that every time you go before God, He doesn't bring up everything in your lifetime and say, "I've *forgiven* you of that, but I'm not going to *forget*!" Aren't you glad that God has *forgotten*!

When the devil comes along and says to God, "Well, you know what Marvin did back in 1960?" God says, "I don't have any record of it. It's not in My book." The devil says, "But don't You remember how he acted?" God says, "No, I don't remember it. I chose to forgive and to forget! 'As far as the east is from the west, so far have I removed his transgressions from him' (Psalm 103:12)."

This is exactly what God wants us to do with individuals. You say,

"Well, but you just don't know what they did to me." Well, you must weigh *what they did to you* against *what God can do for you*. It's kind of like this. If she stole five dollars from you, and somebody came along and said, "If you'll just forgive her, I'll give *you* a million dollars," it would be stupid for you to try to hold on to that five dollars, wouldn't it?

God says to us, "All that I have...all of My blessings, I want to bestow upon you. But the first thing you have to do is get into right relationship with Me. You have to be *right* with Me, and you can't be right until you *forgive!*" Once you and I forgive, we can have a right relationship with God.

Some of you are saying, "Oh, but Brother Gorman! I've just gone through so much! My ex-husband (or my ex-wife) caused me so much hurt!" Hey! Turn the trash loose! If they're *that* bad, why do you want to hold on to all that and miss the blessing of God? Give it up!

Listen to yourself: "Well, bless God! I pay my tithes. I read the Word. I fast." You know what? Just like God doesn't have any record of my sins in heaven, He doesn't have any record of all those good works of yours, either, because they weren't done from the heart. That which is not done by *faith* is not accepted. Am I making sense to you? God wants us to fast and just tear the devil apart! But for us to do that, we have to be right in our spirit.

When we fast sincerely, God responds. For example, when Daniel fasted and prayed, God met him. It took twenty-one days, but Daniel didn't start blaming God. He just kept on believing. Finally, the angel showed up and said, "From the first day that you set your heart to understand, and to humble yourself before your God, your words were heard...but the prince of the kingdom of Persia withstood me twenty-one days; and behold, Michael, one of the chief princes, came to help me....Now I have come to make you understand what will happen to your people in the latter days..." (Dan. 10:12–14, NKJV). What caused that to happen? Fasting and prayer! When you begin to fast and pray, when you really get your spirit right, God responds.

THE FAST THAT GOD HAS CHOSEN

In Isaiah 58:6, God asks: "Is not this the fast that I have chosen? To loose the bands of wickedness, to undo the heavy burdens, and to let the oppressed go free, and that ye break every yoke?" What is God talking about here? He is talking about mercy.

Look at Luke 4:18–19. Jesus says:

> The Spirit of the Lord is upon me, because he hath anointed me to preach the gospel to the poor; he hath sent me to heal the brokenhearted, to preach deliverance to the captives, and recovering of sight to the blind, to set at liberty them that are bruised, To preach the acceptable year of the Lord.

That's what Jesus did! The church is supposed to be doing what Jesus did! He's saying we must show mercy to people who are bound and oppressed. God has dealt very heavily with me about that.

One Monday morning years ago, I had gone in to take a shower and shave before going to church for prayer. As I dressed, God was dealing with me about the homeless who were perhaps sleeping under bridges and were very cold. The wind was blowing, and the wind-chill factor was somewhere around twenty degrees. My heart was aching at the very thought of those out in the cold weather.

When I arrived at the church, there were only a few of us there for prayer. I said, "Let's pray for the homeless." But as I said that, God said to me, "I don't want you to just pray for the homeless. I want you to do something to help them!" So I said, "I don't know whether any of you are going to help me or not, but today—not tomorrow or next week—I am going down to those people with a big pot of soup and some hot chocolate. I'm going to feed those people. I may not be able to feed them *all*, but I can feed *some* of them. Anybody who wants to help me, bring your money up here and lay it down." They brought one of the best offerings I had received in a long time. Out of that handful of people who weren't even expecting to give—because they knew we didn't receive offerings at prayer meetings, we got over 150 dollars.

I asked a faithful woman named Wanda, who was a wonderful cook, to make some calls to get the ingredients needed to make soup. She made about ten gallons of delicious beef soup, and we purchased Styrofoam chests to keep it hot. We also made about eight gallons of hot chocolate. Then we went out in that cold weather that afternoon and fed about 150 people. We also had several coats that other people had given or discarded, and we gave them out. I'll never forget one old man who jumped up and down when he put on one of those warm coats that someone had donated. He said, "Oh, man! Oh, man! I have a coat!" He ran around showing it to other people. To him, that used coat was a treasure.

See, there's no need to pray for those around us in need if we're not willing to go out and give them one of our many coats, or a cup of soup. You say, "Oh, Brother Gorman! That's a rough neighborhood!" Well, what if you had to *live* in it and didn't have any other place to go? We made up our minds that we weren't just going to *preach* about caring for the hungry and homeless, we were going to *do* it!

This is what the Bible is talking about in this scripture. *This* is a true fast. What God is trying to show us here is that there's no need for you and me to be fasting when there are hurting people around us, and we're not showing them any mercy.

Some of the hands of those poor women, who were out there reaching out to us for soup, were cracking from the cold. They asked, "Do you have any gloves?" Hurting people! But you may comment, "If they weren't bums and were real workers…" Let me tell you something. One of the people we served out there, only two years before was a CPA, then went through hard times and a divorce, lost everything, and wound up on the street! There are people reading these words today who would lose their home if they missed three paychecks. You know I'm telling you the truth. So don't point your finger at those people on the street. Yes, some of them are bums. But there are bankers, doctors, and attorneys who are bums, too. They're just dressed in fancy three-pieced suits. They have enough money to dress up, but they're still bums. So, don't point you finger at the homeless just because they're going through a hard time. Many of them would like to have a change, but they'll never get a chance unless you and I reach out to them.

WE MUST SHOW MERCY

We must show mercy to people. Do you know what mercy is? Mercy is extending a helping hand to those who have nothing and have no way to return the favor. That's what the Lord did for us!

What can you do for God? You say, "Well, I can *sing* for Him." Listen, friend. God has angels who can put your singing in the shade. You say, "Oh, but I'll give Him *this*!" What can you give God when He has streets of gold, and jasper and sapphires on His walls? What can you do for God? No matter what you can do for God, He can find someone else who can do it better. The only thing you can do for God is to praise Him from your heart for Who He is, and He lovingly accepts it from you because you are His child.

My wife and I have some drawings that our granddaughter gave us. She has a wonderful, natural talent, and we always knew that someday if she desired to, she could be a great artist. We've kept some of those drawings she gave us when she was a little girl. Did we need them? No, but she was our baby! We could have gone to the store and bought a picture much more beautiful than what she gave us. It's like that with the Lord. He can get something better than what we have, but He takes everything you do for Him if it comes from your heart, holds it close and says, "My child did this for Me!" Why does God do that? Because of His mercy toward us. Anything we give back to God is what *He* has already given us.

What God wants is for us to show mercy to people who are bound, mercy to those in captivity, mercy to those in yokes that you are able to relieve. Whenever you can help a person or take the burden off a person, help them! Take it off! Do it as unto the Lord. Don't be looking for the needy person to give you anything back. We, who went down that cold winter day and served soup to those homeless people, weren't expecting *them* to ever serve us. But we went with the full intention of going back and serving them soup again. I went down there praying that one day God would help us to have a facility where we could get them off the streets, feed and teach them, help them get jobs, and return to their families.

There's an eating place downtown in New Orleans called *Old Dogs, New Tricks*. It's vegetarian, and those people cook those vegetables to where they taste as good as meat! I took a friend there, and when we left I showed him where we used to have *The Caring Place*. It was a place in the French Quarter we opened to witness to people, help them come out of bondage, and move into freedom.

I told the friend how the first person we ever won to God in that facility was a nurse from Chicago. She had two children and went through a miserable divorce. The husband took her for a cleaning. She fought in court, and finally got custody of her children. But while she was going through all that, she started taking pills so she could work two shifts in order to get enough money to pay the attorneys.

She got hooked on drugs. This woman knew that if the hospital where she worked found out, she would be blackballed forever from nursing. Therefore, she left her children with her mother and came to New Orleans with the intention of breaking her drug habit so she could get another nursing job and get her children back. But when she got to New Orleans she had no references and couldn't get a job. The woman wound up turning to prostitution to support her drugs, and went deeper and deeper into bondage. I told my friend how we found her, took her to the Caring Place in the French Quarter, led her to Jesus Christ, and worked with her until she was free from drugs. I told him how I called her mother in Chicago, and said: "We have your daughter!" Only God knew that woman's joy as she wept and thanked me. We took up an offering and sent her back to her mother and children in Chicago. I told my friend that the last time I heard from her, she was back with her children and working again at the hospital she had left. She and her mother and the children were attending church! Why? Because we showed *mercy*!

Oh, she was a sight when we first saw her. Her hair was dirty and tousled. Her complexion was pathetic because she'd been trying to survive, living in the Quarters. Wherever she could sell her body and get a place to stay for the night, that's where she stayed. But today, she's *free* because of mercy!

There's no need for you to fast and pray if you don't have mercy. There's no need for you to pray, "Oh, God, will You give me a job? Will You heal my child?" If you're looking down your nose at other people as though they're tramps, and have no mercy, you can forget about fasting and praying. Hear me today. It's time we show mercy!

When I was a young man, only nineteen years of age, God looked in my heart and said, "I want you to pray for a baptism of compassion and love." I said, "God, I'll pray every day!" I made a covenant with God that every day I would pray forty-five minutes for Him to baptize me with compassion and love. I didn't have a watch—I couldn't afford one. So I'd take my mom's old Big Ben alarm clock out to the barn, and I'd pray forty-five minutes for a baptism of God's compassion and love. Then I would continue my normal prayer time, asking for other things and seeking God's favor upon my life. I did that every day for three months.

One afternoon after I had prayed three or four minutes, something broke inside me and I started weeping uncontrollably. For weeks afterward, I could be driving my car to work and see someone on the street. I'd just start weeping and interceding for them. God answered my prayer by giving me a compassionate love for people. From that day to this, I've never seen a person that I didn't love, and I've never seen a person that I didn't want to help. It changed me. I was selfish until God forgave me, transformed me, and filled me with His love and mercy.

LOVE AND COMPASSION ARE THE KEYS

Remember, we have been looking at Isaiah 58, and I've been talking about fasting. In verse one, God told Isaiah to lift up his voice like a trumpet and show His people their transgressions. What was the message God wanted to get to His people? God wanted the people to know that though they had been fasting, He could not honor it because it wasn't the right kind of fast.

Today we're confronted with all kinds of things that the people who are in authority in our world will not be able to solve. There must be a spiritual shaking that comes from the grass roots. That spiritual shaking will not come except by fasting and prayer.

In the past, we've had fasts that some people didn't benefit from. Why? I see in the Word of God that when Ezra, Nehemiah, or Joel called a fast, it worked. Yet I've seen people who have fasted and it *didn't* work. You know what I'm talking about. Have you ever fasted, yet you didn't get the results you thought you were going to get. To be honest, most of us have.

So I said, "God, take me back and show me what's going on. I know that when we fast and pray Your way, we expect to get results." God spoke to me to go back to the messages on fasting and prayer I had preached from Isaiah 58. I saw again how the first four verses talked about prayers that didn't work. The fifth verse talked about them not getting the response they wanted even though they wrapped themselves in sackcloth and ashes. God couldn't honor them and what they were doing because their motives were wrong, and they had unforgiveness in their hearts.

The same is true for us. Before we start praying and fasting, we must loose the bands of wickedness, undo the heavy burdens, let the oppressed go free, and break every yoke. That's not talking about setting up some kind of counseling session. God is talking about the necessity of you having the right attitude toward people who are going through problems. Don't set yourself up as "Mr. Perfect" or "Miss Holiness." We all have spots on our garments. Admit that you are not too good to get down out of the bleachers and into the arena so you can help people who have burdens and are bound and are going through trouble." You and I can't look at somebody else's child and sneer, "They're a renegade." It could be *your* child. Get in that arena and help break that yoke of drug addiction, alcoholism, gambling, or whatever it is. Break that yoke off so they can go free. Don't point your finger and say, "Oh, if they had done *this* or *that*..." Hey, if they didn't do it, get under the burden with them and help them do it now!

If I'm out on the freeway and I run over a bottle and have a flat, I hope you don't drive by, wave, and yell, "You should have had enough sense to see that bottle and not run over it!" I hope you will get out and help me lift the burden. If you can't do anything else, at least you can stand beside me and encourage me while I change the tire.

God is saying, "Get under the burden with other people! Don't stand back as if you have it all together." Nobody reading this has it all together. Before we go into a fast, we've got to get things right!

Isaiah 58:7 says, "Is it not to deal thy bread to the hungry, and that thou bring the poor that are cast out to thy house? when thou seest the naked, that thou cover him; and that thou hide not thyself from thine own flesh?" Yet we say, "Praise God, I gave fifty cents last week in the offering to help buy beans for those hungry people!"

If your fasting is going to work, as mentioned, you have to get your attitude right. And even when you get an attitude check, deal with repentance, and start praying, there are other things you must do. Notice that God tells us to share our bread with the hungry and to bring into our house those who are poor and have been cast out. He's not telling us to foolishly invite anyone and everyone into our home. He is talking about those who are Christians and who fall on hard times and need a brother or sister to put an arm around them and help. There may be times when you need to bring a person like that into your house for a short time to help them get back on their feet.

God also tells us not to hide ourselves from our own flesh. We are supposed to help the people in the congregation around us, family members and friends in need—not just hurting people off in Ethiopia.

We can't run and hide from our own flesh, our neighbors, or young people our kids went to school with. We dare not turn a deaf ear to our own flesh and to the needy around us.

Isaiah 58:8 declares: "Then shall thy light break forth as the morning, and thine health shall spring forth speedily..." When we obey God and get things in order, He promises that our light will break forth. That means understanding will come to us and health will overtake us. God is saying, "Get it together! When you do, I'm going to cause My understanding to come upon you and your health will spring forth!"

Deuteronomy 28:2 declares that the blessings of God will come upon us and overtake us, if we hearken to the voice of the Lord our God. Health will *spring forth*.

Has there ever been a time when you did something for someone and you got so totally involved in helping them, you forgot all about your own problem? The first thing you knew, you were feeling better than you'd felt in weeks. That's what God is talking about here when He declares that our health will spring forth!

One morning I stopped at a restaurant to eat a bowl of oatmeal. While I was sitting there, I heard a waitress talking to a man and telling him to leave. I glanced back and saw a dirty, ragged man with matted hair. I heard him say, "All I wanted was a piece of toast." The waitress insisted, "You'll have to leave!" The restaurant was packed, and before I could try to make my way toward him, the man was leaving. As he made his way out the door, I and a lot of other people in the place, heard him mutter again, "All I wanted was a piece of toast." He turned, looked at the waitress, and said, "I hope *you* never fall on hard times."

The man hadn't asked for ham and eggs or a steak...just a piece of toast. I didn't know who he was, but I went outside to look for him so I could get him something to eat. I even got in my car and drove around, but he was gone. That was some mother's boy. For all I knew, he could have been a guy with a college education that fell on hard times. I felt so sorry for him. My heart ached. I'd looked at the way he was dressed, his matted hair and ragged beard, and I could tell that he had such low self-esteem that he didn't love himself. He'd been rejected so often, he'd rejected himself. Then he had been humiliated in front of all those people in the restaurant. My heart ached for him. I couldn't get him off my mind. I woke up in the night thinking about him. I said to God, "Forgive me! I should have *jumped* up and *run* over to where he was. I should have said to the waitress, "Give this man whatever he wants to eat, and *I'll* pay for it." But I hesitated too long.

Have *you* ever been rejected? Rejection hurts. Rejection goes deep and is very painful. There went a guy who'd just wanted a piece of toast. How many scraps or pieces of toast did you throw out in the last week or two? How many of you left bread in the refrigerator until it got old and stale?

I don't know how many like him are out there, but you know what? You and I have to listen to the cries of the people out there that are hurting and then respond to them in love. You may be working and not be able to go out with concerned Christians to feed the hungry, but you can donate food or money and become involved in other practical ways. God is checking to see what His people are doing, how we are treating those who are needy. What if He tells us, "I will treat *you* like you treat *them*!"

God's Word says we are to do unto others as we would have them do unto us. (See Matt. 7:12.) God is watching to see how we respond to the needs of other people. He knows every need you have, whether it's for a car, a house, a job, etc. And God has the answer for every one of those needs. He has no problem responding to us when we get it together and involve ourselves in breaking the yoke, setting people free, getting under the burdens of others and helping them bear them. God is speaking to you, me, and His church everywhere about this.

In the first five verses of Isaiah 58, God had His people check their attitudes and repent. Then He told them to start concerning themselves with the needs and pains of others. Notice that there hasn't even been a prayer prayed yet. Then He says in verse nine, "Then..." When? *Then!* After they've put the concerns of the first eight verses in order, "Then shalt thou call, and the Lord shall answer; thou shalt cry, and he shall say, Here I am."

Have you ever been at that point in the night when your load was so heavy and unbearable that you didn't know which way to go, what to do, or how to handle the problem? You'd prayed every prayer you knew how to pray, and all you could do was start crying and crying with tears flowing everywhere? In verse nine, God is telling us, "If you get the first eight verses in order, you will hear God's voice saying,

'Here I am! Don't be crying. I'm close by. I'm going to help you and come to your rescue!'"

It's not going to happen until we get the first eight verses in order. If I were you, I'd get involved in helping the poor. I'd be bringing in food and clothing and blankets. If *we* get things in order and do what's right, God is going to take care of *us*. We need to busy ourselves with getting things in these first eight verses in order like God wants them to be. We need to do what God says, checking off each thing, one by one, to the best of our ability. Then light is going to spring forth. We won't be walking in the dark. We'll have understanding of what's going on.

Back in the late 1980s and early 1990s in the midst of all I was going through, I came to understand that God was sending me to school, and He was paying the bill. I knew I didn't want to flunk a single class, because if I did, I would have to take it over again.

Notice that verse nine says, "If thou take away from the midst of thee the yoke…" In order to take hold of the future, I had to turn loose of the past. According to the scripture, the yoke had to be removed. What is the yoke? The word used for *yoke* here, carries the thought, "Don't stay bound to your past life." It's saying, "Don't keep reminding yourself or others of yesterday's mistakes." God says here, "Get rid of the yoke!"

One of the things I have had to do was get rid of the yoke. Some people constantly wanted to remind me that I'd never make it, and I might as well give up and quit. That's very discouraging when you're already down so low that you have to look up to see bottom! However, a lot of people don't want to let you forget.

If you want God to hear you and say, "Here am I," then get the yoke off of people! Let them go free. Quit reminding them of their pain and failure and the mistakes they made yesterday. Forgive them! Bless them and send them forth!

Some of you need to bless your children who've brought you heart-ache and pain. You need to bless them and let those hurts go. Some need to bless a sister or brother or an ex-mate who sinned against them twenty years ago. You need to break off the yoke. Stop reminding them of their failure. Take off that yoke and let God deal with them. He loves them more than you do, and *He* is big enough to do something about it! You can't change their failure, but you can break off the yoke.

Notice that the last part of verse nine tells us to quit pointing the finger. Quit accusing people. When I was young, if you got mad and told *me* off, *I'd* tell you off too! But I have now come to the conclusion that I don't have to respond. If what you say is untrue, I can let you live with your ignorance. You won't listen to me anyway. But sooner or later if I keep walking in the will of God, you will see that the blessing of God is on me, and you will have to admit it. So, don't be a person who accuses others, and don't let people put a yoke on you with their accusations. Accusations are not necessarily true.

God says in Isaiah 58, "If you do these things, the light is going to come upon you! The blessing of the Lord will overtake you! Your health will spring forth!" When we get out from behind all the gloom, doom, and self-pity and come to God, His blessings will overtake you!

Don't ever forget that your God loves you! He loves you! And He wants you! So obey His Word and dwell in His presence!

Chapter 14

PRAYER AND FASTING

And Jesus being full of the Holy Ghost returned from Jordan, and was led by the Spirit into the wilderness, Being forty days tempted of the devil. And in those days he did eat nothing: and when they were ended, he afterward hungered. And the devil said unto him, If thou be the Son of God, command this stone that it be made bread. And Jesus answered him, saying, It is written, That man shall not live by bread alone, but by every word of God. And the devil, taking him up into an high mountain, shewed unto him all the kingdoms of the world in a moment of time. And the devil said unto him, All this power will I give thee, and the glory of them: for that is delivered unto me; and to whomsoever I will I give it. If thou therefore wilt worship me, all shall be thine. And Jesus answered and said unto him, Get thee behind me, Satan: for it is written, Thou shalt worship the Lord thy God, and him only shalt thou serve. And he brought him to Jerusalem, and set him on a pinnacle of the temple, and said unto him, If thou be the Son of God, cast thyself down from hence: For it is written, He shall give his angels charge over thee, to keep thee: And in their hands they shall bear thee up, lest at any time thou dash thy foot against a stone. And Jesus answering said unto him, It is said, Thou shalt not tempt the Lord thy God. And when the devil had ended all the temptation, he departed from him for a season. And Jesus returned in the power of the Spirit into Galilee: and there went out a fame of him through all the region round about.

—LUKE 4:1–14

FASTING AND TEMPTATION

WANT TO TALK a little more with you about fasting as a key to power in your life and ministry. Please follow me very closely as we go through some things that I believe will challenge and help you.

I want us to go back to the Garden of Eden and think a few moments

229

about Adam and Eve. The first temptation that came to man upon this earth was to eat of the forbidden fruit in the Garden of Eden. When tempted by Satan, Adam and Eve sold us out for some kind of fruit that grew on a tree. Adam and Eve disobeyed and ate something they should not have eaten. That was what caused them to be cast out of the Garden and brought sin upon all men. Their fall wasn't murder or going out and committing some other hideous crime. All they did was eat something they had been forbidden to eat.

Jesus Christ, as He began His ministry, defeated the same devil that tempted Eve and persuaded her to eat of the forbidden fruit and give the fruit to her husband Adam. That same devil met Jesus in the wilderness after Jesus had fasted forty days and was hungry. (Notice it doesn't say Jesus was *thirsty*; it says He was *hungry*. We know that the desire for water is far greater than the desire for bread. Therefore, we believe that Jesus had drunk water during His fast, though He had eaten no food.)

When Jesus was tempted by the devil in the wilderness after fasting forty days, Satan's first temptation was that Jesus turn a stone into bread (Luke 4:3). But Jesus defeated Satan by fasting and put a block to Satan's efforts. After He had fasted, Jesus was tempted. We'll come back to that in a minute, but first let's go a step further.

Many of the temptations that come to us, come when we have plenty. Matthew 24:38 tells us that before the flood in the days of Noah, before he entered into the ark, people were eating, drinking, and being merry. Remember Esau? He had a brother named Jacob. What did Esau do? He was hungry and sold his birthright for a bowl of Jacob's lentil stew (Gen. 25:33–34). Isn't it amazing that food is involved again? And when the fingers of a man's hand came and wrote upon the wall before King Belshazzar, what was he doing? Eating, drinking, and being merry (Daniel 5:1–5). It seems that when people get caught up in eating and drinking and satisfying their fleshly desires, somehow we lose our sense of the value of being obedient unto God. King Belshazzar even had the holy vessels from the house of God brought in and he and his guests started drinking out of them! As a result, judgment came and he was wiped out.

When King Herod's wife Herodias destroyed the imprisoned John the Baptist by instructing her daughter to demand his head on a platter, what were Herod and his guests doing? Eating and drinking to celebrate Herod's birthday (Matt. 14:6–11).

Don't get me wrong. God isn't against celebrating. He isn't against eating and drinking. But when your life is not what it ought to be with God and you begin to just satisfy the cravings of your flesh, you open yourself up to temptation from Satan. One of the best ways to bring the old body under control is to deny yourself and fast. Fasting not only helps us spiritually, it helps us keep our flesh—our old man—under control.

Notice that in Luke 4:1 it says, "And Jesus being full of the Holy Ghost returned from Jordan, and was led by the Spirit into the wilderness." Why? *For a fast.* Many times our temptations and testing come to us when we are full of the Holy Spirit. Jesus had just been baptized in water. The Spirit had descended upon Him in the form of a dove, and the Spirit never departed from Him. But notice in this passage that you shouldn't think that temptation is going to come to you only when things are going bad. Matthew tells us that *the Spirit* led Jesus into the wilderness. There in the wilderness, while Jesus was fasting, He was tempted.

When you fast, you're going to be tempted. You will be tested. Don't expect everything to go easy for you. There will be days when you feel as if you're floating, but there will also be days when it feels like every demon in the whole area has come to your house. There will be things that surface when you fast that you hadn't thought about in years and years. Satan will try to block you somehow because he knows that when people repent, fast, pray, and seek the face of God, it moves heaven. It never fails.

Let's go back to the Old Testament and let me show you a couple of things. Do you need guidance? Ezra had been commanded by God to take the vessels and the treasury back to Jerusalem, but for him to get those things back there, he was going to have to travel through an area infested by thieves and robbers. He knew that his life and the lives of the people with him were in danger. He was confused and didn't know what to do. So in Ezra 8:21–22, we read:

> Then I proclaimed a fast there, at the river of Ahava, that we might afflict ourselves before our God, to seek of him a right way for us, and for our little ones, and for all our substance.

> For I was ashamed to require of the king a band of soldiers and horsemen to help us against the enemy in the way: because we had spoken unto the king, saying, The hand of our God is upon all them for good that seek him; but his power and his wrath is against all them that forsake him.

Ezra had been given the option of asking the king for soldiers and horsemen to help him and the people with him, but he had told the king that God fought and protected those who served Him. Now, these godly people were faced with a very difficult, seemingly impossible, situation. So Ezra and the people prayed and fasted, seeking God for divine direction.

You have been trying to witness to your family and friends, but you've found yourself in a very difficult situation and you don't know what to do. The people around you are watching to see how you're going to handle it. Oh, you could turn to the arm of flesh for help. You wouldn't sin by doing that, but you wouldn't bring the glory to God that He deserves. You have an opportunity, and you don't want to fail the Lord. You want to have a better relationship with God, be closer to Him, and love Him more. You need His guidance and direction. Like Ezra, you need God to speak to you and open your understanding so you know what to do. What should you do? Do what Ezra did. Ezra 8:23 declares: "So we fasted and besought our God for this: and he was intreated of us." God heard them, and He answered!

Go with me to Jonah so I can show you what's happening here. Some of you feel that the reason you're not being blessed is that some kind of judgment is on you. How do you get that judgment off? Some Christians think: "Well, I'm going through this because I failed God, there's judgment on me, and I'm reaping what I sowed." As we read chapter one, we see that Jonah had been commissioned by God to go to Nineveh and tell them that in forty days they were going to be wiped off the face of the earth. That's literally what God had told him to do. However, Jonah knew that if he went and told the people of Nineveh what God said, there was a strong possibility that they might repent, be forgiven, and escape death. That was a problem because Jonah didn't *like* Nineveh. He wanted Nineveh in hell. So Jonah decided to run from the presence of God. He went down to Joppa and caught a ship sailing to Tarshish.

But Jonah 1:4 says the Lord sent out a great wind into the sea. The storm and wind and waves were so great that it looked as if the ship was about to be broken. The desperate crew on the boat cried to their gods and cast the ship's goods into the sea to lighten the ship, but Jonah lay fast asleep, totally unaware of what was going on. When the terrified crew cast lots to see who was responsible for bringing all that evil upon them, the lot fell on Jonah. He told them he was fleeing from the presence of the Lord, and counseled them to cast him into the sea so it would become calm once again. The compassionate men kept battling the violent waves and struggling to bring the boat to land, but finally they took Jonah up and cast him into the sea. When they did, the waters ceased their raging and became calm.

However, the Bible says the Lord had prepared a great fish to swallow Jonah. He remained in its belly three days and three nights. In chapter two, Jonah tells us that down in the depths of the sea with weeds wrapped about his head in the belly of that fish, he remembered the Lord. Perhaps you feel like you're in the belly of a fish, too, and you can identify with how he felt. Jonah's desperate, repentant cries and his promise to pay what he had vowed reached God in His holy temple. The Lord spoke to the fish, and it vomited out Jonah upon the dry land.

Jonah—soggy, pitiful mess that he was, lay coughing and gasping on that beach. And the word of the Lord came unto Jonah the second time, telling him to go to the great city of Nineveh and preach unto it what God told him to say. This time, Jonah obeyed!

Nineveh was huge, sixty miles in circumference, but Jonah began to go through the city one day's walk, crying out, "In forty more days, Nineveh will be overthrown!" Jonah 3:5–6 declares that the people of Nineveh believed God, proclaimed a fast, and *everyone*—from the greatest to the least of them—put on sackcloth.

How about you? Do you believe that God will hear *you* when you pray? If you do, that's the first key.

In Nineveh, they didn't have a *feast*—they had a *fast*. Even the king rose from his throne, laid aside his robe, covered himself with sackcloth, and sat in ashes. He laid aside his pride—one of the number one problems with humanity. And throughout all Nineveh he issued a decree that no man or beast, flock or herd, was to eat or drink. Furthermore, he declared that both man and beast be covered with sackcloth, and men were to cry mightily to God and turn from their evil way and the violence in their hands. The king said, "Who can tell if God will turn and repent, and turn away from His fierce anger so we won't perish?" (Jonah 3:9).

I want you to get the picture of how serious this king was. If you'd lived in Nineveh and had a poodle, you would have put sackcloth on that little dog and not let it have any water or food. It was the same for your cats. They wore sackcloth, and they didn't eat or drink, either. In that entire city, neither beast nor man ate or drank. This was a *total* fast—probably for about twelve to twenty-four hours—and every person and all their animals took part. All the people cried out to God, for the king had said, "Who can tell? God *may* hear us and turn away from His anger so we won't perish?"

Jonah 3:10 tells us that when God saw their works, that they turned from their wicked way, He relented concerning the calamity which He had declared He would bring upon them, and He didn't do it. You see, when we get serious with God, it moves His great heart.

Like those people in Nineveh, some of you and your loved ones are facing desperate situations, and you're going to have to get serious with God. When you get desperate with God and deny yourself and fast before Him, your merciful God will see it and move on your behalf!

Oh, I know. Some of you are protesting, "Brother Gorman, you don't know what so and so said!" Well, what if you had a preacher who got mad and pouted because you repented? Jonah, who hadn't wanted to preach to Nineveh in the first place, had to be forced into obeying and coming to declare the word of the Lord. He was afraid the people of Nineveh would repent and believe and God would honor it. He knew God was a God of mercy, and if they repented and cried out to Him, He would answer. But Jonah didn't *want* them blessed! What I'm trying to show you is that there is no one who can keep you from your blessing except *you*. It doesn't matter what your mother-in-law, your father-in-law, or your wife says. It doesn't matter what your neighbor, your employer, or your employees say. Nobody but *you* can stop your blessing! When you get down to business with God, it doesn't matter if your pastor, the board, and everybody else is against you. When you get serious with the Lord, *none* of them can keep the blessing of God from coming upon your life!

You and I look for people to endorse us, but we don't need *people* to endorse us. We need *God's* endorsement. It's wonderful to have friends and people who love us, but we serve God because He loves us, and we love Him! So when you fast, quit wondering about what somebody else is doing. What do you need God to do for *you*?

You can pray. If you have to go to work, get up early enough to pray first and then go on to work. I'm talking about being serious with this thing. I'm talking about getting down and plowing through! You may need some miracles. We're serving a miracle-working God! You say, "Why are you saying all that, Brother Gorman?"

I'm saying these things because Jonah got mad and pouted when God didn't do what he wanted. Jonah went out of the city, made himself a booth to shield himself from the hot sun, and sat there in the shade until he could see what would become of Ninevah. To Jonah's delight, God prepared a gourd vine and let it grow up over the prophet's head to help shade him from the blazing sun and deliver him from his grief. But when the morning sun dawned the next day, God prepared a cutworm to attack the gourd plant and make it wither and die. Then God prepared a scorching east wind, and the blazing sun beat down on Jonah's head. The prophet grew faint and begged with all his soul to die rather than live. Yet Jonah was the one who had kept himself from being blessed. Unlike his God, Jonah had no love, pity, or compassion for a great city that had more than 120,000 persons not spiritually bright enough to know their right hand from their left, as well as many cattle and other animals not accountable for sin (Jonah 4:11).

Matthew 6:14–16 declares:

> For if ye forgive men their trespasses, your heavenly Father will also forgive you: But if ye forgive not men their trespasses, neither will your Father forgive your trespasses. Moreover when ye fast, be not, as the hypocrites, of a sad countenance; for they disfigure their faces, that they may appear unto men to fast. Verily I say unto you, They have their reward.

Some believer goes out to work and somebody asks, "Why do you look so downcast?" The believer replies piously, "Well, our church has called a fast, and I'm fasting." He got his reward right there. He killed it. It's over. Another believer who is fasting says, "I just can't stand so and so!" The moment that believer utters those words—or even if he or she only *thinks* the words—that believer's fasting is dead. So the first thing you need to do before you ever begin to fast, as I said in the first chapter on fasting, is to forgive everybody who ever hurt you. I am repeating this because it is so important for your spiritual break-through, and for the power that you seek.

Forgive them to the extent that you can say, "God, bless them! Bless them financially! Bless their children! Bless them with the necessary vehicles! Bless them with new clothes! Bless them with a new home, if they need it! Bless them, Lord!" When you can sincerely pray like that, you know in your heart that you've forgiven them.

Isn't it strange that the Lord first talks about forgiveness, and then adds, "When you fast…" Why? Because forgiveness has to come first, or else there is no need to fast. It won't help. Also notice that Jesus says *when* you fast…not, *if* you fast. Obviously, the Lord knew and expected that all Christians would fast. He didn't say, "I want you to fast on this day, that day, or some other day."

Let me show you how serious this thing of fasting is with God. In the Old Testament they had a time of fasting when all Israel was called to fast. Anyone who didn't fast was cut off. God was serious about fasting. Yet in the New Testament, fasting is a matter of grace. There's no set day, no set number of days, no set time. Jesus just says, "When you fast…" The Lord knew that when you and I really fell in love with Him, the time would come when our love for Him would be greater than our desire for food.

Think about it. Have you ever fallen in love with someone so deeply that you lost your appetite? You didn't have time to eat. You had to rush so you could get to wherever they were because you wanted to be with them. That's what Jesus is talking about when He says, "When you fast…"

There are two things I want to point out to you before you go into a fast. I've already talked to you about one of them: *forgiveness*. For the other, go with me to Psalm 35:13, where it says: "But as for me, when they were sick, my clothing was sackcloth: I humbled my soul with fasting; and my prayer returned into mine own bosom." Notice that God says I am to humble myself. That's what I am to do when *I* fast and what you are to do when *you* fast. You and I are to humble our souls with fasting. If we will humble ourselves, if we will forgive people, and if we will go into the fast repenting, the heavens will open, and we will see great things!

ENTER WITH PRAYER

We go into fasting seeking, first of all, His presence. That doesn't mean we can't ask for something from God, but the *first* thing we do is seek His presence. In Zechariah 7:5 we read:

> Speak unto all the people of the land, and to the priests, saying, When ye fasted and mourned in the fifth and seventh month, even those seventy years, did ye at all fast unto me, even to me?

Zechariah and Haggai were prophets to Judah after the Babylonian exile. These men of God were contemporaries of Zerubbabel who led the first group of Jews back from Babylon. Zechariah's ministry began just two months after Haggai began his. Both prophets made it clear that the returning exiles were to rebuild the temple. But in contrast to Haggai, Zechariah's message was primarily one of encouragement. He made it clear that rebuilding the temple was a spiritual work, and they could expect God's help and direction in their task. The true builder of the temple was God Himself. The people were just laborers with Him to accomplish the task.

You see, for seventy years the Jews had been in captivity. For seventy years they had sought God. For seventy years, on the fifth and seventh month of each year, they had fasted. But when they fasted, they fasted for their own personal needs. They didn't fast because they wanted the presence of God. They were concerned about their needs and getting out of captivity. They were more concerned about God delivering them than they were about God's presence coming in. Now it was time for the people to put their priorities straight by putting God and His work first; then they would be blessed.

Like the Jews of Zechariah's day, so much of *our* praying and fasting is in behalf of our own needs. Please pay close attention to what I'm saying because this is a word to believers today. When you go to prayer, I want you to start watching how you pray. When the average person begins to pray, they start listing all the things they need God to do for them. "I need You to take care of this situation…Lord, we're having problems with this…" Believers start listing their needs as they come to God in prayer. That's what the children of Israel had been doing while they were in captivity.

God had a word He wanted Zechariah to give these returning

exiles. He wanted them to know that He had been very unhappy and displeased because they had sought His hand instead of His presence. They had not sought for Him to come near to them and for them to draw near to Him. They had wanted God's help and what He had, but they hadn't really wanted *Him*. God wanted them to know that He was disappointed in that kind of fasting. God wasn't condemning them for asking help for their needs, but He didn't want that to be the main reason they fasted.

He wanted them to fast because they wanted to dwell in His presence and know what it was like to stay in close communion with Him.

Read 2 Chronicles 7:14 with me:

> If my people, which are called by my name, shall humble themselves, and pray, and seek my face, and turn from their wicked ways; then will I hear from heaven, and will forgive their sin, and will heal their land.

Did you notice that God said "seek My face" before He said anything about turning from their wicked ways? God's face represents His presence. God is more concerned about you seeking His presence before you ask Him to deliver you from some sin or habit. He knows that if His presence is not there, you will not have the strength or power to give up the sin or habit.

You may say, "That's in the Old Testament." Well, let's go to Acts 13:1–2:

> Now there were in the church that was at Antioch certain prophets and teachers... As they ministered to the Lord and fasted, the Holy Ghost said, Separate me Barnabas and Saul for the work whereunto I have called them.

These prophets and teachers had come together to fast, pray, and minister to the Lord. What does it mean to *minister* to the Lord? It means to worship and praise Him and minister in obedience to the Lord and what He is saying. To worship the Lord means to obey and submit to Him, acknowledging Him as the Lord and authority over your life. Therefore, as they began to minister to the Lord with fasting, the Holy Spirit spoke to them.

Do you need a word directly from God? Minister to the Lord and fast. Take your eyes off yourself and focus them on the Lord. Worship and give glory to the Lord and exalt His name. Submit to Him and make Him Lord of your life.

I want to ask you something. How can you minister to the Lord if you haven't been obedient with your tithes and offerings? If you are behind on your tithes, catch them up. If you have to, set a date when you will have them paid up, then pay your tithes off in installments as quickly as possible. You cannot expect the presence of the Lord to come down into your heart and your dwelling place if you are stealing from Him. When you pay your tithes and give offerings, you are ministering to the Lord. You are taking what is His and bringing it to Him in obedience. When you are obedient unto the Lord, you are ministering unto Him.

In Zechariah, God was unhappy because His people had not sought His presence. In Acts 13:2, as these prophets and teachers were fasting and seeking the Lord's presence, He showed up and began talking to them! Do you know what would have happened when the people of God were in captivity if they had sought His *face* instead of His *hand*? God might not have brought them out of captivity any quicker, but He would have come into captivity with them and spoken with them heart-to-heart.

Sometimes God doesn't deliver us *out* of the situation we find ourselves in, but He comes *into* the situation with us and walks through it with us, making us more than conquerors in the midst of everything going on around us. He did not deliver Daniel out of the lions' den, but He got in the den with Daniel and locked the mouths of the lions! He did not deliver the three Hebrew children out of the fiery furnace, but He got in and walked through the fire with them because they focused on Him!

So I'm not telling you that God is going to instantly deliver you out of your trouble. He may. He can. But I am going to tell you that where you've been walking in that thing alone, you're not going to walk alone anymore because He's going to come down and walk through it with you! That's what fasting and prayer does. It brings God down into your situation to minister to you, help you, and be near you!

I don't know about you, but there have been times I was going through such difficult circumstances, all it took was just one word from God and it was as if a load lifted off me. It didn't change the circumstances, but that word He spoke gave new strength. As you seek *first* His presence, God will give you a word and speak to your heart. He will give you direction and show you what to do.

God delights when His people seek His face in fasting and prayer. He appreciates it so much, that in Isaiah 58:9 He says: "Then shalt thou call, and the Lord shall answer; thou shalt cry and he shall say, Here I am." What if this week you were praying in the middle of your storm—going through your trial and battle, facing that impossible situation, and all at once you heard a voice speaking deep inside you saying, "Here I am! I am with you! You're not going under; You're going over because I am in the midst of this thing with you!" That's what fasting and prayer does when we get down to business with it and really begin to seek His face.

You know, sometimes people "get under the eight ball," so to speak, and they're in such difficulty that they begin to think that everybody—including God, is against them. Have you ever felt that way? Have you ever reached the place where you think, "God, are You even listening to me? Are you even hearing what I'm saying? Do You even know where I am? What's going on, Lord? What's happening?" If so, why don't you agree to let that verse I just quoted from Isaiah 58:9, be one of those verses we stand on together?

Let's also agree on Jeremiah 29:11. Now remember, Jeremiah was raised up by God to be a prophet when the first five books of the Bible, called the Pentateuch, had been completely disregarded. The people were in deep backsliding, idolatry was in the land, and Satanic worship such as sorcery and divination were practiced instead of following the Word of the Lord. The ten northern tribes of Israel had been carried away by the Assyrians into captivity. Ruthless Nebuchadnezzar would come to tear down Jerusalem's walls, destroy the temple, and lead many of the people into captivity to his kingdom, Babylon. Remember how a group fled from King Nebuchadnezzar to Egypt and forced Jeremiah to accompany them?

This group was in great difficulty. They were at the place where they thought everybody was against them. No Babylonian guard that came along had a good word to say to them; all the guards knew to do was talk down to them because they were a bunch of Jews and everybody hated Jewish people. So the Jews were treated roughly and unkindly while they were in Babylonian captivity. Yet in the midst of all that was going on around them, they'd come to wonder if anyone, any-where, even knew or thought about them and where they were. The voice of the prophet Jeremiah rose to call the people back to God! "For I know the thoughts that I think toward you, saith the Lord, thoughts of peace, and not of evil, to give you an unexpected end" (Jeremiah 29:11). You see, God wasn't thinking about them and their terrible ending, and neither is He thinking about *you* regarding how bad it's all going to turn out. When God looks at you He remembers that His thoughts toward you are good, not evil! His thoughts are for peace. He looks at you and thinks how He can bring you into His blessings!

Some people are under the curse of feeling that they're never going to get out of where they are. They think, "My grandfather before me was like this, and my father was like this. I've been in poverty, nobody ever did anything to help me, and I can't come out of my circumstances." But I want you to know that when God looks at you, He thinks of ways He can bless you and bring you out! He's thinking of ways He can prosper you and lift you up! He's thinking of ways He can cause you to be triumphant instead of in a state of gloom and doom. God's thoughts toward you are not those of leaving you where you are, but of bringing you into that state of blessing and refreshing where He wants you to be! That's the kind of thoughts God has toward you!

Jeremiah 29:12 declares: "Then shall ye call upon me, and ye shall go and pray unto me, and I will hearken unto you." When you call, He is going to answer! God wants you to believe Him for big, mighty things! He wants to show Himself exceedingly great in your life. He wants your family members and friends to see that He hasn't cut you off because of your failure, or because you might have been nasty to someone or snapped at them. God's Word says that He can bring you out into the glory and blessing He has provided for you.

The next verse, verse 13, promises, "And ye shall seek me, and find me, when ye shall search for me with all your heart." When you turn to Him, praying and fasting, searching for God with all your heart, you will find Him! And in verse 14, God declares that He will be found of you when you pray to Him. He will turn away your captivity. He will gather you and cause you to return to the place you belong!

Your neighbor or someone at your work may be thinking badly toward you. Your mate or family member may be thinking wrongly toward you. But *God* is thinking *good* about you! He's thinking how

He can help you. However, you may be saying, "Well, He has a real opportunity to help me! I'm in really bad shape. Why doesn't He hurry up?" It's because God responds to *faith*. He wants you to come to the place where you *believe* He will do it! He wants you to believe that He is a good God and that He's not thinking bad thoughts about you.

You know, there are times when you can hear what other people are saying, or a person will come and tell you what somebody said. You can get to the place where you think, "Well, *nobody* thinks anything good about me!" But I want you to remind yourself every day that there is One thinking about you, and He is more powerful than all the rest of the world put together! That's your God! That's my God! He is thinking *good* of you and me. Our God is looking for a way that He can help us move to a place of faith so He can release all the various blessings that He has for us! That's the kind of God we serve!

I want to take us a little further here. When the Israeli scribe Ezra and other children of Israel—priests, Levites, singers, porters, etc.,—left their Babylonian captivity and undertook their four-month journey back to Jerusalem, they needed protection. They needed protection not only for themselves, but also for the enormous amount of silver, gold, and vessels which the king, his counselors and lords, and all Israel had given them to carry with them as an offering. Ezra 8 tells us that Ezra and these people were in a dangerous situation where they didn't know how or what to do. They needed divine direction.

You may need direction about a legal matter or a child of yours. You may need direction about a position that has opened to you. You may need direction about any number of things, and at the same time you may need protection. I want to tell you about the sure way to get direction and protection from God for you and your family. When I must have divine direction and emergency situations are threatening, I not only fast food and spend the extra needed time in prayer. I also fast when it comes to reading the newspaper and watching television.

Ezra the prophet was well acquainted with prayer, seeking God, and fasting. Ezra knew that they, their women and children, and all their goods required God's divine intervention and protection. He knew they had to have guidance. So what did Ezra do? The Bible says in Ezra 8:21, that he proclaimed a fast. And when they fasted and besought God, He was entreated of them. He heard and answered their prayers.

He intervened, protected, and guided them because they fasted and sought His presence and intervention.

If you will cry out to God, spending the first twenty to thirty minutes of your prayer time seeking His face and His presence and then beseeching Him for His guidance and divine intervention, He will hear and help. Stop running in and telling God about all your troubles and going through all your lists of needs as if He is unconcerned and hasn't noticed! I used to do that very thing. Then one day God said to me, "I know your needs before you ask. I know what you're going to pray before you say it. I know all of that."

"Lord," I responded, "if that's the case, why should I pray? Why should I do it?" He answered, "Ask and pray because you show faith when you ask! But above all else, I want you to desire Me and love Me, to walk before Me, and be in My presence. In My presence is fullness of joy!"

Understand? You and I must first move into the presence of almighty God and *then* make known our requests and petitions. Let's put it this way. Say you went to the bank tomorrow morning to ask the banker for a loan to help tide you over for certain things. You sat in your car, laid it all out, and prepared your speech to tell the banker everything you wanted him to know...before the banker ever got to the bank. You're not going to get that loan. Why? The banker wasn't even there!

That's the way it is when you and I rush into prayer, voicing our requests. We start talking to God before we've even entered His presence. First, we have to come into God's presence, face to face, heart to heart, worshipping and waiting before Him. *Then* we can present our needs.

"Oh," you say, "I thought God was everywhere!"

Yes, God *is* everywhere. But while you are rushing in to lay out your needs and requests, you're not really into prayer. Stop that! First, begin to praise Him. Lift up your hands before Him. Sometimes you will find yourself leaping for joy. Begin to get excited about what the Lord has already done. Begin to praise His holy name! Why? Because the Lord *inhabits*—He dwells in—the praises of His people! (Psalm 22:3). God perks up His ears and pays close attention to what we are saying as we speak His name and praise and worship Him.

I remember a young man years ago, who was married and had four or five children. He had been convicted of drug use and distribution and had been sentenced to seventeen years. He was going to a hearing, appearing before a judge. The young man had come to us for prayer, and a number of us had entered into a time of fasting and prayer on his behalf because we had seen the change in his life. We knew he had been delivered and was on the right road. We hated to see him have to leave his family for seventeen years. The judgment had already been issued, but we were interceding.

As the young man stood before that judge who was reading him the riot act, telling him how he deserved his punishment, he watched as the judge took the folder and went to lay it on his desk. As he did so, a letter that I had written to the judge fell out. The judge's clerk had placed the letter inside the folder, but the judge had never read it. So the judge paused, picked up the letter, and read through it. Then he turned to the young man and asked, "Do you go to this church?"

"Yes, your honor. I do," the young man replied.

The judge persisted, "Do you go there regularly?"

"Yes, your honor. I do."

The judge turned his back and looked over the letter again. Then he said slowly, "I'm going to do something I have never done before." (The District Attorney on the case said later that he had never seen the judge do anything of that nature.) The judge continued: "I am going to reverse my decision and give you five years suspended sentence. But if I hear that you are not going to that church, I will sentence you to the maximum!"

You see, there comes a time when judgment has been set. There may be someone reading this who has a judgment hanging over your head. I want you to know that there is a God who can reverse it!

Look at 1 Kings 21:1–26, and let me show you from the Bible. After scheming Queen Jezebel lied and had godly Naboth the Jezreelite murdered and his land possessed because he had refused to sell wicked King Ahab his vineyard, you'd think that God would have let that evil king have whatever he deserved. God had even told Elijah the prophet that judgment was upon Ahab and sent him to tell the king that the same dogs who licked up dead Naboth's blood would lick up Ahab's blood in the same place.

But when King Ahab heard the words of God's judgment coming upon him, proclaiming his punishment and death, Ahab rent his clothes, put sackcloth on his flesh, fasted, lay in sackcloth and went softly (v. 27). All those things were acts of humility and repentance. The sentence had been rendered. King Ahab was doomed. But when

Ahab heard Elijah's words, that king started repenting before almighty God and crying out to Him. He humbled himself and started praying. What happened? The word of the Lord came to Elijah, saying: "Seest thou how Ahab humbleth himself before me? Because he humbleth himself before me, I will not bring the evil in his days: but in his son's days will I bring the evil upon his house" (1 Kings 21:28–29).

In other words, God reversed His decision. He didn't do what He had just said He was going to do. Instead, God delayed the evil and brought it upon his house in the days of Ahab's son.

You may be under the gun. But if you will fast, pray, and humble yourself, you serve a God in heaven who will do the same for you! You may be thinking, "Oh, but I was wrong about this, and I was wrong about that…" How could you be more wrong than King Ahab was? Yet when he humbled himself and began to repent, pray, and fast, God said: "I'm going to reverse this thing. I'm going to put a hold on it. I'm not going to let it happen. I will not bring the evil in King Ahab's days, but in his son's days I will bring the evil upon his house."

When you study the Word of God you will find that there were few kings who even came close to being as wicked as King Ahab was. But when Ahab repented, God reversed and delayed the words of judgment He had spoken. How the God we serve could hold up judgment already spoken on a man as wicked as Ahab is difficult for us to grasp or accept. We don't want something to come upon our children. But we see in the New Testament that God's curse can be reversed. Jesus Christ, who knew no sin, took the curse for us on the cross of Calvary. Because He took that curse for us, it can be reversed when we understand what God has for us and we repent. Then the curse Jesus bore for us doesn't come upon us or upon our children. Thank God, the curse can be broken!

So I say to you today—whoever you are that's under the gun—don't let this week continue to roll on as it has been going. Prepare your heart. Pour out your soul before God. Let Him minister to you and do His holy, healing work in you.

I want to deal with two more issues that are tied together. In 2 Chronicles 20, there was a king. He was told that there were several armies coming against him, and they would destroy and wipe him out. First of all, King Jehoshaphat, the king of Judah, did not have a trained, powerful military force. His men and his people were no match for what was coming against them. Jehoshaphat knew it and said, "What can I do? They will wipe us out completely!"

Listen to this. It will be one of the most important areas that I've dealt with. Notice that Jehoshaphat said he was going to appeal to the mercy of almighty God. What is mercy? Mercy is when you get help that you can't pay for, you don't deserve, and you don't have any right to it whatsoever. What you really deserve is judgment, but instead, God gives you mercy. So Jehoshaphat appealed to the mercy of God. Second Chronicles 20:3 tells us that he called a fast. All the people came together and began to fast. As they fasted and sought the face of God, the Almighty's heart was moved. God spoke to the people and told them what to do. He showed mercy.

The people didn't have a military force. They didn't *want* to fight. Furthermore, they couldn't have fought a war even if they had wanted to! Yet here the enemy was coming against them. The people said, "Dear God, please show mercy!" They began to fast and seek God for mercy, and as they sought Him, He was moved.

God said to them, "The battle is not yours. It's Mine!" That's mercy! They didn't deserve it. They didn't have any way to pay Him. But God stepped in and took over. All He asked them to do was believe Him and put their trust in Him. Then He would fight their battle for them!

God said, "Here's the way we're going to fight the battle. Get your choir ready. So they obeyed, got the choir ready, and out went their choir leading the people! What little military force they had was behind the choir. The choir led the way. When that choir began to sing and praise, the presence of God came down upon the enemies' armies and confused them. The enemy forces turned and started killing one another! Not one Israelite—not one—lifted a sword, but all of their enemies' forces were killed. There was such a slaughter, it took the Israelites three days to strip off and gather up all the enemies' jewels and gold and riches and haul them away. *Three days* to gather up all that spoil because God fought their battle!

Why did God fight their battle? Because they threw themselves upon His mercy! Some of you have fumbled the ball so badly and made so many mistakes that you are saying, "God, there's no way I can believe that You can forgive me. I haven't been faithful, or loyal, or done the things I should have done." But the Lord is saying to you today, "Believe Me and throw yourself upon My mercy!"

I am inviting *you* to throw yourself upon God's mercy! Don't come in like you're a holy Joe. No! Say, "I know I don't deserve it or have a right to it, but I'm throwing myself on the mercy of almighty God! I'm going to seek His face, ask Him for His help, and believe that in His *mercy*, God is going to help me!"

In the second and ninth chapters of Daniel, he needed revelation. That's what some of you need in order to understand what's going on with you. Daniel received the revelation he needed because he fasted and prayed. If I asked, some of you would say, "I don't know *what* is happening to me! I don't know why it's happening or what's going on. I just don't understand it."

King Darius was going through a battle, and Daniel faced a situation that he did not understand and for which he did not have the answer. Daniel fasted and prayed. Like Daniel, do you find yourself in a situation today where you realize that you desperately need God? You may need guidance. You may need protection or provision. You may need God to stay the hand of judgment. You may need God's mercy. You may need God to intervene in your behalf and close the mouths of those who are lying about you or judging you wrongly. I don't know. But you have reached a decision, and you're crying out to the Lord. "God, I need you today, and I want to make a commitment. I've seen Your words in my own Bible, and Your word can't lie. God, I'm going to throw myself upon Your mercy. I'm going to seek You with all My heart. I may not be able to fast like some other people fast, but I can fast one meal or two meals, or I can go on the Daniel fast, or fast one meal a day. But God, I'm going to do whatever You tell me to do this week because I'm appealing to Your mercy."

If you're facing a situation similar to something I've described, talk to God about it. Make a commitment to Him right there where you are. This is something between you and God. It is God who is going to intervene for you. Move into this situation as I have shown you from the scripture. Stand upon God's Word and let it speak to you. Begin to talk to God. Worship Him for who He is and all He has done! Tell Him where you are, what you need, and why you need it. Declare His promises! Then stand still and see the salvation of the Lord!

FASTING: A FINAL NOTE

One more thing. If you have not already read *The 21 Day Fast* by Rev. Bob Rodgers, I urge you to order it immediately from Bob Rodgers Ministries, P. O. Box 19229, Louisville, Kentucky 40259. I found the book to be invaluable, I ordered 5,000 of them and gave them to ministers in Africa. I also bought 5,000 to sell on my book and CD table. I recommend it highly!

Chapter 15

THE COMING REVIVAL

THE VISION

IT WAS AUGUST 3, 1983, and approximately 1:30 p.m. I had just finished lunch, returned to my office at First Assembly of God in New Orleans, and sat down at my desk. My mind was focused on the work I needed to complete that afternoon. God, however, had something else in mind.

Just before tackling the first item on my "To Do" list, I leaned back in my chair, stretched out both arms, and rolled back my head to relax the tight muscles in my neck and shoulders. I was leaning back like that— relaxing, stretching, casually gazing upward with my mind in "neutral"— when suddenly the whole ceiling above my head seemed to turn into a movie screen. I realized I was experiencing an open vision!

For the next three hours I watched scene after astounding scene of the most incredible move of God I've ever witnessed—a worldwide panorama of miraculous events! Astonishing healings of all kinds of afflictions and diseases. Cancer eradicated by the power of God. Blind eyes and deaf ears opening. People literally jumping out of wheelchairs. Powerful deliverances from demonic spirits.

I kept looking to see who was in charge—who was leading this ministry. None of the works I witnessed was being done by preachers. As a matter of fact, *no one* seemed to be in charge. In one huge auditorium in the United States where such healings and deliverances were taking place I saw several men standing on a platform. However, I soon realized they were simply observing. God said, "This is a work of the Holy Spirit!"

It seemed to be the same worldwide—a mighty move of God where all the work was being done by the body of Christ itself—by lay people! And these lay people being so marvelously used by God were of *all ages.*

I watched as *children*, who looked to be about seven or eight years old, prayed for people in wheelchairs to be healed. People with bodies twisted and ravaged by disease. Paralyzed people. Hopeless cripples.

249

Every affliction imaginable. Yet *children* prayed, and people literally *shot* out of their wheelchairs, instantly healed! I saw children confront adults and reveal things in their lives that their elders needed to repent of. The adults would fall to their knees, crying and repenting!

As I watched, the Lord spoke openly to me regarding how men had hindered the work of the Holy Spirit by their programs and secular knowledge. He spoke plainly to me about their pre-conceived ideas of how things must be done or conducted. The Spirit emphasized to me that *God's ways are not man's ways*!

The vision went on to show me the great revival that will take place among the youth. I gawked in amazement at teenagers receiving instantaneous, visible, totally miraculous answers to simple, powerful prayers of faith. People were raised up from gurneys. The crippled took off braces. Blind eyes opened. The demon-possessed were liberated as, in the name of Jesus, teenagers took authority over evil spirits.

It was the same for young adults, the middle-aged, and elderly who were laying hands on people, one after another. The people praying and ministering with such power and authority were *lay people*—the body of Christ! Lay people working miracles. Lay people binding up the bruised and broken. Lay people setting at liberty those who were bound.

For three hours I sat totally transfixed, staring at that screen. Marveling! Rejoicing! Weeping! Desperately hungering to be part of what was taking place before my eyes! And then I was made to understand the vivid images of *future events* I had been watching. God was allowing me to see what will happen in the end-time revival, the last day move of the Holy Spirit. I saw the Spirit's supernatural gifts that will be so evident—*especially* the word of knowledge, the word of wisdom, discerning of spirits, gifts of healings, and the gift of miracles. I realized that God was letting me know that this great revival will not come by even the best efforts of men and their organizations.

God said that a great awakening would be coming soon. He said the emphasis of the awakening would be on repentance, holiness, the supernatural, Holy Spirit empowerment, and leadership. However, it appeared that God was greatly disturbed. He said, "No longer will we look to programs and man-produced emphases. The Holy Spirit will be in control. The teaching and preaching will be Word-centered and will be delivered with power and revelation given by the Holy Spirit."

I continued to stare at the massive crowds and witness many people of all ages praying as miracles of every kind took place. I saw thousands of crippled people healed. People came out of wheelchairs by the thousands. All types of braces were removed and thrown aside, no longer needed. Multitudes of deaf, dumb, and blind people immediately received their healing. Many twisted and deformed individuals began shouting and praising God for their instant restoration. God said: "This is My church in ministry. Personalities are coming down. The eyes of the world will not be on personalities, but on My Church."

The Lord said: "I will pour out My Spirit on all people and all denominations." He named several religious denominations: Methodist, Lutheran, Presbyterian, Catholic.... Then He added, "Especially the Baptists."

"Lord," I asked, "why are You showing partiality to the Baptists?"

He responded, "There will be many workers needed because the harvest will be so great. The Baptists know My Word, but they do not know My power. I will pour out My Spirit upon them."

Even as I watched, somehow I knew a split would come among Pentecostals. It would be a split between the traditional and the supernatural. A split between Pentecostals who *turn away from* the gifts and power of the Holy Spirit and Pentecostals who *covet and cherish* the Spirit's holy presence, power, and miraculous manifestations whenever and wherever He chooses.

I was sitting there, grappling with the staggering implications of such a division among Pentecostals, wondering why I was seeing all I was witnessing, when the Lord said to me: "Most men witness only one mighty revival in their lifetime. Every time I try to do a new thing, they try to put it in the old mold. I don't do any two things exactly alike."

Anguish and dread slashed through my heart. I could not bear the thought, yet I had to know! I swallowed hard, blinking back tears. "Do You mean I won't see the coming world-wide revival because I witnessed the mighty revival in New Orleans?"

"If you will be true to Me," the Lord replied, "I will let you be part of another great move. The church will become powerful and the world will recognize she is a force to contend with. The world will look to the church for answers."

The Lord talked to me at length about repentance and holiness, emphasizing the importance of *inner* holiness. He warned against judging others and told me that God looks on the heart.

As the Lord spoke, I kept staring at the miraculous events taking place before my eyes. Multitudes being born again. Much weeping and repenting. People lying on pads and gurneys (people who for years had been unable to walk) jumping to their feet, running, and shouting! For a long time—I judge it was close to an hour, I continued watching the great things taking place all around me.

Then God spoke, breaking the silence: "The coming of Jesus is soon. It is important to watch for His return and prepare yourself for that hour! In the last days I will pour out My Spirit upon all flesh. The church is going to be prepared to end this journey and leave this world a powerful, prophetic, Holy Ghost directed and empowered body of believers!"

When the vision was finished, I struggled to pull myself up from my desk. My body was very weak. I stood and managed to get over to my recliner. Then I laid back and rehearsed in my mind all the things God had shown me.

A NIGHT VISION/DREAM

Elmer Nugent, who is my spiritual son, pastored First Assembly of God in Camden, Arkansas. Elmer has now been promoted to be with the Lord.

Elmer contacted me and asked me to preach for him on a particular Sunday. I told him I could be there for only that one day because I had promised my wife that we would take a few days off. I explained that we had been heavily booked for many months.

During the Sunday morning service, nothing special happened. However, Sunday night when I walked into the building that would seat about 450 people, it was practically filled. I was pleasantly surprised at the crowd.

During that evening service, twenty-eight people were baptized in the Holy Spirit and two women were miraculously healed. One of the women was scheduled for surgery the following Tuesday. On Monday she went to her doctor. After examining her, the surgery was cancelled.

Elmer persuaded me to stay longer. On Monday night there was a capacity crowd and a great move of God. On Tuesday night there was a miraculous healing of a deaf lady. Several people accepted Jesus as Savior, and I ministered a long time in the altar service. The crowds continued to grow as the meeting continued. Many nights the building was filled with people.

Thursday night there was a well-dressed gentleman seated to my right. Feeling that he was a minister, I walked back and introduced myself to him. He was very reserved. I told him I felt he was a preacher. At first he did not acknowledge it. However, when I started to walk away, he said, "I am the pastor of First Baptist Church, and I came here to check this out. That was my mother-in-law who was healed of deafness on Tuesday night."

On Saturday night, we had a service, and he and his wife were present. They responded to the altar invitation. Both were slain in the Spirit, received the Holy Spirit and spoke in tongues.

One night, through a word of knowledge, I called for a person whose right foot had been seriously injured. The man was unable to work. His foot was turned sideways. As I prayed for him, we watched his foot as God straightened it and totally healed it before our eyes.

His buddies, who were truck drivers like him, learned of his healing and talked about it on their CB radios. People from as far away as Nevada came to Camden to attend the revival. Truckers judged their timing so they could pull off the Interstate and attend the services. They parked their 18-wheelers along the road by the church. There is no way for me to know how many miracles took place during that nine-week revival.

When the revival began, my mother had just been admitted to a nursing home. Her former house was where my wife Virginia and I were staying during that series of meetings. During one of those nights after Virginia and I had gone to bed, I experienced what I determined to be a *night vision/dream*. It was as vivid as if I were actually experiencing it in real life.

I saw a very black line, the blackest black I had ever seen. In the vision/dream, I was lifted up and saw that the line started in New Orleans. It came through El Dorado, Arkansas, and then continued near Jonesboro, Arkansas. The black line worked its way up through Missouri, and on up to the Chicago area. I identified Chicago, but I didn't recognize any area beyond it.

Beginning against the black line and moving its way out toward the west, there was a raging fire. The fire was so great that it frightened me! I asked, "Lord, are you going to destroy those areas?"

The Holy Spirit responded by saying, "These are the Last Day revival fires. They will spread throughout the world. There will be no country that is not touched. This revival will produce repentance and holiness, followed by great manifestations of My Spirit. You will see healings and creative miracles, greater than you have ever witnessed. I am going to bring My Church back to its roots!"

Knowing that the church had been birthed in an outpouring of the Holy Spirit, I immediately began to think in terms of the early church in the book of Acts. As I reflected, the Spirit kept emphasizing to me how *holiness, repentance*, and *a hunger for miracles* would be a great part of this coming end-time revival. He told me that multitudes would turn to Christ. Then the Spirit said to me: "Persecution will be the theme, urging people to prepare for Christ's return!"

THE MODERN-DAY CHURCH GROWTH MOVEMENT

With that in mind, please think about the following with me. Much of our modern day church growth movement has been on the rise because of certain recently published books and "*the seeker-sensitive*" message. I see two major problems here.

Problem #1

The first problem of the church growth movement is that we are in danger of believing that a crowd constitutes a church.

The true measure of a church is *not* the size of its membership roll. If the ministry that Jesus began—the ministry that was *continuous* through the book of Acts—is not taking place in a church, then we have only a social fellowship. If we're not careful, we will find ourselves denying the power of the Holy Spirit.

The enormous *crowd* that gathers in the stands at Texas Stadium to watch the Dallas Cowboys play football is not a *church*. Why not? They gather at that big, expensive stadium on Sundays, don't they? They are excited and enthusiastic, aren't they? They help support the Dallas Cowboy's organization with their money and attendance, don't they? They talk about the Cowboys and invite people to attend the games with them, don't they? So what's the big deal? Why can't we call the crowd that meets on Sundays at Texas Stadium a *church*?

You know the answer. It's simple. It takes more than *a big crowd of people*—more than *a growth in numbers*—to constitute a church. It also takes more than *a big crowd of people carrying on religious activities* to have a church, too, doesn't it? So, I ask you: If the ministry that Jesus began—the ministry that was continuous through the book of Acts—is *not* taking place inside and outside a church building, should we call the group of people who meet there a *church*?

Problem #2

The second problem of the church growth movement is that ministers are in danger of seeking growth while sacrificing the move and power of the Holy Spirit.

We'd better take another look at the church in the New Testament. The early church wasn't birthed or built on what *people* wanted, but on what the *Holy Spirit* desired. Peter and Paul didn't try to *protect* people *from* the power and demonstration of the Spirit. They weren't afraid people might be *offended* by the manifestation of the gifts of the Spirit.

Those apostles, prophets, teachers, pastors, and evangelists of the early church knew that mere growth in numbers does not constitute a church. They understood that if the supernatural ministry that Jesus began and that continued throughout the book of Acts and the New Testament was *not* taking place in a church, it was only *a social fellowship*…even if that congregation happened to be growing in numbers. They also understood that if that social fellowship were not careful, it would find itself *denying* the power of the Holy Spirit.

A WARNING AND CHALLENGE

Just think of the dreadful mess our world is in right now. Every day another horror story appears in the news. Drugs and alcohol. Murder. Child abuse. Unnatural sexual activities. Incest, fornication, adultery. Homosexuality out of the closet and in front of the camera. Refusal to marry. Divorce running rampant. The filth of pornography streaming like an open sewer down the middle of our streets and seeping into our homes through television and the internet. Our land stained by the blood of millions of aborted babies. Disobedience and disrespect in our homes and our schools. Terrorism at home and abroad. Disasters of every description. And it all seems to be escalating!

Who is the sick, twisted mastermind behind all this? His name is *Satan*! And naive, complacent Christians think they can *ignore* him?

Yeah, right. *They* may not know much about *him*, but I can guarantee that *he* knows all about *them*! If it's the same devil I fight, they'd better sleep with one eye open!

Surely the Lord is about to bring His true church to a moment in time when we will boldly confront the powers of hell. *But we're not ready!* Look around you. What do you see? Are we preparing for war? Do we know how to use the mighty weapons that God has given His Church? Do we even know what those weapons are?

The Bible declares that "the weapons of our warfare are not carnal, but mighty through God to the pulling down of strongholds" (2 Cor. 10:4). What are those weapons? The sword of the Spirit, which is the Word of God! The authority of Jesus' name! The power of His precious blood! The baptism in the Holy Spirit! Prayer and travail! The gifts of the Holy Ghost! God has given us these mighty weapons of mass destruction to use against hell and all its forces, yet we're running around with cap guns and water pistols! We've been so busy competing to see who's the greatest, that we've forgotten who the real enemy is! It's not each other! It's not the church down the street that's outgrowing us! Never forget that your real enemy is Satan, and he wants *you*!

I've been preaching the Gospel most of my life. I go a lot of places, and I see a lot of things. With a breaking heart I tell you that in many Pentecostal churches today the manifestation of the gifts of the Spirit and times of intercession around the altar are fast becoming things of the past. Many of our pastors and people are perfectly content to have church whether the Holy Spirit shows up or not. Who needs *Him* when they can have their slick, seeker-friendly services, and comfortable rituals? Who wants demon-possessed people coming in and causing disturbances and running off the visitors? I'm not trying to sound harsh. I'm stating facts, not finding fault. It's a great source of grief to me that much of the church is totally unprepared for the things that are coming.

I want to ask you this question: What would happen if every person who names the name of Jesus and who claims to be Spirit-filled were to unite in fasting and prayer against the demonic spirits wrecking many segments of our society and many of our churches? Believe me when I tell you that unless we return to old-fashioned fasting and prayer, spending hours in meditation and heart-searching under the guidance of the Holy Spirit, we will be unable to usher in the great revival God is trying to send.

Some reading this will yawn and say, "If God wants to send a revival, He'll send it." That's like some of the lukewarm, complacent people I've spoken to over the years who have said, "God knows where I am. If He wants to deliver me, or heal me, or bless me, He'll do it. He's God, and He doesn't need any help from you or me to do what He wants to do."

If you even halfway know your Bible, you'll have to admit that such statements are untrue. It is only those in the church who are willing and obedient—submissive and responsive to the will and purpose of God—who will experience the great, empowering manifestations of God.

The Word of God plainly tells us that in the last days He will pour out His Spirit upon all flesh. He first gives us the promise in Joel 2:28–32, then repeats it through Peter in Acts 2:16–21 on the Day of Pentecost after the miraculous outpouring of the Holy Spirit in the Upper Room. We've read it. Many of us have preached it and heard it preached. But do we really *believe* it?

Read what Peter said, won't you? Notice that the Lord emphasizes the fact that we will witness supernatural manifestations, not only through adults of all ages, but through *our children*—our sons and daughters! That's what I saw in the vision God gave me!

> But this is what was spoken by the prophet Joel: 'And it shall come to pass in the last days, says God, That I will pour out of My Spirit on all flesh; Your sons and your daughters shall prophesy, Your young men shall see visions, Your old men shall dream dreams. And on My menservants and on My maidservants I will pour out My Spirit in those days; And they shall prophesy.
>
> —Acts 2:16–18

Are we nearing that time? Notice that when Peter got to Acts 2:18, he didn't stop quoting. He continued in verses 19 through 21 that I've included below. Peter didn't know what it all meant, and you and I don't know what it all means, but God said all these things will come to pass in the last days immediately preceding the return of Christ. Read it. It all sounds pretty ominous and awesome to me!

And I will shew wonders in heaven above, and signs in the earth beneath; blood, and fire, and vapour of smoke: The sun shall be turned into darkness, and the moon into blood, before the great and notable day of the Lord come: And it shall come to pass, that whosoever shall call on the name of the Lord shall be saved

THE COMING REVIVAL

We can read about what the revival in Jesus' day and the revivals in the New Testament were like. The coming revival will be a supernatural revival that will affect not just a single area or a few spots in a country. It will encompass the world!

It is no secret that today in our time many churches on foreign soil are experiencing phenomenal manifestations of the Holy Spirit such as healings, deliverances, and people raised from the dead. Many of these supernatural manifestations have been documented. What is the key?

Those experiencing such miraculous manifestations are not depending on *their own* abilities and education. Like Paul, they are declaring to know nothing among them save *Jesus Christ and Him crucified*. They are seeing the *anointed, biblical messages* they preach confirmed by *supernatural demonstrations*.

When the Lord spoke to me in my office in that powerful vision back on August 3, 1983, He let me know that the mighty coming revival will not be to a segment of this country or to just a few countries. Through committed Christian people who pay the price for revival, that mighty move of God will impact the entire world! The Church will leave this world as God's prophetic, Holy Spirit directed and empowered body of believers!

WILL GOD DO IT AGAIN?

It is my belief that we are presently on the verge of this great outpouring of the Holy Spirit that will enable us to take the full gospel message to the ends of the earth, and then we will see the coming of our Lord and Savior. I call upon you now to join with me in persevering in Spirit-empowered prayer that you and I and our loved ones will see and be a part of that revival in our lifetime that will shake the world!

The Spirit of God did it for the second-century church, didn't He? Can He do it for us? Of course He can! That's not the issue. The questions before us are: Will we *let* Him do it again? Do we *want* Him to do it again? Oh, how we need to cry out to God until the church of our day is wholly filled and flooded with the Spirit Himself! *Deluged! Soaked! Saturated! Submerged* in the glory of God and totally reformed and transformed by His mighty power! *We're* not waiting on God: *He* is waiting on *us!*

NOTES

PREFACE

1. Donald Gee, *Concerning Spiritual Gifts*, (BookMasters, Kindle Edition), 1.

CHAPTER 1: STRANGERS TO THE SUPERNATURAL

1. Smith Wigglesworth, *Smith Wigglesworth on Spirit-filled Living* (New Kensington, PA: Whitaker House, 1998), 7–9, 11.
2. Shared by Pastor George Stormach, a close friend of Wigglesworth's, on a tape reproduced by Sure Word Ministries.

CHAPTER 2: STRANGERS TO THE SUPERNATURAL

1. Carol Vogel, *The New York Times*, Art & Design, "One Person's Trash is Another Person's Lost Masterpiece" (Oct. 23, 2007), 1.
2. David B. Barrett's work, "A Chronology of Renewal in the Holy Spirit," appears as the Appendix in Vinson Synan's book, *The Century of the Holy Spirit, 100 Years of Pentecostal and Charismatic Renewal, 1901–2001* (Nashville: Thomas Nelson Publishers, 2001, Appendix copyright 2001 by David B. Barrett).

CHAPTER 4: THE GIFT OF THE WORD OF WISDOM

1. Howard Carter, Spiritual Gifts and Their Operation (Springfield, MO: Gospel Publishing House, 1968), 17.
2. Ibid., 18.
3. Harold Horton, *The Gifts of the* Spirit (Springfield, MO: Gospel Publishing House, 1934), 56.
4. Lester Sumrall, *The Gifts and Ministries of the Holy Spirit* (New Kensington, PA: Whitaker House, 1982), 62–64.
5. Ibid.
6. Ibid., 65.
7. Harold Horton, *The Gifts of the Spirit* (Nottingham, England: The Assemblies of God Publishing House, 1934), 57.
8. Howard Carter, *Questions and Answers on Spiritual Gifts* (Tulsa, Oklahoma: Harrison House, 1976), 33–34.
9. Ibid., p. 34.
10. Lester Sumrall, *The Gifts and Ministries of the Holy Spirit* (New Kensington, PA: Whitaker House, 1982), 65, 66.
11. Howard Carter, *Questions and Answers On Spiritual Gifts* (Tulsa, Ok: Harrison House, 1976), 34.
12. Lester Sumrall, *The Gifts and Ministries of the Holy Spirit* (New Kensington, PA: Whitaker House, 1982), 66.

13. Ibid., 66–67.

14. Harold Horton, *The Gifts of the Spirit* (Nottingham, England: The Assemblies of God Publishing House, 1934), 61–67.

15. Ibid., 64–65.

16. Ibid., 65–66.

17. Ibid., 66.

18. Howard Carter, *Questions and Answers on Spiritual Gifts* (Tulsa, Oklahoma: Harrison House, 1976), 20–22.

19. Harold Horton, *The Gifts of the Spirit* (Nottingham, England: The Assemblies of God Publishing House, 1934), 57.

20. Ray McCauley, *The Gifts of the Holy Spirit* (The Republic of South Africa: Conquest Publishers, ©1988), 39.

21. Howard Carter, *Questions and Answers on Spiritual Gifts* (Tulsa, Oklahoma: Harrison House, 1976), 36.

CHAPTER 5: THE GIFT OF THE WORD OF KNOWLEDGE

1. Lester Sumrall, *The Gifts and Ministries of the Holy Spirit* (New Kensington, PA.: Whitaker House, 1982), 67.

2. Ralph M. Riggs, *The Spirit Himself* (Springfield, MO.: Gospel Publishing House, 1949), 125–126.

3. Ray McCauley, *The Gifts of the Holy Spirit* (Randburg 2125 Republic of S. Africa: Conquest Publishers, 1988), 36–37.

4. Ken and Lorraine Krivohlavek, *Desire Spiritual Gifts* (Pasig City, Philippines: ICI Ministries, 2004), 63, 67.

5. Howard Carter, *Spiritual Gifts and Their Operation* (Springfield, MO: Gospel Publishing House, 1968), 27–30, 34.

6. Ken and Lorraine Krivohlavek, *Desire Spiritual Gifts*, (Pasig City, Philippines: ICI Ministries, 2004), 64.

7. Gordan Lindsay, *Commissioned with Power*, (Dallas, TX: Christ for the Nations, 2001), 102.

8. Howard Carter, *Spiritual Gifts and Their Operation*, (Springfield, MO: Gospel Publishing House, 1968), 35–36.

9. Paraphrased from the Krivohlavek's, *Desire Spiritual Gifts*, and Howard Carter's, *Spiritual Gifts and Their Operation*.

10. Harold Horton, *The Gifts of the Spirit*, (Nottingham, England: Assemblies of God Publishing House, 1934), 52.

11. Ibid., 53.

CHAPTER 6: THE GIFT OF DISCERNING OF SPIRITS

1. This speech, though not addressed to Satan in his own person, seems to be ironically spoken of his evil genius fulfilling itself in and through a human ruler (the king of Tyre) who appropriates to himself the honors due only to God, as in the case of the king of Babylon (Isa. 14:12–15). Here is to be seen a foreshadowing of "the beast" who is to attribute to himself divine

rights in the time of the end (Dan. 7:8–28; 2 Thess. 2:1–12; Rev. 13; 19:20). (Quoted from a footnote in the Amplified Bible, Ezek. 28:13).

2. Gordon Lindsay, *Commissioned with Power: An Overview of the Gifts of the Spirit* (Dallas, TX: © 2001), 156.

3. Ken and Lorraine Krivohlavek, *Desire Spiritual Gifts* (Pasig City, Philippines, ICI Ministries, © 2004), 84–85.

4. Harold Horton, *The Gifts of the Spirit* (Nottingham, England: The Assemblies of God Publishing House, © 1934), 74–78.

PART 3: THE 3 GIFTS OF POWER

1. Lester Sumrall, *The Gifts and Ministries of the Holy Spirit,* (Whitaker House: New Kensington, PA, © 1982), 85.

CHAPTER 7: THE GIFT OF FAITH

1. Lester Sumrall, *The Gifts and Ministries of the Holy Spirit*, (Whitaker House: New Kensington, PA., © 1982), 88.

2. Ibid., 86.

3. Ibid., 87.

4. Gordon Lindsay, *Commissioned With Power—An Overview of the Gifts of the Spirit*, (Christ for the Nations: Dallas, TX, © 2001), 166.

5. Howard Carter, *Spiritual Gifts and Their Operation,* (Gospel Publishing House: Springfield, MO, © 1968), 39.

6. Ken and Lorraine Krivohlavek, *Desire Spiritual Gifts*, (ICI Ministries: Pasig City, Philippines, © 2004), 89.

7. Gordon Lindsay, *Commissioned With Power—An Overview of the Gifts of the Spirit,* (Christ for the Nations: Dallas, TX, © 2001), (See Lindsay's title for chapters 15–20, each stating a reason the gift of faith may be imparted.).

8. Ibid., 167–169.

9. Ibid., 168.

10. Ibid.

11. Ibid.

12. Gordon Lindsay, *The John G. Lake Sermons*, (CFNI Ministries: Dallas, TX, © 1949), 10–11.

13. Dr. Eddie Hyatt, ministering at Christ for the Nations Institute: "The Prayer of Dedication," (CFNI Ministries: Dallas, Texas, in *The Voice of Healing,* Aug. 2007 issue), 8–9.

14. W. Van Deventer and W.S. Weeden, "I Surrender All."

15. Dr. Lester Sumrall, *The Gifts and Ministries of the Holy Spirit*, (Whitaker House: New Kensington, PA, © 1982), 96–97.

16. Taken from Mel Montgomery Communications International, Media Files, *Howard Carter: A Man of Whom the World Was Not Worthy.*

17. John G. Lake, *The John G. Lake Sermons on Dominion Over Demons, Disease, and Death,* (The Voice of Healing Publishing Company–now Christ for the Nations, © 1949), 104–105, 107–108.

CHAPTER 8: THE GIFTS OF HEALINGS

1. Howard Carter, *Questions and Answers on Spiritual Gifts* (Tulsa, OK: Harrison House, © 1976), 98.

2. Harold Horton, *The Gifts of the Spirit* (Nottingham, England: The Assemblies of God Publishing House, © 1934), 94.

3. Howard Carter, *Questions and Answers on Spiritual Gifts* (Tulsa, OK: Harrison House, © 1976), 99.

4. Smith Wigglesworth, *Smith Wigglesworth on Spiritual Gifts* (New Kensington, PA: Whitaker House, © 1998), 91.

5. Howard Carter, *Spiritual Gifts and Their Operation* (Springfield, MO: Gospel Publishing House, © 1968), 49.

6. Harold Horton, *The Gifts of the Spirit* (Nottingham, England: The Assemblies of God Publishing House, © 1934), 96.

7. Ibid.

8. Smith Wigglesworth, *Smith Wigglesworth on Spiritual Gifts* (New Kensington, PA: Whitaker House, © 1998), 91.

9. Ibid., 93.

10. Ibid., 93, 95, 96.

11. Ibid., 96, 97.

12. Ibid., 98, 99.

CHAPTER 9: THE GIFT OF THE WORKING OF MIRACLES

1. Ray McCauley, *The Gifts of the Holy Spirit* (Randburg, Republic of South Africa: Conquest Publishers, 1988), 10.

2. Howard Carter, *Spiritual Gifts and Their Operation.* (Springfield, MO: Gospel Publishing House, 1968), 65.

3. Ibid., 60.

4. Lester Sumrall, *The Gifts and Ministries of the Holy Spirit,* (New Kensington, PA: Whitaker House, 1982), 107.

5. Howard Horton, *The Gifts of the Spirit.* (Springfield, MO: Gospel Publishing House, U.S. edition published 1975), 109.

6. Lester Sumrall, *The Gifts and Ministries of the Holy Spirit.* (New Kensington, PA: Whitaker House, 1982), 106.

7. Gordon Lindsay, *Commissioned with Power: An Overview of the Gifts of the Spirit.* (Dallas, TX: Christ for the Nations, 2001), 261.

8. Howard Carter, *Spiritual Gifts and Their Operation,* (Springfield, MO: Gospel Publishing House, 1968), 63.

9. Ibid., 65–66.

10. Ibid., 66.

11. Gordon Lindsay, *Commissioned with Power: An Overview of the Gifts of the Spirit,* (Dallas, TX: Christ for the Nations, 2001), 261.

12. Ibid., 261–262.

13. Howard Carter, *Spiritual Gifts and Their Operation,* (Springfield, MO: Gospel Publishing House, 1968), 61–62.

14. Corrie Ten Boom, *The Hiding Place* (Grand Rapids, MI: Chosen Books, 1971).

15. Howard Carter, *Spiritual Gifts and Their Operation* (Springfield, MO: Gospel Publishing House, 1968), 67–68.

16. Smith Wigglesworth, *Smith Wigglesworth on Spiritual Gifts* (New Kensington, PA: Whitaker House, 1998), 98–99.

CHAPTER 10: THE GIFT OF PROPHECY

1. Harold Horton, *The Gifts of the Spirit* (Nottingham, England: The Assemblies of God Publishing House, © 1934), 159.

2. Ibid.

3. Ibid.

4. Gordon Lindsay, *Commissioned with Power: An Overview of the Gifts of the Spirit* (Dallas, TX: Christ for the Nations, © 2001), 327.

5. Harold Horton, *The Gifts of the Spirit* (Nottingham, England: The Assemblies of God Publishing House, © 1934), 169.

6. Ken and Lorraine Kivohlavek, *Desire Spiritual Gifts* (Pasig City, Philippines, ICI Ministries, © 2004), 58.

7. Harold Horton, *The Gifts of the Spirit*, (Nottingham, England: The Assemblies of God Publishing House, © 1934), 170.

8. Lester Sumrall, *The Gifts and Ministries of the Holy Spirit* (New Kensington, PA: Whitaker House, © 1982), 116.

9. Ibid., 116–117.

10. Ibid., 117.

11. Lester Sumrall, *The Gifts and Ministries of the Holy Spirit* (New Kensington, PA: Whitaker House, © 1982), 118.

12. Ken and Lorraine Krivohlavek, *Desire Spiritual Gifts* (Pasig City, Philippines: ICI Ministries, © 2004), 52.

13. Ibid.

14. Donald Gee, *Now That You've Been Baptized In The Spirit* (Springfield, Missouri: Gospel Publishing House, © 1972), 123–124.

15. Howard Carter, *Questions & Answers On Spiritual Gifts* (Tulsa, Oklahoma: Harrison House, © 1976), 122.

16. Donald Gee, *Now That You've Been Baptized In The Spirit* (Springfield, Missouri: Gospel Publishing House, © 1972), 124.

17. Ibid.

18. Donald Gee, *Now That You've Been Baptized In The Spirit*, (Springfield, MO: Gospel Publishing House, © 1972), 125.

19. Lester Sumrall, *The Gifts and Ministries of the Holy Spirit*, (New Kensington, PA: Whitaker House, ©), 118.

20. Ken and Lorraine Krivohlavek, *Desire Spiritual Gifts*, (Pasig City, Philippines: ICI Ministries, © 2004), 49–51.

21. Ibid., 54.

22. Ibid.

23. Lester Sumrall, *The Gifts and Ministries of the Holy Spirit* (New Kensington, PA: Whitaker House, © 1982), 114.

24. Howard Carter, *Questions & Answers on Spiritual Gifts*, (Tulsa, Oklahoma: Harrison House, © 1976), 123.

25. Ken and Lorraine Krivohlavek, *Desire Spiritual Gifts*, (Pasig City, Philippines: ICI Ministries, © 2004), 56.

26. Harold Horton, *The Gifts of the Spirit* (Nottingham, England: The Assemblies of God Publishing House, © 1934), 163–164.

CHAPTER 11: THE GIFT OF TONGUES

1. Phil Taylor, *The Person and Work of the Holy Spirit* (Tulsa, Oklahoma: Carbondale A/G, 1992), 81.

2. Gordon Lindsay, *Commissioned with Power* (Dallas, TX: Christ for the Nations, Inc., 2001), 392.

3. Ibid., 391.

4. Lester Sumrall, *The Gifts and Ministries of the Holy Spirit* (New Kensington, PA: Whitaker House, 1982), 128–129.

5. Howard Carter, *Spiritual Gifts and Their Operation* (Springfield, MO: Gospel Publishing House, 1968), 86.

6. Ibid., 88.

7. Harold Horton, *The Gifts of the Holy Spirit* (Nottingham, England: Assemblies of God Publishing House, 1934), 133.

8. Ray McCauley, *The Gifts of the Holy Spirit* (Randburg, Republic of South Africa, Conquest Publishers, 1988), 61.

9. Ken and Lorraine Krivohlavek, *Desire Spiritual Gifts* (Pasig City, Philippines: ICI Ministries, 2004), p. 19.

10. Ibid., 20.

11. Lester Sumrall, *The Gifts and Ministries of the Holy Spirit* (New Kensington, PA: Whitaker House, 1982), 121–122.

12. Ken and Lorraine Krivohlavek, *Desire Spiritual Gifts* (Pasig City, Philippines: ICI Ministries, 2004), 26.

13. Lester Sumrall, *The Gifts and Ministries of the Holy Spirit* (New Kensington, PA: Whitaker House, 1982), 121.

14. Robert L. Brandt, *Spiritual Gifts* (Brussels, Belgium: International Correspondence Institute, 1978), 163.

15. Ken and Lorraine Krivohlavek, *Desire Spiritual Gifts* (Pasig City, Philippines: ICI Ministries, 2004), 20.

16. Ken and Lorraine Krivohlavek, *Desire Spiritual Gifts* (Pasig City, Philippines: ICI Ministries, 2004, 21–23.

17. Ibid., 23–24.

CHAPTER 12: THE GIFT OF INTERPRETATION OF TONGUES

1. Lester Sumrall, *The Gifts and Ministries of the Holy Spirit* (New Kensington, PA: Whitaker House, 1982), 126.

2. Gordon Lindsay, *Commissioned With Power—An Overview of the Gifts of the Spirit* (Dallas, TX: Christ for The Nations, 2001), 506–507.

3. Ken and Lorraine Krivohlavek, *Desire Spiritual Gifts* (Pasig City, Philippines, ICI Ministries, 2004).

4. Ibid., 33.

5. Gordon Lindsay, *Commissioned With Power—An Overview of the Gifts of the Spirit* (Dallas, TX: Christ for the Nations, 2001), 511.

6. Lester Sumrall, *The Gifts and Ministries of the Holy Spirit* (New Kensington, PA: Whitaker House, 1982), 130.

7. Howard Carter, *Questions & Answers on Spiritual Gifts* (Tulsa, OK: Harrison House, Inc., 1976), 183.

8. Lester Sumrall, *The Gifts and Ministries of the Holy Spirit* (New Kensington, PA: Whitaker House, 1982), 131.

9. Gordon Lindsay, *Commissioned With Power—An Overview of the Gifts of the Spirit* (Dallas, TX: Christ for the Nations, 2001), 511–512.

10. Lester Sumrall, *The Gifts and Ministries of the Holy Spirit* (New Kensington, PA: Whitaker House, 1982), 131.

11. Ibid., 132.

12. Ibid., 129.

13. Ken and Lorraine Krivohlavek, *Desire Spiritual Gifts* (Pasig City, Philippines: ICI Ministries, 2004), 35–37.

14. Ibid., 43.

15. Harold Horton, *The Gifts of the Spirit* (Nottingham, England: The Assemblies of God Publishing House, 1934), 149–151. (Note: The U.S. edition was published in Springfield, MO: Gospel Publishing House, 1975).

16. Ken and Lorraine Krivohlavek, *Desire Spiritual Gifts* (Pasig City, Philippines: ICI Ministries, 2004), 41–43.

17. Ibid., 43.

18. Howard Carter, *Spiritual Gifts and their Operation* (Springfield, MO: Gospel Publishing House, 1968), 94–96.

19. Lester Sumrall, *The Gifts and Ministries of the Holy Spirit* (New Kensington, PA: Whitaker House, 1982), 128.

20. Howard Carter, *Spiritual Gifts and Their Operation* (Springfield, MO: Gospel Publishing House, 1968), 93–94.

21. Jackie Pullinger, *Chasing the Dragon* (Ventura, CA: Published by Regal Books from Gospel Light, 1980), 74.

22. Ibid., 130–131.

23. Howard Carter, *Spiritual Gifts and their Operation* (Springfield, MO: Gospel Publishing House, 1968), 96.